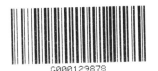

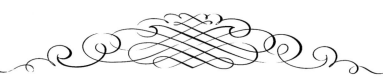

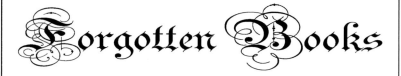

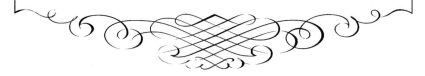

ISBN 978-1-333-88774-2
PIBN 10696840

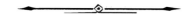

THE

SOUTHERN HARMONY, AND MUSICAL COMPANION:

CONTAINING A CHOICE COLLECTION OF

TUNES, HYMNS, PSALMS, ODES, AND ANTHEMS;

SELECTED FROM THE MOST EMINENT AUTHORS IN THE UNITED STATES:

TOGETHER WITH

NEARLY ONE HUNDRED NEW TUNES, WHICH HAVE NEVER BEFORE BEEN PUBLISHED;

SUITED TO MOST OF THE METRES CONTAINED IN WATTS'S HYMNS AND PSALMS, MERCER'S CLUSTER, DOSSEY'S CHOICE, DOVER SELECTION, METHODIST HYMN BOOK, AND BAPTIST HARMONY;

AND WELL ADAPTED TO

CHRISTIAN CHURCHES OF EVERY DENOMINATION, SINGING SCHOOLS, AND PRIVATE SOCIETIES:

ALSO, AN EASY INTRODUCTION TO THE GROUNDS OF MUSIC, THE RUDIMENTS OF MUSIC, AND PLAIN RULES FOR BEGINNERS

BY WILLIAM WALKER.

Sing unto God, ye kingdoms of the earth: O sing praises unto the Lord.—DAVID.
Speaking to yourselves in psalms, and hymns, and spiritual songs, singing and making melody in your hearts to the Lord.—PAUL.

NEW EDITION, THOROUGHLY REVISED AND MUCH ENLARGED.

PHILADELPHIA:

PUBLISHED BY E. W. MILLER, 1102 AND 1104 SANSOM STREET.

AND FOR SALE BY

J. B. LIPPINCOTT & CO., AND BOOKSELLERS, GENERALLY, THROUGHOUT THE UNITED STATES.

PREFACE TO NEW EDITION.

The Author, feeling grateful to a generous public for the very liberal patronage which they have given the former editions of the Southern Harmony, has endeavoured to remedy the only deficiency which he has heard mentioned, by adding a large number of good tunes for church use, together with several excellent new pieces never before published, which has enlarged the work about forty pages, and makes it one of the largest Music Books ever offered at the same price. Therefore he hopes to secure that continued and increased patronage which it may merit from those who love the Songs of Zion.

WILLIAM WALKER.

Spartanburg, S. C., January, 1847.

PREFACE TO REVISED EDITION.

Since the Southern Harmony was first published, many of the tunes having gone out of use, the *Author* determined to revise the work, and leave out those pieces, and supply their places with *good new tunes*, which have been selected for their intrinsic worth, and great popularity, and highly devotional character. He has also enlarged the work with thirty-two pages of excellent music, many of the tunes being suitable for revival occasions. All of which he hopes will be found entirely satisfactory to the many friends and patrons of the *Southern Harmony*.

The Author now tenders his grateful thanks to a generous and enlightened public for the very flattering manner in which the former editions of this work have been received, and hopes that this revised edition may be duly appreciated, and the demand for it increase as its merits may deserve.

WILLIAM WALKER.

Spartanburg, S. C., July, 1854.

PREFACE TO FORMER EDITION.

THE compiler of this work, having been solicited for several years by his brother teachers, pupils, and other friends, to publish a work of this kind, has consented to yield to their solicitations.

In treating upon the rudiments of Music, I have endeavoured to lead the pupil on step by step, from A, B, C, in the gamut, to the more abstruse parts of this delightful science, having inserted the gamut as it should be learned, in a pleasing conversation between the pupil and his teacher.

In selecting the Tunes, Hymns, and Anthems, I have endeavoured to gratify the taste of all, and supply the churches with a number of good, plain tunes, suited to the various metres contained in their different Hymn Books.

While those that are fond of fuged tunes have not been neglected, I have endeavoured to make this book a complete Musical Companion for the aged as well as the youth. Those that are partial to ancient music, will here find some good old acquaintances which will cause them to remember with pleasure the scenes of life that are past and gone; while my youthful companions, who are more fond of modern music, I hope will find a sufficient number of new tunes to satisfy them, as I have spared no pains in trying to select such tunes as would meet the wishes of the public.

I have also selected a number of excellent new Songs, and printed them under the tunes, which I hope will be found satisfactory.

Some object to new publications of music, because the compilers alter the tunes. I have endeavoured to select the tunes from original authors. Where this could not be done, and the tune having six or seven basses and trebles, I have selected those I thought most consistent with the rules of composition.

I have composed the parts to a great many good airs, (which I could not find in any publication, nor in manuscript,) and assigned my name as the author. I have also composed several tunes wholly, and inserted them in this work, which also bear my name.

The compiler now commends this work to the public, praying God that it may be a means of advancing this important and delightful science, and of cheering the weary pilgrim on his way to the celestial city above.

WILLIAM WALKER

Spartanburg, S. C., September 1835

THE GAMUT, OR RUDIMENTS OF MUSIC.

PART FIRST.

OF MUSIC.

PUPIL. What is Music?

TEACHER. Music is a succession of pleasing sounds.

P. On what is music written?

T. On five parallel lines including the spaces between them, which is called a stave; and these lines and spaces are represented by the first seven letters in the alphabet, A, B, C, D, E, F, and G. These letters also represent the seven sounds that belong to each key-note in music: when eight letters are used, the first is repeated.

P. How many parts are there used in vocal music?

T. Commonly only four; viz. Bass, Tenor, Counter, and Treble; and the letters are placed on the staves for the several parts in the following order, commencing at the space below the first line in each stave.

BASS STAVE NATURAL.

	B	me ◇	Space above.
A		law ▢	Fifth line.
	G	sol ○	Fourth space.
	F	faw △	Fourth line.
E		law ▢	Third space.
	D	sol ○	Third line.
	C	faw △	Second space.
B		me ◇	Second line.
A		law ▢	First space.
G		sol ○	First line.
F		faw △	Space below.

F Clef

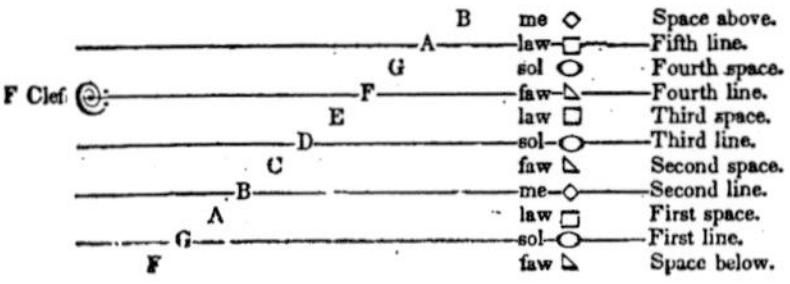

TENOR OR TREBLE STAVE NATURAL.

G Clef

	G	sol ○	Space above.
F		faw △	Fifth line.
	E	law ▢	Fourth space.
D		sol ○	Fourth line.
	C	faw △	Third space.
	B	me ◇	Third line.
A		law ▢	Second space.
	G	sol ○	Second line.
	F	faw △	First space.
E		law ▢	First line.
D		sol ○	Space below.

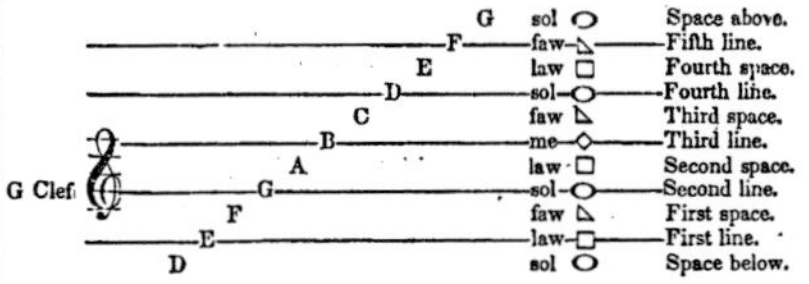

COUNTER STAVE NATURAL.

C Clef

	A	law ▢	Space above
G		sol ○	Fifth line.
	F	faw △	Fourth space.
E		law ▢	Fourth line.
	D	sol ○	Third space.
	C	faw △	Third line.
B		me ◇	Second space.
A		law ▢	Second line.
	G	sol ○	First space.
	F	faw △	First line.
E		law ▢	Space below.

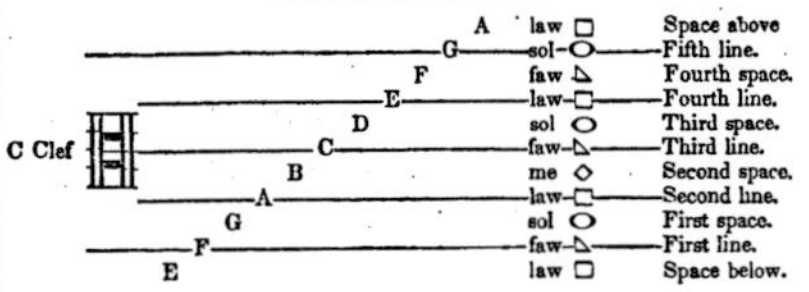

You may observe that the letters are named or called by the names of the four notes used in music. You see in the above staves that F is named faw, C sol, A law, B me, O faw, D sol, E law, and F faw again; every eighth letter being the first repeated, which is an octave; for every eighth is an octave.

P. How many notes are there used in music, what are their names, and how are they made?

THE GAMUT. OR RUDIMENTS OF MUSIC

T. All notes of music which represent sounds are called by four names, and each note is known by its shape, viz.; the me is a diamond, faw is triangle, sol is round, and law is square. See the example.

EXAMPLE.

P. But in some music books the tunes are written in round notes entirely. How do we know by what names to call the notes in these books? *

T. By first finding the me for me is the governing and leading note; and when that is found, the notes on the lines and spaces in regular succession are called, faw, sol, law, faw, sol, law, (twice,) and those below the me, law, sol, faw, law, sol, faw, (twice;) after which me will come again. Either way, see the following—

EXAMPLE.

This is the rule for singing round notes. You must therefore observe that the natural place for the me in parts of music is on that line or space represented by B.

But if B be flat, ♭ *me* is on..E
B ♭ and E ♭ it is on..A
B ♭ E ♭ and A ♭ it is on..D
B ♭ E ♭ A ♭ and D ♭ it is on..G
If F be sharp, ♯ *me* is on..F
F ♯ and C ♯ it is on..C
F ♯ C ♯ and G ♯ it is on..G
F ♯ C ♯ G ♯ and D ♯ it is on..D

* For singing Doe, Rae, See, seven syllables and numerals, see p. xxxi.

As in the following example, viz.:

Me in its NATURAL ♮ place. Tenor or treble ME.
Me, transposed by flats.
B flat, *me* is in E.
B and E flat *me* is in A.
B, E, and A flat, *me* is in D.
B, E, A, and D flat, *me* is in G.
Me, transposed by sharps.
F sharp, *me* is in F.
F and C sharp, *me* is in C.
F, C, G, sharp, *me* is in G.
F, C, G, D, sharp, *me* is in D.
Counter ME.
ME.
Bass ME.

P. How many marks of sound or kinds of notes are there used in music?

T. There are six kinds of notes used in music, which differ in time. They are the semibreve, minim, crotchet, quaver, semiquaver, and demisemiquaver.

SCALE OF NOTES.

The following scale will show, at one view, the *proportion* one note bears to another.

One Semibreve — is equal in time to

Two — Minims,

Four — Crotchets,

Eight — Quavers,

Sixteen — Semiquavers,

Thirty two — Demi-semi-quavers.

Explain the above scale.

T. The semibreve is now the longest note used. it is white, without a stem, and is the measure note, and guideth all the others.

The minim is but half the length of a semibreve, and has a stem to it.

The crotchet is but half the length of the minim, and has a black head and straight stem.

The quaver is but half the length of the crotchet, has a black head, and one turn to the stem, sometimes one way, and sometimes another.

The semiquaver is but half the length of the quaver, has also a black head and two turns to the stem, which are likewise various.

The demisemiquaver is half the length of a semiquaver, has a black head, and three turns to its stem, also variously turned.

P. What are rests?

T. All rests are marks of silence, which signify that you must keep silent so long a time as takes to sound the notes they represent, except the semibreve rest, which is called the bar rest, always filling the bar, let the mood of time be what it may.

THE RESTS.

P. Explain the rests.

T. The semibreve, or bar rest, is a black square underneath the third line.
The minim rest is the same mark above the third line.
The crotchet rest is something like an inverted figure seven.
The quaver rest resembles a right figure of seven.
The semiquaver rest resembles the figure seven with an additional mark to the left.
The demisemiquaver rest is like the last described, with a third mark to the left.
The two bar rest is a strong bar reaching only across the third space.
The four bar rest is a strong bar crossing the second and third space and third line.
The eight bar rest is two strong bars like the last described.

NOTE.—These notes are sounded sometimes quicker, and sometimes slower, according to the several moods of time. The notes of themselves always bear the same proportion to each other, whatever the mood of time may be.

OF THE SEVERAL MOODS OF TIME.

P. Please tell me how many moods of time there are in music.

T. There are nine moods of time used; four of common, three of triple, and two of compound.

P. Why are the first four moods called common time moods?

T. Because they are measured by even numbers, as 2, 4, 8, &c.

P. Why are the next three called triple moods?

T. Because they are measured by odd numbers, having either three minims, three crotchets, or three quavers, in each bar.

P. Why are the last two called compound time moods?

T. Because they are compounded of common and triple; of common, as the bar is divided equal, the fall being equal to the rise in keeping time; and of triple, as each half of the bar is three fold; having either three crotchets, three quavers, or notes to that amount, to each beat.

P. Please explain the several moods of time in their order.

MOODS OF COMMON TIME

The first mood is known by a plain C, and has a semibreve or its quantity in a measure, sung in the time of four seconds—four beats in a bar, two down and two up.

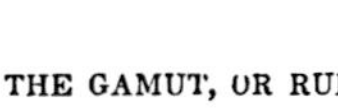

The second mood is known by a C with a bar through it, has the same measure, sung in the time of three seconds—four beats in a bar, two down and two up.

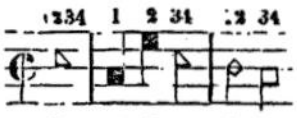

The third mood is known by a C inverted, sometimes with a bar through it, has the same measure as the first two, sung in the time of two seconds—two beats in a bar. This mood is sometimes marked with the figure 4 above 4, thus, 4/4

The fourth mood is known by a figure 2 over a figure 4, has a minim for a measure note, sung in the time of one second—two beats in a bar, one down and the other up.

MOODS OF TRIPLE TIME.

The first mood of triple time is known by a figure 3 over a figure 2, has a pointed semibreve, or three minims in a measure, sung in the time of three seconds—three beats, two down and one up.

The second mood is known by a figure 3 over a 4, has a pointed minim or three crotchets in a measure, and sung in 2 seconds—three beats in a bar, two down and one up.

The third mood is known by the figure 3 above figure 8, has three quavers in a measure, and sung in the time of one second—three beats in a bar, two down and one up

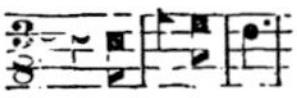

MOODS OF COMPOUND TIME

The first mood of compound time is known by the figure 6 above figure 4, has six crotchets in a measure, sung in the time of two seconds—two beats in a bar, one down and one up.

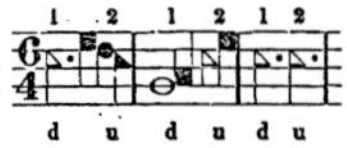

The second mode of compound time is known by the figure 6 above an 8, has six quavers in a measure, sung in the time of one second and a half—two beats in a bar, one down and one up.

P. What do the figures over the bar, and the letters *d* and *u* unde it, in the above examples of time, mean ?

T. The figures show how many beats there are in each bar and the letter *a* shows when the hand must go down, and the *u* when up.

P. What *general* rule is there for beating time ?

T. That the hand fall at the beginning, and rise at the end of each bar, in all moods of time.

P. Do you suppose those moods, when expressed by figures, have any particular signification, more than being mere arbitrary characters ?

T I think they have this *significant* meaning, that the lower figure shows how many parts or kinds of notes the semibreve is divided into, and the upper figure signifies how many of such notes or parts will fill a bar—for example, the first mood of compound time, (6 above 4,) shows the semibreve is divided into four parts—*i. e.* into crotchets, (for four crotchets are equal to one semibreve;) and the upper figure 6 shows that six of these parts, viz. crotchets, fill a bar. So of any other time expressed by figures.

P. How shall we with sufficient exactness ascertain the proper time of each beat in the different moods ?

T. By making use of a pendulum, the cord of which, from the centre of the ball to the pin from which it is suspended, to be, for the several moods, of the following lengths :—

For the first and third moods of common time, the first of triple and first of compound, [all requiring second beats,]............	39 2-10 inches
For the second mood of common, second of triple, and first of compound,..	22 1 10
For the fourth of common	12 4-10
For the third of triple time,'	5 1-21

Then for every swing or vibration of the ball, count one beat, accompanying the motion with the hand, till something of a habit is formed, for the several moods of time, according to the different lengths of the cord, as expressed above.

NOTE.—If teachers would fall upon this or some other method, for ascertaining and keeping the true time, there would not be so much difficulty among singers, taught at different schools, about timing music together; for it matters not how well individual singers may perform, if, when several of them perform together, they do not keep time woll, they disgust, instead of pleasing their hearers.

OF ACCENT

P. What is meant by accent ?

T. Accent is a particular emphasis or swell of voice on a certain part of the measure which is according to the subdivision of it, and is essential to a skilful performance of music, as the chief intention of accent is to mark emphatical words more sensibly, and express the passions more feelingly. If the poetry be good, and the music skilfully adapted, the important words will fall upon the accented parts of the bar. Should emphatical words happen on the unaccented part, the music should always bend to the words.

P. What part of the measure is accented in the several moods of time ?

T. The first three moods of common time are accented on the first and third notes in the measure when the bar is divided into four equal parts; and the fourth mood is accented on the first part of the measure when only two notes are in a bar; if four, accent as in the first three. In triple time, when the measure is divided into three equal parts, the accent is on the first and third; if only two notes are in a bar, the accent is always on the longest note. In compound time the accent is on the first and fourth notes in the measure, when the bar is divided into six equal parts. Couplet accent is when two notes are accented together, as two quavers in the first three moods in common time, or two crotchets in the first mood of triple time. &c. In keeping time the accent is always strongest with the down beats

DIRECTIONS FOR BEATING TIME

P. How must I beat time?

T. In the first two moods of common time, for the first beat, lightly strike the end of your finger on whatever you beat upon; second, bring down the heel of your hand; third, raise your hand a little and shut it partly up; fourth beat, raise it up even with your shoulder, and throw it open at the same time, which completes the bar. The third and fourth moods, for the first beat let the hand fall; second, raise it up. The first two beats in triple time are the same as in the first of common time; third beat, raise the hand up. Compound time is beat in the same manner as in the third of common. Be careful that the motion of the hand should be always gentle, graceful, and regular, and never raise it much above a level with your shoulder.

CHARACTERS USED IN MUSIC.

NAMES.	EXAMPLES.	EXPLANATION.
A Stave Ledger line	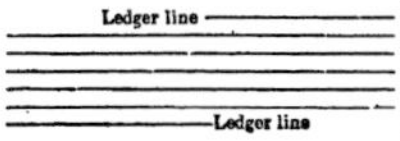	Is five parallel lines with their spaces, on which notes and other musical characters are written, and the ledger line is added when notes ascend or descend beyond the stave.
A Brace		Is drawn across the first end of the staves, and shows how many parts are sung together. If it include four parts, the order of them are as follows. The lowest and first part is the bass, the second is tenor, the third counter, and the fourth and upper part is treble; if only three parts, the third is treble.
The F Clef		Is placed on the fourth line of the stave, and belongs to the bass or lower part in music; it is sometimes used in counter.
The G Clef	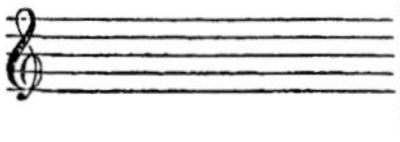	Stands on G, second line of the tenor or treble stave, and crosses that line four times. It is always used in tenor and treble, and sometimes in counter.
The C Clef		Stands on C, middle line; is used only in counter.
A single bar		Is a plain line or mark across the stave, and divides the time into equal parts according to the mood of time and measure note.
A measure note		Is a note that fills a measure; i. e. from one bar to another, without any other note or rest.
Bars,		Any quantity of music written between two of these marks or bars, is called a bar of music.

A Dot, or point of addition,

Set at the right hand of a any note, adds to it half its length, or causes it to be sounded half as long again as it would be without the dot; thus, a pointed semibreve is sung as long as three minims, &c.

A Flat,*

Set immediately preceding or before a note, sinks it half a tone; i. e. causes it to be sung half a tone lower than it would be without the flat.

A Sharp,

Set before a note, raises it half a tone; i. e. causes it to be sung half a tone higher than it would be without the sharp.

A Natural

Restores a note from flat or sharp to its natural sound.

A Slur

To raise

Over or under any number of notes, shows that they must be sung to one syllable, gliding softly from one sound to the other. The tails of the notes are often joined together, which answers the same purpose as a slur.

* We recommend singers to omit accidental flats and sharps, unless they understand them properly

Figure 3,

Over or under three notes, is a mark of diminution, and shows that they must be sung in the time of two of the same kind without a figure.

A Trill

Shows that the note over which it is placed should be warbled with a soft roll.

A Direct

Shows the place of the succeeding note on the stave.

A Hold:

Notes thus marked are sounded one fourth longer than their usual time.

A Staccato

Is seldom used in vocal music. The notes over which it is placed should be sounded distinct and emphatical.

Appogiatura, or grace notes,

Are small extra notes, added and set before or after regular notes, to guide the voice more gracefully into the sound of the succeeding [illegible]

Mark of accent and half accent

┬ Shows the place which is accented in each measure.
ı Shows the half accent.

Double Bar

Shows the end of a strain; it also shows when to repeat.

Repeat

Shows that the tune is to be sung twice from it to the next double bar or close.

Figure 1, 2, or double ending.

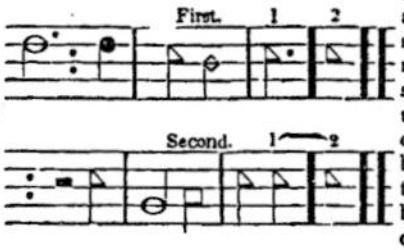

At the end of a strain, or at the end of a tune, shows that the note or notes under 1 are to be sung before you repeat, and those under 2 after omitting those under 1; but if the notes are tied together with a slur, both are sung the second time, as in the second example.

A Close

Shows the end of a tune or anthem.

A Prisma :‖: Denotes a repetition of preceding words

OF CHOOSING NOTES.

P. What are choosing notes, and how must I sing them?

T. They are notes set immediately over each other on the same stave; either of which may be sung, but not by the same voice; (in bass the lower notes are termed ground bass.) If two persons are singing the same part, one may sing the upper notes, and the other the lower notes. See the example on the bass stave.

EXAMPLE OF CHOOSING NOTES.

OF SYNCOPATION.

P. What is meant by syncopation, or syncopated notes?

T. Syncopation is any number of notes set on the same line or space included by a slur; sometimes driven across or through the bar, and sometimes in the middle; one of such notes only are to be named, but sound the time of all the notes, whether driven across the bar or not, swelling the voice a little at the usual place of the accent.

EXAMPLES OF SYNCOPATION.

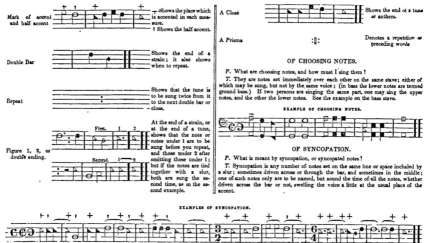

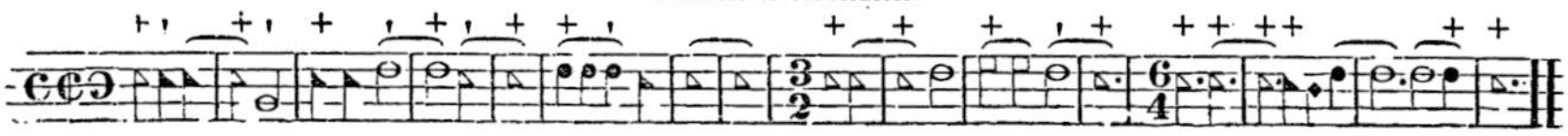

OF SYNCOPE OR SYNCOPEED NOTES.

P. What is meant by syncope, or syncopeed notes?

T. It is when a note is set out of its usual order, requiring the accent to be upon it, as though it were in the usual place of the accent, as in common time having half the time of the measure in the middle; as a minim between two crotchets, or a crotchet preceding a pointed minim, or a crotchet between two quavers, &c.

EXAMPLES OF SYNCOPEED NOTES.

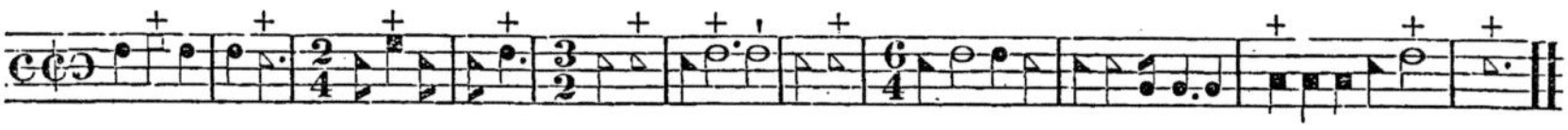

OF THE KEYS OR KEY NOTES.

P. What is meant by the keys in music, how many are there, and how are they known?

T. The key note of every correct piece of music is the leading note of the tune, by which all the other sounds throughout the tune are compared, and is always the last note in the bass, and generally in the tenor. If the last note in the bass be faw immediately above me, the tune is on a sharp or major key; but if law immediately below me, it is a flat or minor key.

There are but two natural places for the keys, A and C. A is the natural place of the flat key, and C the natural place of the sharp key. Without the aid of the flats and sharps at the beginning of the stave, no tune can rightly be set to any other than these two natural keys; but by the help of these, me, the centre, leading and governing note, and of course the keys, are removed at pleasure, and form what are called artificial keys, producing the same effect as the two natural keys; i. e. by fixing the two semi or half tones equally distant from the key notes. The difference between the major and minor keys is as follows; the major key note has its 3d, 6th, and 7th intervals, ascending half a tone higher than the same intervals ascending from the minor key note; and this is the reason some tunes are on a sharp key, and others on a flat key. This also is the reason why music set to the major or sharp key is generally sprightly and cheerful; whereas music set to the minor or flat key is pensive and melancholy. Sharp key tunes suit to sing hymns and psalms of praise and thanksgiving, and flat key tunes those of prayer and supplication.

OF TONES AND SEMITONES.

P. What is meant by tones and semi or half tones?

T. There are said to be but seven sounds belonging to every key note in music, every eighth being the same, and is called an octave. Therefore these sounds are represented by only seven letters. These sounds in music are called tones; five of them are called whole tones, and two of them semitones or half tones. The natural places for the semitones are between B and C, and between E and F, and they are always between me and faw, and law and faw, find them where you may.

P. Are the semitones always between the same letters in every tune?

T. No; although the natural situation of semitones are between B C and E F yet their situations, as well as the two keys, are very often altered by flats and sharps set at the beginning of the tune. You therefore remember that the natural place for the me is on B, but if B be flat, me is on E, &c.; and if F be sharp, me is on F, &c. Of course, if the me is removed, the semitones are as the semitones are always, between me and faw, and law and faw.

P. Well, my good teacher, I am very much obliged to you for this explanation for I have studied a great deal about them, but it is now plain to me.

T. Well, my studious pupil, as you understand these rules pretty well, you may now proceed to singing.

OF SOUNDING THE EIGHT NOTES.

P. Please tell me how to sound the eight notes, and where I must commence?

T. Commence first on faw, the major or sharp key note on the tenor and treble stave; than ascend softly from one sound to another till you sing the eighth note on the fifth line, which is an octave; then descend, falling softly from one sound to the other till you end at the close. Then commence on law, the minor or flat key note, ascend and descend in the same manner till you come to the close. By this you learn the difference between the major and minor moods or keys.

After having sounded the eight notes several times, you may go on to sing the other lessons for tuning the voice, and then some plain tunes.

LESSONS FOR TUNING THE VOICE.

Eight notes. MAJOR KEY. *Common Time.* Eight Notes. MINOR KEY.

Triple Time, Major Key.

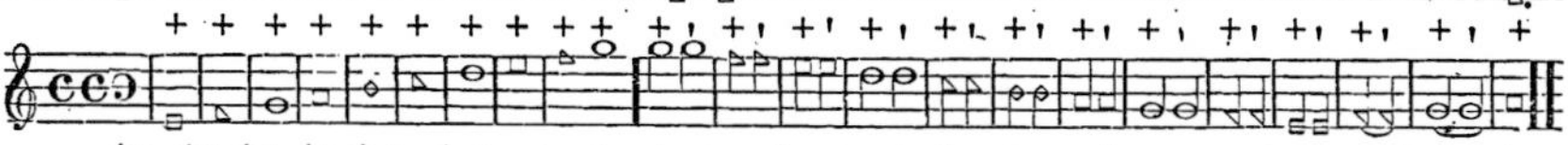

INTERVALS

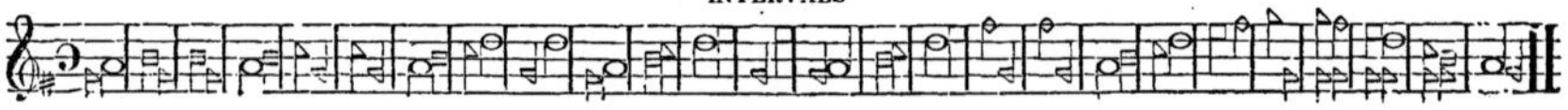

NOTE.— + stands over the usual place of the accent, and ' over the half accent.

PART SECOND.

INTRODUCTION TO THE GENERAL SCALE, AND RULES FOR PITCHING OR KEYING MUSIC.

THE following is a representation of the general scale, showing the connexion of the parts, and also what sound of the general scale each letter, line, or space in either of the octaves represents: for instance, A the minor key, occupies the 2d, 9th, and 16th sounds of the general scale: C, the natural major key, the 4th, 11th, and 18th. Thus, it will appear that every octave being unison, are considered one and the same sound. Although the last in the bass is the key note, and in case the me is not transposed, will either be on the 2d and 4th degrees as above stated, yet with the same propriety we may suppose them on the 9th, 11th. &c. degrees; for when we refer to a pitchpipe for the sound of either of the foregoing keys, if it be properly constructed, it will exactly correspond to the 9th, 11th, &c. sounds of the general scale. Then by descending the octave, we get the sound of the natural key; then by ascending a 3d, 4th, or 5th, as the tune may require, we readily discover whether the piece be properly keyed. If we find, after descending the octave, we can ascend to the highest note in the tenor or treble, and can pronounce them with ease and freedom, the piece may be said to be properly keyed; but if, on the contrary, after descending, we find it difficult to ascend as above, the piece is improperly keyed, and should be set lower.

NOTE.—This method of proving the keys is infallible to individuals, and will hold good in choirs, when we suppose the teacher or leader capable of judging for the commonality of voices.

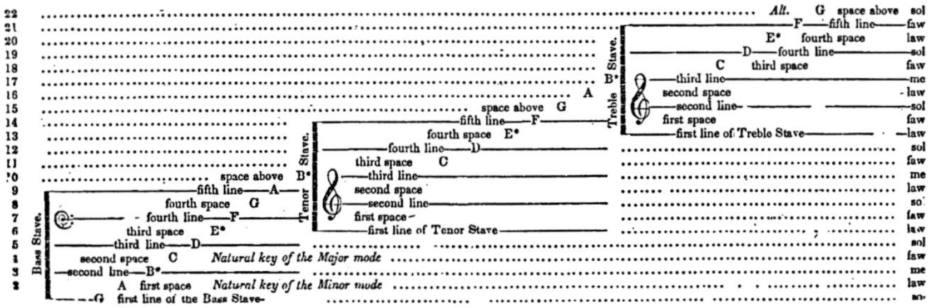

The foregoing scale comprises three octaves, or twenty-two sounds.

The F clef, used on the fourth line in the bass, shows that that line is the 7th sound in the general scale.

The G clef, used on the second line in the tenor and treble, shows that that line, in the tenor, is the eighth sound in the general scale, and in the treble, (when performed by a female voice,) the fifteenth sound; for if the treble, as well as the tenor, were performed entirely by men, the general scale would comprise only fifteen sounds: hence, the treble stave is only raised an octave above that of tenor, in consequence that female voices are naturally an octave above men's, and to females the treble is usually assigned. The stars (*) show the natural places of the semitones.

When the C clef is used, (though it has now become very common to write counter on either the G or F clefs,) the middle line in the counter is in unison with the third space in tenor, (C,) and a seventh above the middle line in the bass, &c.

Three octaves being more than any common voice can perform, the bass is assigned to the gravest of men's voices, the tenor to the highest of men's, and the treble to the female voices: the counter (when used) to boys, and the gravest of the female voices.

Two sounds equally high, or equally low, however unequal in their force, are said to be in unison, one with the other. Consequently, E on the lower line in the treble stave, is in unison with E on the fourth space in the tenor; and E on the third space in bass, is in unison with E on the first line of the tenor, and an octave below E, the lower line in the treble. ☞ See the General Scale. From any one letter in the general scale, to another of the same name, the interval is an octave—as from B to B, D to D, &c.

Agreeably to the F and G clefs used in the general scale, a note on any line or space in the bass, is a sixth below a note on a corresponding line or space in the tenor, and a thirteenth below a note in the treble occupying the same line or space, (when the treble is performed by females.) ☞ See the General Scale. Suppose we place a note on D, middle line of the bass, another on B, the middle line of the tenor or treble, the interval will appear as just stated: and to find any other interval, count either ascending or descending, as the case may be.

EXAMPLE.

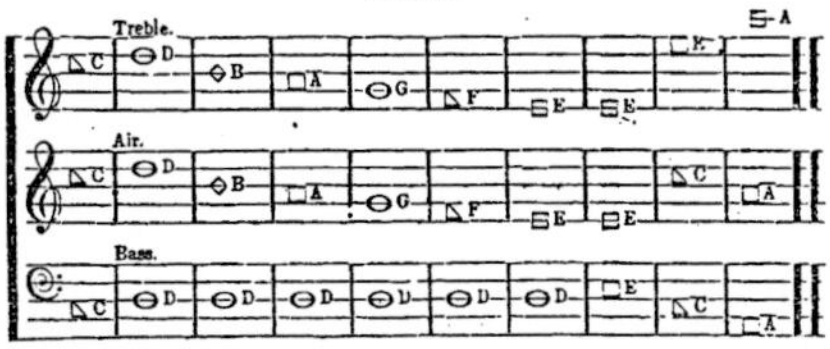

Octave. Ditto. 6th. 5th. 4th. 3d. 2d. Unison. Octave. Double Oct

In counting intervals, remember to include both notes or letters—thus, in counting a sixth in the above example, D is one, E is two, F is three, G is four, A five, and B six.

In the above example, the notes in the treble and air are placed in unison with each other. But assigning the treble to female voices, and the air to men's voices, (as is customary,) an octave must be added to the notes in the treble, (as previously observed of a woman's voice being an octave more acute than a man's,) the interval then being the bass and treble—in the first bar, would be a fifteenth or double octave, in the third bar, the note on B in the treble, a thirteenth above D in the bass, &c. Observe that an octave and a second make a ninth; an octave and a third make a tenth; an octave and a fourth make an eleventh; an octave and a fifth make a twelfth; an octave and a sixth, a thirteenth; an octave and a seventh, a fourteenth; two octaves, a fifteenth, &c. always including both the first and last note.

When a ledger line is added to a treble stave, a note occupying it is said to be in *alt*; and when the notes descend below the bass stave, they are termed *doubles*.

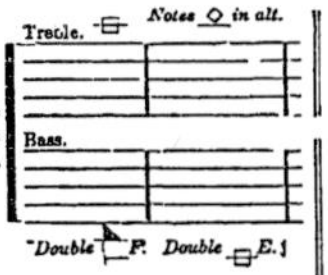

TERMS BY WHICH THE DIFFERENT INTERVALS IN THE GAMUT ARE DENOMINATED.

1. An interval composed of a tone and a semitone, as from B to D, is called a minor third.

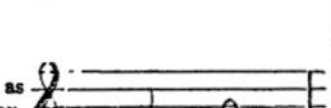

2. An interval composed of two full tones, as from faw to law, is called a third major.

3. An interval composed of two full tones and a semitone, as from me to law; i. e. from B to E, is called a fourth.

4. An interval composed of three full tones, as from faw to me, i. e. from F to B, is called a triton, or fourth redundant.

5. An interval composed of three tones and a semitone, as from faw to sol, i. e. from C to G, or from G to D, is called a fifth.

6. An interval composed of three tones and two semitones, as from law to faw, i. e. from E to C, is called a sixth minor.

7. An interval composed of four tones and a semitone, as from faw to law, i. e. from C to A, is called a sixth major.

8. An interval composed of four tones and two semitones, as from sol to faw, i. e. from D to C, is called a 7th minor. [*See next example.*]

9. An interval composed of five tones and a semitone, as from faw to me, i. e. from C to B, is called a seventh major.

10. An interval composed of five tones and two semitones, is called an octave, (as has already been observed.) ☞ *See examples of the three last mentioned intervals.*

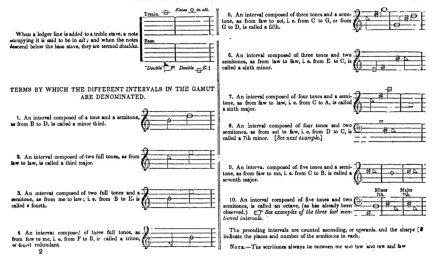

The preceding intervals are counted ascending, or upwards, and the sharps (#) indicate the places and number of the semitones in each.

NOTE.—The semitones always lie between me and faw, and law and faw

OF HARMONY AND COMPOSITION

Having given an explanation of the different intervals contained in the octave, and the manner in which the parts of music are connected, I proceed to show how they may be used in composition to produce harmony.

Harmony consists in the proportion of the distance of two, three, or four sounds, performed at the same time, and mingling in a most pleasing manner to the ear.

The notes which produce harmony, when sounded together, are called *concords*, and their intervals, *consonant intervals*. The notes which, when sounded together, produce a disagreeable sound to the ear, are called *discords*, and their intervals, *dissonant intervals*. There are but four concords in music—viz.: *unison, third, fifth*, and *sixth*; (their eighths or octaves are also meant.) The unison is called a perfect chord, and commonly the fifth is so called; if the composer please, however, he may make the fifth imperfect, when composing more than two parts. The third and sixth are called imperfect, their chords being not so full, nor so agreeable to the ear, as the perfect: but in four parts the sixth is often used instead of the fifth so in effect there are but three concords, employed together, in composition.

N B. The meaning of imperfect, signifies that it wants a semitone of its perfections, to what it does when it is perfect: for as the lesser or imperfect third includes but three half tones, the greater or major third includes four, &c. The discords are a *second*, a *fourth*, a *seventh*, and their octaves; though the greater fourth sometimes comes very near to the sound of an imperfect chord, it being the same in ratio as the minor fifth. Indeed some composers (the writer of these extracts is one of them) seem very partial to the greater fourth, and frequently admit it in composition. The following is an example of the several concords and discords, and their octaves under them:

	CONCORDS.				DISCORDS.		
Single Chords.	1	3	5	6	2	4	7
Their Octaves.	8	10	12	13	9	11	14
	15	17	19	20	16	18	21
	22	24	26	27	23	25	28

Notwithstanding the 2d, 4th, 7th, &c., are properly discords, yet a skilful composer may use them to some advantage, provided a full chord of all the parts immediately follow: they will then answer a similar purpose to acid, which being tasted immediately previous to sweet gives the latter a more pleasing flavour. Although the 4th is really a discord, yet it is very often used in composition. The rough sound of the 4th may be so mollified by the sweetness of the 5th and 8th as to harmonize almost as well as any three sounds in nature; and it would be reasonable to suppose that where we have two perfect chords, a discord may be introduced with very little violation to the laws of harmony; but as it is the most difficult part of composition to use a discord in such a manner and place as to show more fully the power and beauty of music, we think composers should only use them sparingly, (as it is much better to have all sweet than to have too much sour or bitter,) and always let them be followed by a perfect chord.

ON THE TRANSPOSITION OF KEYS.

The reason why the two natural keys are transposed by flats and sharps at the beginning of the stave, is to bring them within the stave, and to bring the music within the compass of the voice. The key notes or places of the keys are always found in the last note of the bass of a correct tune, and is either faw immediately above me the sharp key—or law immediately below me the flat key. The reason why one tune is on a sharp, lively key, and another on a flat, melancholy key, is, that every third, sixth and seventh, ascending from the sharp key, are half a tone higher than the same intervals ascending from the flat key note. For instance, a third ascending from the sharp key note faw, (being a major third,) is very different from a third ascending from law the flat key note, (a minor third,) and so of other intervals. Any person may be convinced of this by hearing a tune sung first in a flat and afterwards in a sharp key; when if the parts are correctly carried on, the chords will be entirely changed, and the tune as first sung, will scarcely be recognised or thought to be the same; we will give one example. Let Windham tune be sung on its proper flat key, and then on a sharp key, and the intervals will be entirely changed, and so with any other tune. (See the example.)

EXAMPLE.

WINDHAM—on the flat key law, its proper key.

WINDHAM—on the sharp key faw.

EXAMPLES OF THE KEYS.

Major Key. Minor Key.

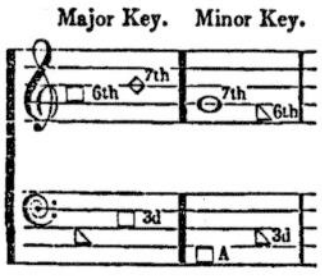

In the Major key, from law to faw, its third, the interval is two tones, [a Major third]—from faw to law, its sixth, the interval is four tones and a semitone, [a Major sixth]—and from faw to me, its seventh, the interval is five tones and a semitone, [a Major seventh.]

In the Minor key, from law to faw, its third, the interval is one tone and a semitone, [Minor third]—from law to faw, its sixth, the interval is three tones and two semitones, [a Minor sixth] and from law to sol, its seventh, the interval is four tones and two semitones, [a Minor seventh.]

To prove the utility of removing the key, I will produce two examples. First, Let the tune "*Suffield*" be written on key note A, (natural flat key,) instead of E, its proper key—and, besides the inconvenience of multiplying ledger lines, few voices would be able to perform it—the treble in particular.

SUFFIELD—on E, its proper key, from the repeat.

The same on A, the assumed, or natural key A.

Second, Let "*Complainer*" be written on key note C, (natural sharp key,) instead of G, its proper key, and there are but few that could perform it,—the tenor in particular.

COMPLAINER—on G, its proper key, from the repeat.

The same on the assumed, or natural key C.

The *me*, and consequently the *keys*, is removed either by sharping its fifth or flatting its fourth, thus:

BY SHARPS.

1. A fifth from B me, its natural place, will bring us to..............F
2. A fifth from F me, will bring us to...............................C
3. A fifth from C me, will bring us to...............................G
4. A fifth from G me, will bring us to...............................D
5. A fifth from D me, will bring us to...............................A
6. A fifth from A me, will bring us to...............................E
7. A fifth from E me, will bring us back to..........................B

BY FLATS.

1. A fourth from B me, will bring us to..............................E
2. A fourth from E me, will bring us to..............................A
3. A fourth from A me, will bring us to..............................D
4. A fourth from D me, will bring us to..............................G
5. A fourth from G me, will bring us to..............................C
6. A fourth from C me, will bring us to..............................F
7. A fourth from F me, will bring us home to.........................B

This accounts for the customary rules of transposition, viz.

The natural place for me is..B
If B is ♭, me is on..E
If B and E is ♭, me is on..A
If B, E, and A is ♭, me is on..D
If B, E, A, and D is ♭, me is on.......................................G
If B, E, A, D, and G is ♭, me is on....................................C
If B, E, A, D, G, and C is ♭, me is on.................................F
If F be ♯, me is on..F
If F and C be ♯, me is on..C
If F, C, and G be ♯, me is on..G
If F, C, G, and D be ♯, me is on.......................................D
If F, C, G, D, and A is ♯, me is on....................................A
If F, C, G, D, A, and E is ♯, me is on.................................E

> "By flats the me is driven round,
> Till forced on B to stand its ground;
> By sharps the me's led through the keys,
> Till brought to B its native place."

A SCALE, SHOWING THE SITUATION OF BOTH KEYS IN EVERY TRANSPOSITION OF THE ME BY SHARPS AND FLATS.

A SCALE, SHOWING THE SITUATION OF THE SEMITONES IN EVERY TRANSPOSITION OF THE ME BY FLATS AND SHARPS.

Natural place of the Semitones.

BY FLATS

B C. E F.　　E F. A B.　　A B. D E.　　D E. G A.　　G A. C D.　　C D. F G　　F G. B C

Natural place of the Semitones.

BY SHARPS.

Observe that, by six flats or six sharps, (including the natural place,) both of the keys are placed on every letter in the stave, and by the same number of either character, (including the natural place,) the whole octave is divided into semitones; and it is impossible to use another flat or sharp in transposition, for seven flats or sharps would only put them in their natural places. You may also observe, that one flat, or six sharps, places the keys and semitones precisely in the same situation; and that one sharp, or six flats, has the same effect, and two flats or five sharps, and two sharps or five flats, &c.; and with six flats, or one sharp, one of the semitones is in its natural place; i. e. between B and C. Also with six sharps, or one flat, one of the semitones is in its natural place, i. e. between E and F, as the natural places of the semitones are between B and C, and E and F; and we suppose the reason why both of these characters are used in transposing music, is to save the trouble and time of making so many of either character; for a person can make one flat much quicker than six sharps, or one sharp quicker than six flats, &c.

Thus I think I have showed satisfactorily how the keys are removed, and how the octave is divided into semitones by flats and sharps, and why both characters are used in transposition.

C 8th or 1st △ 3d		
B 7th ◇ 2d		
A 6th □ 8th or 1st		
G 5th ○ 7th		
F 4th △ 6th		
E 3d □ 5th		
D 2d ○ 4th		
C 1st △ 3d		
B ◇ 2d		
A □ 1st		

SCALE OF KEYS

The figures at the left hand of the column of notes shows the degrees of the sharp key, those at the right hand show the degrees of the flat key. This scale shows that the ◇ is between the two keys, and that the first degree of the sharp key is the first note above the ◇, and that the first degree of the flat key is the first note below the ◇

Every sharp key has its relative flat key a third below; and every flat key has its relative sharp key a third above.

These admit of an easy and natural transition from one to the other.

Every sharp at the beginning of a tune takes the place of me, the fourth degree from the sharp key, and raises that note half a tone, and removes the me and the key to the fifth above or to the fourth below.

Every flat at the beginning of a tune takes the place of the me, sinks that note half a tone, and removes the me and the key to the fourth above, or to the fifth below.

The seven sounds have also distinct names from their situation and effect in the scale. The key note is called the tonic; the next above, or its second, the supertonic—its third, the mediant—its fourth, the subdominant—its fifth, the dominant—its sixth, the submediant—its seventh, the leading note.

Tonic.
Tonic.
Supertonic.
Mediant.
Subdominant.
Dominant.
Submediant.
L. note.

The tonic is so called from its being the principal or pitch of the tune.

The supertonic is so called from its being the note above the tonic.

The mediant is so called from its being in the middle way between the tonic and dominant.

The subdominant is so called from its being the fifth below the tonic, as the dominant is the fifth above.

The dominant is so called from its being a principal note, and requires the tonic generally to be heard after it, especially at a close, and is therefore said to govern it.

The submediant is so called from its being in the middle way between the tonic and its fifth below.

The leading note is so called from its leading to the tonic, and is the sharp seventh of the scale, and therefore in the minor mode is necessarily sharpened in ascending.

There are also fourteen intervals in the scale bearing distinct names, viz.; Unison, Minor second, Major second, Minor third, Major third, Perfect fifth, Minor sixth, Major sixth, Minor seventh, Major seventh, Octave.

Perfect chord.
Dischord.
Dischord.
Imperfect chord.
Imperfect chord.
Dischord.
Concinnous sound.
Unison
Minor 2d
Major 2d.
Minor 3d.
Major 3d
Perfect 4th.
Sharp 4th.

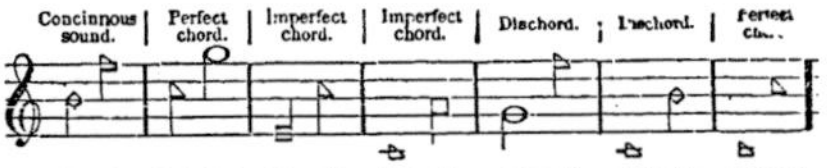

As the scale admits of only twelve semitones, so an octave although by counting the first and last note, which are octaves to each other, and really one and the same sound in effect; it contains thirteen sounds, yet it has but twelve intervals, because the unison cannot properly be called an interval; and the sharp fourth and flat fifth, although necessarily distinguished in harmony, are performed on keyed instruments with the same keys, and make but one interval.

ON THE MODULATION OF KEY.

The modulation or changing of the key note from one letter or given tone to another, being so frequent in every regular composition, particularly Anthems, that the performers will be very often embarrassed, unless they endeavour to acquire a knowledge or habit of discerning those changes.

The transition from one letter or key is sometimes effected by gradual preparation, as by accidental flats, sharps, or naturals. When the change is gradual, the new key is announced by flats, sharps, or naturals. When the change is sudden, the usual signs or signature at the beginning of the stave are either altered or removed, as in the tune called the Christian's Song, or the Judgment Anthem.

EXAMPLE.

TRANSITION IN THE MAJOR MODE FROM ONE KEY OR LETTER TO ANOTHER.

Key of C, into G, by a sharp on F. *Key of G, into D, by an additional sharp on C.*

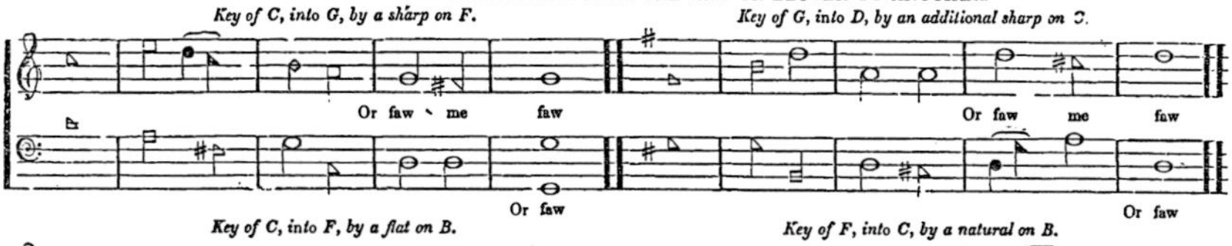

Key of C, into F, by a flat on B. *Key of F, into C, by a natural on B.*

TRANSITION IN THE MINOR MODE, FROM ONE KEY OR LETTER TO ANOTHER.

Key of A, into E, by one sharp. *Key of E, into B, by an additional sharp on C.*

Key of D, into A, by a natural on B

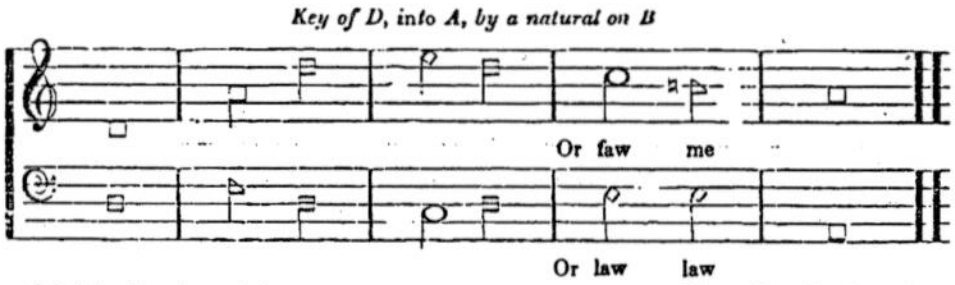

Major Key of C, into the minor of A *Minor Key of A, into the major of C.*

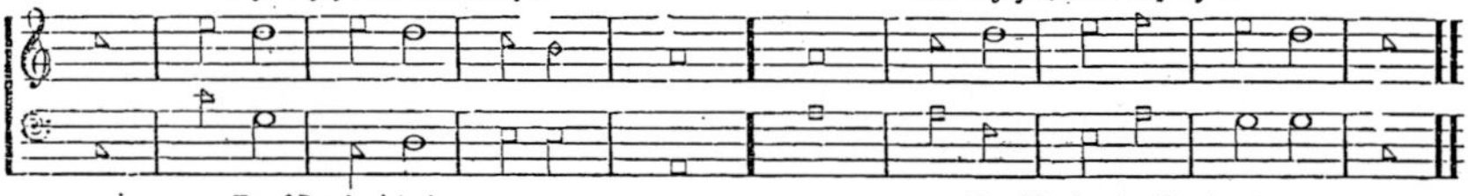

Key of D major, into B minor *Key of B minor, into D major.*

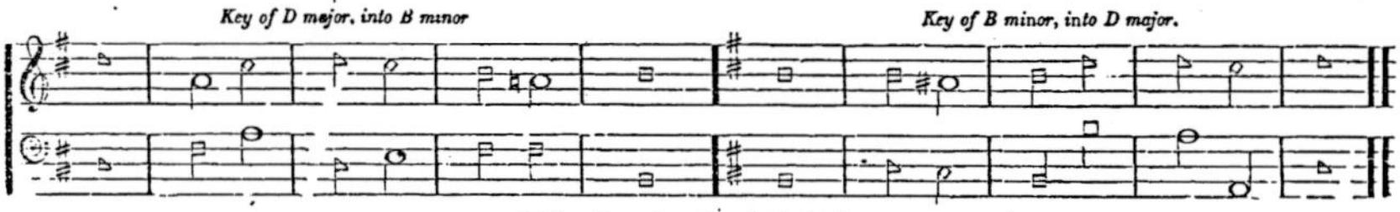

Sudden change from C major, to C minor.

To aid those who wish further information with respect to the best method of modulation by retaining the sol fawing system, the following observations are added.

In order to do this, the syllables must follow into the new key and take the same place there which they held in the original key; i. e. faw must be the new key note, sol its dominant or fifth, and me its leading note, if changing from the minor to the major mode or key. If changing from major to minor, law must be the new key, and law mediant to the major key its dominant, and me also its leading note.

There are four different pitches which the composer may consistently change to form any given pitch; viz. the fifth of the given pitch may be changed to the key note by adding such flats, sharps, or naturals, as will place the semitones in their regular degrees in the diatonic scale, (the scale in common use,) to the fourth, observing the same order of semitones, or to the sixth, its relative minor key, or change itself into a minor key if previously major, (see the example,) from C major to C minor. In order to modulate into the fourth of the key, the major 7th is made flat. For example, in the key of C major, by flatting B, F becomes the key note. To apply the syllables in this case, let C immediately preceding the flat be called sol, preserving the tone of faw, its former name, then by falling a whole tone to B, calling it faw, you come into the key of F. In modulating into the fifth of the key, the fourth is made sharp, and becomes the leading note or sharp seventh of the new key. Example:—In the key of C major by sharping F you make G the key note. In order to apply the syllables in this case, let G immediately preceding the sharp be called faw, preserving the tone which it held as sol, then by falling half a tone, and calling F me, you arrive at the key of G.

This is the method most common to be used in psalmody in modulating from one key to another.

Having gone thus far with our subject, we feel willing to close by making a few observations on the ornamental part of singing, or what are generally termed graces. This is the name generally given to those occasional embellishments which a performer or composer introduces to heighten the effect of a composition. It consists not only in giving due place to the apogiatura turn, shake, or trill, and other decorative additions, but in that easy, smooth, and natural expression of the passages which best conveys the native beauties and elegancies of the composition, and forms one of the first attributes of a cultivated and refined performer

A person or persons may be well acquainted with all the various characters in psalmody, (or music;) they may also be able to sing their part in true time, and yet their performance be far from pleasing; if it is devoid of necessary embellishments, their manner and bad expression may conspire to render it disagreeable. A few plain hints, and also a few general and friendly observations, we hope will tend to correct these errors in practising of vocal music.

GENERAL OBSERVATIONS.

1. Care should be taken that all the parts (when singing together) begin upon their proper pitch. If they are too high, difficulty and perhaps discords will be the consequence; if too low, dulness and languor. If the parts are not united by their corresponding degrees, the whole piece may be run into confusion and jargon before it ends; and perhaps the whole occasioned by an error in the pitch of one or more of the parts of only one semitone.

2. It is by no means necessary to constitute good singers that they should sing very loud. Each one should sing so soft as not to drown the teacher's voice, and each part so soft as will admit the other parts to be distinctly heard. If the teacher's voice cannot be heard it cannot be imitated, (as that is the best way to modulate the voice and make it harmonious,) and if the singers of any one are so loud that they cannot hear the other parts because of their own noise, the parts are surely not rightly proportioned, and ought to be altered.

3 When singing in concert the bass should be sounded full, bold, and majestic, but not harsh; the tenor regular, firm, and distinct; the counter clear and plain, and the treble soft and mild, but not faint. The tenor and treble may consider the German flute; the sound of which they may endeavour to imitate, if they wish to improve the voice.

4. Flat keyed tunes should be sung softer than sharp keyed ones, and may be proportioned with a lighter bass; but for sharp keyed tunes let the bass be full and strong, but never harsh.

5. The high notes, quick notes, and slurred notes, of each part, should be sung softer than the low notes, long notes, and single notes, of the same parts. All the notes included by one slur should be sung at one breath if possible.

6. Learners should sing all parts of music somewhat softer than their leaders do, as it tends to cultivate the voice and give them an opportunity of following in a piece with which they are not well acquainted; but a good voice may be soon much injured by singing too loud.

7. When notes of the tenor fall below those of the bass, the tenor should be sounded strong, and the bass soft.

8. While first learning a tune it may be sung somewhat slower than the true time or mood of time requires, until the notes can be named and truly sounded without looking on the book.

9. Learners are apt to give the first note where a fuge begins nearly double the time it ought to have, sounding a crotchet almost as long as a minim in any other part of the tune, which puts the parts in confusion by losing time; whereas the fuges ough to be moved off lively, the time decreasing (or the notes sung quicker) and the sound

of the engaged part or parts increasing in sound as the others fall in. All solos or fuges should be sung somewhat faster than when all the parts are moving together.

10. There are but few long notes in any tune but what might be swelled with propriety. The swell is one of the greatest ornaments to vocal music if rightly performed. All long notes of the bass should be swelled if the other parts are singing short or quick notes at the same time. The swell should be struck plain upon the first part of the note, increase to the middle, and then decrease softly like an echo, or die away like the sound of a bell.

11. All notes (except some in syncopation) should be called plain by their proper names, and fairly articulated; and in applying the words great care should be taken that they be properly pronounced and not torn to pieces between the teeth, nor forced through the nose. Let the mouth be freely opened, but not too wide, the teeth a little asunder, and let the sound come from the lungs and be entirely formed where they should be only distinguished, viz. on the end of the tongue. The superiority of vocal to instrumental music, is that while one only pleases the ear, the other informs the understanding.

12. When notes occur one directly above another, (called choosing notes,) and there are several singers on the part where they are, let two sing the lower note while one does the upper note, and in the same proportion to any other number.

13. Your singers should not join in concert until each class can sing their own part correctly.

14. Learners should beat time by a pendulum, or with their teacher, until they can beat regular time, before they attempt to beat and sing both at once, because it perplexes them to beat, name time, and sound the notes at the same time, until they have acquired a knowledge of each by itself.

15. Too long singing at a time injures the lungs.*

16. Some teachers are in the habit of singing too long at a time with their pupils. It is better to sing but only eight or ten tunes at a lesson, or at one time, and inform the learners the nature of the pieces and the manner in which they should be performed, and continue at them until they are understood, than to shun over forty or fifty in one evening, and at the end of a quarter of schooling perhaps few beside the teacher know a flat keyed tune from a sharp keyed one, what part of the anthem, &c requires emphasis, or how to give the pitch of any tune which they have been learning unless some one inform them. It is easy to name the notes of a tune, but it requires attention and practice to sing them correctly.

17. Learners should not be confined too long to the parts that suit their voices best, but should try occasionally the different parts, as it tends greatly to improve the voice and give them a knowledge of the connexion of the parts and of harmony as well as melody.* The gentlemen can change from bass to tenor, or from tenor to bass, and the ladies from treble to tenor, &c.

18. Learners should understand the tunes well by note before they attempt to sing them to verses of poetry.

19. If different verses are applied to a piece of music while learning, it will give the learners a more complete knowledge of the tune than they can have by confining it always to the same words. Likewise applying different tunes to the same words will have a great tendency to remove the embarrassment created by considering every short tune as a set piece to certain words or hymns.

20. When the key is transposed, there are flats or sharps placed on the stave, and when the mood of time is changed, the requisite characters are placed upon the stave.

21. There should not be any noise indulged while singing, (except the music,) as it destroys entirely the beauty of harmony, and renders the performance very difficult, (especially to new beginners;) and if it is designedly promoted is nothing less than a proof of disrespect in the singers to the exercise, to themselves who occasion it, and to the Author of our existence.

22. The apogiatura is placed in some tunes which may be used with propriety by a good voice; also the trill over some notes; but neither should be attempted by any one until he can perform the tune well by plain notes, (as they add nothing to the time.) Indeed no one can add much to the beauty of a piece by using what are generally termed graces, unless they are in a manner natural to their voice.

23. When learning to sing, we should endeavour to cultivate the voice so as to make it soft, smooth, and round, so that when numbers are performing in concert, there may on each part (as near as possible) appear to be but one uniform voice. Then, instead of confused jargon, it will be more like the smooth vibrations of the violin, or the soft breathings of the German flute. Yet how hard it is to make some be-

* A cold or cough, all kind of spirituous liquors, violent exercise, too much bile on the stomach, long fasting, the veins overcharged with impure blood, &c. &c. are destructive to the voice of one who is much in the habit of singing. An excessive use of ardent spirits will speedily ruin the best voice. A frequent use of some acid drink, such as purified cider, vinegar, and water mixed and sweetened a little with honey, or sugar with a little black or cayenne pepper, wine, and loaf sugar, &c. if used sparingly, are very strengthening to the lungs.

* Melody is the agreeable effect which arises from the performance of a single part of music only. Harmony is the pleasing union of several sounds, or the performance of the several parts of music together.

neve soft singing is the most melodious, when at the same time loud singing is more like the hootings of the midnight bird than refined music.

24. The most important ornament in singing is strict decorum, with a heart deeply impressed with the great truth we utter while singing the lines, aiming at the glory of God and the edification of one another.

25. All affectation should be banished, for it is disgusting in the performance of sacred music, and contrary to that solemnity which should accompany an exercise so near akin to that which will through all eternity engage the attention of those who walk in climes of bliss.

26. The nearest perfection in singing we arrive at, is to pronounce the words* and make the sounds as feeling as if the sentiments and sounds were our own. If singers when performing a piece of music could be as much captivated with the words and sounds as the author of the music is when composing it, the foregoing directions would be almost useless; they would pronounce, accent, swell, sing loud and soft where the words require it, make suitable gestures, and add every other necessary grace.

27. The great Jehovah, who implanted in our nature the noble faculty of vocal performance, is jealous of the use to which we apply our talents in that particular, lest we use them in a way which does not tend to glorify his name. We should therefore endeavour to improve the talent given us, and try to sing with the spirit and with the understanding, making melody in our hearts to the Lord.

* In singing there are a few words which should vary a little from common pronunciation, such as end in i and y; and these should vary two ways. The following method has been generally recommended: In singing it is right to pronounce majesty, mighty, lofty, &c. something like majestee, mightee, loftee, &c.; but the sense of some other words will be destroyed by this mode of expressing them; such as sanctify, justify, glorify, &c. These should partake of the vowel O, rather than EE, and be sounded somewhat like sanctifay, justifay, glorifay, &c. It would indeed be difficult to describe this exactly; however, the extreme should be avoided on both sides.

INTRODUCTORY REMARKS,

FROM THE COLUMBIAN HARMONY.

There is a charm, a power, that sways the breast,
Bids every passion revel or be still;
Inspires with rage, or all your cares dissolves;
Can soothe distraction, and almost despair:
That power is music.

Armstrong.

So great is the empire of music over all the faculties of human nature, and so loud have been the ingenious in celebrating its power and praises, that they have left nothing in heaven, not at all in the air, sea, or on the earth, but what in excess of fancy or merit they have subjected to its dominion for the better. Its harmony ravishes the soul and carries it beyond itself; helps, elevates, and extends it. It exterminates fear and fury, abates cruelty, alleviates sorrow and heaviness, and utterly destroys spleen and hatred. In short, music cures disease, sweetens the labourer's toil, and adds new courage to the soldier.

Divine music must be allowed by all who practise it to be an emanation from the Deity; it is admirably calculated to raise the mind above the sublunary enjoyments of this life, in gratitude to our beneficent Benefactor and Creator. When I consider upon the divine nature and power of music on the affections, I am wrapped up in admiration, love, and praise, and cannot but adore the Almighty Giver of so good and glorious a gift; and that it has pleased him to bestow upon me and my fellow beings faculties to sing his praise. It is in the performance of sacred music that we assimilate ourselves to the angelic choirs of glory, more nearly than in any other employment upon earth besides. Most of the arts and employments of this life will accompany us no farther than the grave; but this will continue an employment with the redeemed of God while eternal ages roll. It had its origin in God, and from God it was communicated to angels and men. Long before this world's foundations were laid, angels and archangels sang their grateful praises to the eternal Jehovah, encircling his throne and infinitely exulting. When God had created this lower world and all its appendages, the angelic hosts and seraphim above, like bright morning stars shining with the most serene brilliancy, sang together: and the archangels, the chief cherubim heaven, and sons of God, shouted for joy, to behold the new-creation so well accomplished.

Since then the cherubim and seraphim of heaven sing their ceaseless lays to their Creator, and consider music as one of the most noble and grand vehicles for conveying their love to him, shall man, mortal man, presume to look with haughty scorn, derision, and contempt upon that science which dignifies those exalted beings above? Ungrateful to God, and unmindful of his transcendent privilege, must he be that is possessed of the voice of melody, who delights not to celebrate the praises of the Most High, by singing hymns and anthems to his name. When amazing pity had seized the compassionate breast of our Redeemer; when it had prevailed upon him to resign his royal diadem of glory and robes of light into the hands of his eternal Father, with filial submission and humility; when he condescended to leave the throngs of adoring angels who cluster around the throne of God; and when he voluntarily left the realms of bliss that he might veil his divinity in humble clay, and become the sufferer for all sin against an incensed God, to appease his flaming wrath for a wretched world of men; I say well might shining legions of angels descend through the portals of the skies at his nativity, at so amazing condescension, and proclaim the joyful news to man, that a God on earth was born, and sing while hovering over the Redeemer's humble manger, and around the vigilant shepherd, "Glory to God in the highest, peace on earth, and good will towards men." Before his unparalleled sufferings, while in humble state, he rode upon the foal of an ass towards Jerusalem, well might his followers strew the way with their clothes and branches of palm trees, and shout, "Hosanna! blessed is he that cometh in the name of the Lord! Hosanna in the highest!" After he had administered his memorable supper to his disciples he sang with them a hymn, as the last consolation to them till he should have passed through the gloomy vale of death and all its horrors.

Soon after his agonizing passion, while the infernal powers roared their loud acclamations through the gloom of hell, and black despair triumphing at the bloody horrid deed, he breaks the bands of death asunder, and rose triumphant, and was escorted by myriads of hymning angels to the bosom of his Father God, from whose paternal hands he again received his diadem of glory and robes of eternal effulgence, there to be our Advocate, Mediator, and Redeemer, until he shall come the second time from heaven, not as before in humility, but with all the grandeur of heaven, with the shout of the archangel and with the trump of God, to judge the world; and till then, and eternally after, the choirs of glory will ever worship him with songs of endless praises, and sing, "Hallelujah, for the Lord God omnipotent reigneth, and he shall reign for ever and ever, King of kings and Lord of lords! Hallelujah!" "Worthy is the Lamb that was slain," shall the saints of glory for ever sing, "and hath redeemed us to God by his blood, to receive power, and riches, and wisdom, and strength, and honour, and glory, and blessing. Blessing, and honour, glory, and power be unto him that sitteth upon the throne, and unto the Lamb for ever and ever! Amen." No art in nature is better calculated to interest the feelings and command the passions of the soul than sacred music when well performed. It raises within the soul a kind of seraphic pathos, and almost transports the soul to the paradise of God, far, far beyond the contaminations of this gross sphere of nature, to a sphere of elevated glory. Were the soul to expand her wings, and take her flight to the realms of bliss, what would she behold among those celestial choirs less than ten thousand times ten thousand saints and angels, clad in robes of purest white, and interstreaked with shining gold, and exulting in the all-glorious praises of God. What would be her raptures to hear the chief cherubim of heaven sweeping the cerulean strings of their golden lyres symphoniously, and then the whole chorus of heaven, both vocal and instrumental, to fall in with them in one full burst of heavenly harmony! she would not behold a single being in so august a throng as millions, indifferent in the praises of God, nor hear one languid tone from the meanest seraph's tongue; if such be the harmony of heaven, let it raise the flame of emulation in every bosom to imitate the blest above. Let each singer perform in church properly, enchoired, and in the manner that it ought to be done, and grand effects will be the unavoidable result, if the music itself be good. By hearing good music well performed, we are ready to say, "O! ye enchanting, ecstatic, and delightful sons and daughters of harmony! O! that I could take the wings of the morning, and soar aloft with your sublime strains to the mansions of glory."

ON THE DIFFERENT PLANS OF NOTATION.

There are seven plans of notation used now in various parts of the world, which are to some extent national. The *English*, faw, sole, law, faw, sole, law, me. *Italian*, doe, rae, me, faw, sole, law, see. *French*, ut, rae, me, faw, sole, law, see. *Sweeds and Danes*, Dae, rae, nae, faw, sole, law, tee. In Germany, (among the peasantry,) and in some parts of the United States, the numerical 1, 2, 3, 4,

5, 6, 7. *Spanish*, perhaps, faw, sole, law, bae, doe, naw, me:—All repeating the first name, to make the eighth or octave sound: A very respectable number of my patrons being rather partial to the *Italian*, and also to the *numerical* system of seven syllables, I introduce a few examples, to make them plain to those who may wish to use them in learning to sing.

EXAMPLES.

Doe, rae, me, faw, sole, law, see, doe, doe, see, law, sole, faw, me, rae, doe. Doe, rae, me, faw, sole, law, see, doe.

C D E F G A. B C C B A G F E D C   F G A B C D E F

Doe, rae, me, faw, sole, law, see, doe, doe, see, law, sole, faw, me, rae, doe. Doe, rae, me, faw, sole, law, see, doe.

C D E F G A B C C B A G F E D C   G A B C D E F G G F E D C B A G

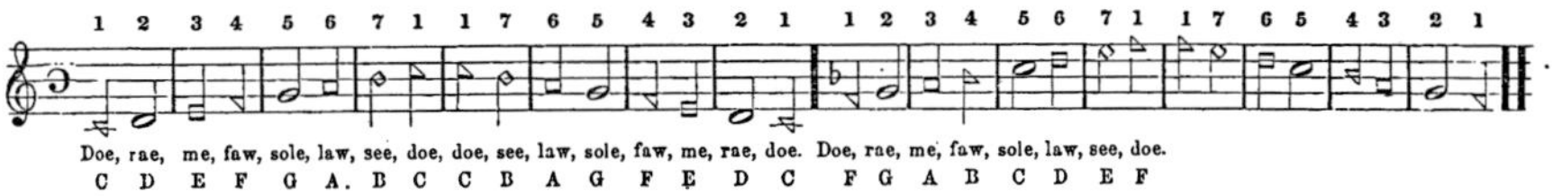

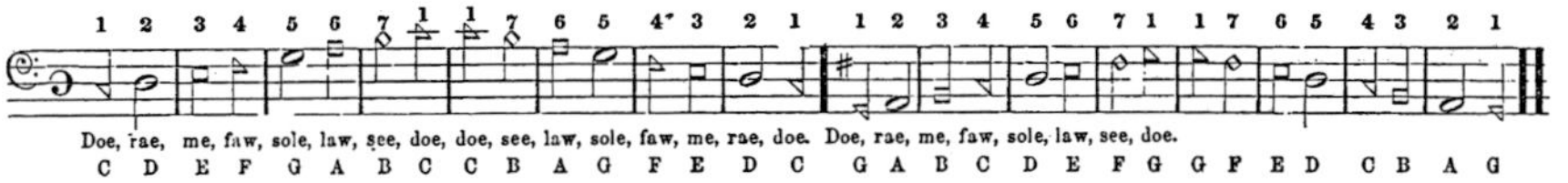

I suppose the above will be sufficient, always observing the same order in other transpositions, remembering that the major or sharp key-note faw, is called doe; sing the scale thus, doe, rae, me, &c., ascending; and doe, see, law, &c. descending: numerical sing 1, 2, 3, &c. ascending; and 1, 7, 6, &c. descending. For singing seven syllables *Italian* and the *numerical*, the transposition tables are generally written thus:

The natural place for doe or 1 is on...C
But if B be flat, the place for doe or 1 is on..F
If B and E be flat, the place for doe or 1 is on...B
If B, E, and A be flat, the place for doe or 1 is on....................................E
If B, E, A, and D be flat, the place for doe or 1 is on...............................A
If F be sharp, the place for doe or 1 is on..G
If F and C be sharp, the place for doe or 1 is on.....................................D

If F, C, and G be sharp, the place for doe or 1 is on................................A
If F, C, G, and D be sharp, the place for doe or 1 is on...........................E

In singing the seven syllables in our patent-note books, no regard is had to the shape of the notes, but name them as laid down in the rule and examples; and in singing numerals, call the major key doe, or faw, 1, and the other notes by the numerical distance they are from the major key; and if you wish to use the other plans, sing as herein directed.

Some contend that no one can learn to sing correctly without using the seven syllables. Although I have no objections to the seven syllable plan, I differ a little with such in opinion, for I have taught the four syllables patent notes, the Italian seven syllables, and the numerals also, and in twenty-five years' experience, have always found my patent note pupils to learn as fast, and sing as correct as any. Consequently I think that the main thing is to get *good teachers*, who understand the science of music well, and teach it faithfully, and who always keep good order in their schools; and that the various plans of notation or solmization may be considered more a matter of taste than necessity.

THE AUTHOR.

July, 1854.

DICTIONARY OF MUSICAL TERMS.

Adagio, very slow, the first mood in common time C.
Allegro, lively, quick, the third mood in common time C.
Accent, a stress of the voice on a particular note or syllable.
Acrostic, a poem, the first letters of the lines of which form a name.
Air, the tenor part, the inclination of a piece of music.
Alt, high above the stave.
Alto, or *Altus*, high counter.
Appetone, between a tone and semitone.
Affettuoso, tender, affecting, mournful, plaintive.
Andante, moderate.
Bass, the lowest part of music, grove, solemn.
Bassoon, a kind of wind instrument for bass.
Bass Viol, a large or bass fiddle.
Breve, an ancient note II, equal to two semibreves.
Blank verse, a poem without rhyme.
Canticles, divine or pious poems, songs.
Chant, to sing praises.
Conorous, loud and harmonious.
Chord, a sound, a concord, proportional vibrations.
Chorus, all the parts together.
Clefs, characters representing particular sounds or degrees.
Comma, a small part, as 1 4, 1-5th, &c. of a tone.
Crescendo, increasing in sounds, &c.
Compose, to make tunes or set notes for music.
Concert, many singers or instruments together.
Counter, is high treble performed in a female voice.
Diagram, the gamut or rudiments of music.
Diapason an octave, an eighth degree.
Dissonance, discord, disagreement.
Drama, a tragical piece for the stage to be acted.
Duet, two parts only moving together.
Diminuendo, diminishing in sound, becoming louder.
Forte, or *For*, full, loud, or strong.
Fuge, or *Fugha*, the parts of music following each other in succession.
Gamut, the scale or rudiments of music.
Grand, full, great, complete, pleasing.
Grave, slow, solemn, mournful, most slow.
Guido, a direct.
Harmony, a pleasing union of sounds.
Harmonist, a writer of harmony, a musician.
Hexameter, having six lines to a verse.
Hautboy or *Hoboy*, a kind of wind instrument.

Inno, a hymn or song.
Intonation, giving the pitch or key of a tune.
Interval, the distance between two degrees or sounds.
Ionic, light and soft.
Keys, pieces of silver, ivory, &c. for the fingers, on an instrument.
Key note, the principal or leading note of each octave.
Largo, one degree quicker than the second mood in common time.
Lima, the difference between major and minor.
Lento, slow.
Major mood, the sharp key, the great third, high, cheerful.
Major chord, an interval having more semitones than a minor chord of the same degrees.
Medius, is low treble performed in a man's voice.
Moods, certain proportions of time, &c.
Modulate, to regulate sounds, to sing in a pleasing manner.
Musica, the art of music, the study or science of music.
Music, a succession of pleasing sounds, one of the liberal sciences.
Necessario, continuing like thorough-bass.
Notes, seven characters representing the degrees or sounds of music
The syllables applied by the Italians are as follows, viz.

Ut Re Mi Faw Sol La Si	But this plan has not been finally adopted for the
C D E F G A B	English music.

Octave, an eighth degree, six tones and two semitones.
Ode, a poem.
Organ, the largest of all musical instruments.
Pastoral, rural, a shepherd's song, something pertaining to a shepherd.
Piano, or *Pia*. directs the performer to sing soft, a kind of instrument.
Pentemeter, five lines to each verse.
Pitchpipe, a small instrument for proving sounds.
Satire, a poem written to expose vice and folly.
Selah, a note often used in the Psalms of David, the true import of which is unknown perhaps it may be a musical character requiring attention, or signifying *amen*.
Serenade, a night song, music played in the evening to entertain a friend or lover.
Solo, one part alone.
Symphony, a piece of music without words, which the instrument plays while the voices rest.
Syncope, cut off, disjointed, out of the usual order
Syncopation, notes joined in the same degree in one position.
Trill, or *Tr.*, a tune like a shake or roll.
Transposition, the changing the place of the key note.
Trio, a tune in three parts.
Violoncello, a tenor viol, 1-8th above a bass viol

PART I.

CONTAINING

MOST OF THE PLAIN AND EASY TUNES COMMONLY USED IN TIME OF DIVINE WORSHIP.

LIVERPOOL. C. M.

M. C. H. Davis. Mercer's Cluster, page 146

Young people all, at - ten - tion give, And hear what I shall say; I wish your souls with Christ to live, In ev - er - last - ing day.
Remember you are hast'ning on To death's dark, gloomy shade; Your joys on earth will soon be gone, Your flesh in dust be laid.

2 Death's iron gate you must pass through,
Ere long, my dear young friends;
With whom then do you think to go,
With saints or fiery fiends?
Pray meditate before too late,
While in a gospel land,
Behold King Jesus at the gate,
Most lovingly doth stand

3 Young men, how can you turn your face
From such a glorious friend;
Will you pursue your dang'rous ways?
O don't you fear the end?
Will you pursue that dang'rous road
Which leads to death and hell?
Will you refuse all peace with God,
With devils for to d-ell?

4 Young women too, what will you do,
If out of Christ you die?
From all God's people you must go,
To weep, lament, and cry:
Where you the least relief can't find,
To mitigate your pain;
Your good things all be left behind,
Your souls in death remain

5 Young people all, I pray then view
The fountain open'd wide;
The spring of life open'd for sin,
Which flow'd from Jesus' side;
There you may drink in endless joy,
And reign with Christ your king,
In his glad notes your souls employ,
And hallelujahs sing.

INVITATION 8 7 4. *Wm Walker.* Baptist Harmony, p 249

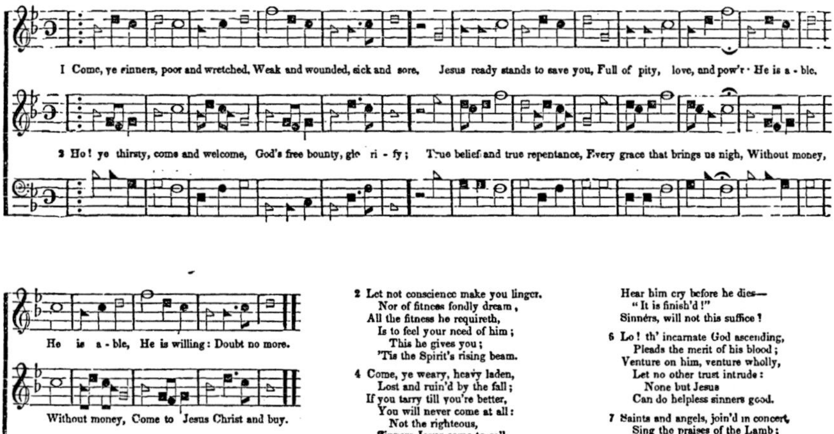
1 Come, ye sinners, poor and wretched, Weak and wounded, sick and sore, Jesus ready stands to save you, Full of pity, love, and pow'r · He is a - ble,
3 Ho! ye thirsty, come and welcome, God's free bounty, glo ri - fy; True belief and true repentance, Every grace that brings us nigh, Without money,

He is a - ble, He is willing: Doubt no more.
Without money, Come to Jesus Christ and buy.

2 Let not conscience make you linger,
Nor of fitness fondly dream,
All the fitness he requireth,
Is to feel your need of him;
This he gives you;
'Tis the Spirit's rising beam.

4 Come, ye weary, heavy laden,
Lost and ruin'd by the fall;
If you tarry till you're better,
You will never come at all:
Not the righteous,
Sinners Jesus came to call.

6 View him prostrate in the garden,
On the ground your Saviour lies
On the bloody tree behold him
Hear him cry before he dies—
"It is finish'd!"
Sinners, will not this suffice?

6 Lo! th' incarnate God ascending,
Pleads the merit of his blood;
Venture on him, venture wholly,
Let no other trust intrude:
None but Jesus
Can do helpless sinners good.

7 Saints and angels, join'd in concert,
Sing the praises of the Lamb;
While the blissful seats of heaven
Sweetly echo with his name
Hallelujah!
Sinners here may sing the same

PRIMROSE C. M.

Chapin. Hymn 88. B. 2. Watts 3

1 Sal - vation! O the joyful sound! 'Tis pleasure to our ears; A sovereign balm for every wound, A cor - dial for our fears
2 Buried in sor - row and in sin, At hell's dark door we lay, But we a - rise by grace di - vine, To see a heav'nly day
3 Sal - vation! let the echo fly The spacious earth around, While all the ar - mies of the sky Conspire to raise the sound.

KEDRON. L. M.

Dare.

Thou Man of grief, remember me; Thou never canst thy - self for - get Thy last ex - piring ag - o - ny—Thy fainting pangs and bloody sweat.

MEDITATION. L. M

Dover Selection, p. 9

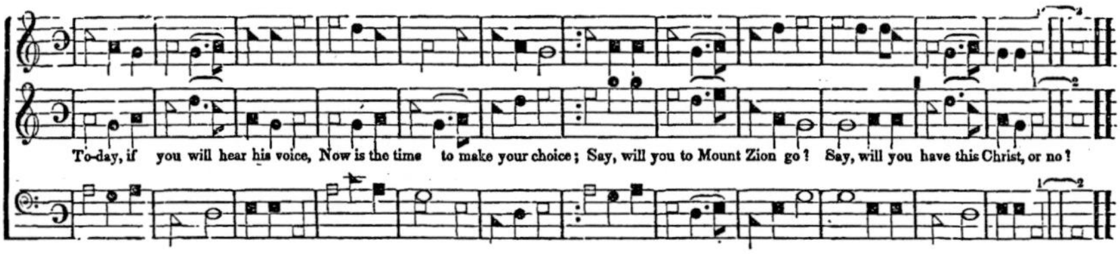
To-day, if you will hear his voice, Now is the time to make your choice; Say, will you to Mount Zion go? Say, will you have this Christ, or no?

HANOVER. C. M.

Baptist Harmony, p. 247.

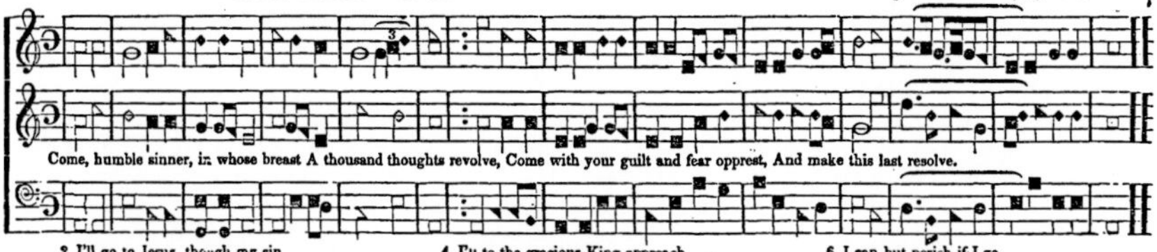
Come, humble sinner, in whose breast A thousand thoughts revolve, Come with your guilt and fear opprest, And make this last resolve.

2 I'll go to Jesus, though my sin
Hath like a mountain rose;
I know his courts, I'll enter in
Whatever may oppose.

3 Prostrate I'll lie before his throne,
And there my guilt confess,
I'll tell him I'm a wretch undone
Without his sovereign grace

4 I'll to the gracious King approach,
Whose sceptre pardon gives;
perhaps he may command my touch,
And then the suppliant lives.

5 Perhaps he may admit my plea,
Perhaps will hear my prayer;
But if I perish, I will pray,
And perish only there

6 I can but perish if I go,
I am resolv'd to try;
For if I stay away, I know
I must for ever die.

7 But if I die with mercy sought,
When I the King have tried,
This were to die (delightful thought
As sinner never died.

SUPPLICATION. L. M.

51st Psalm. Watts

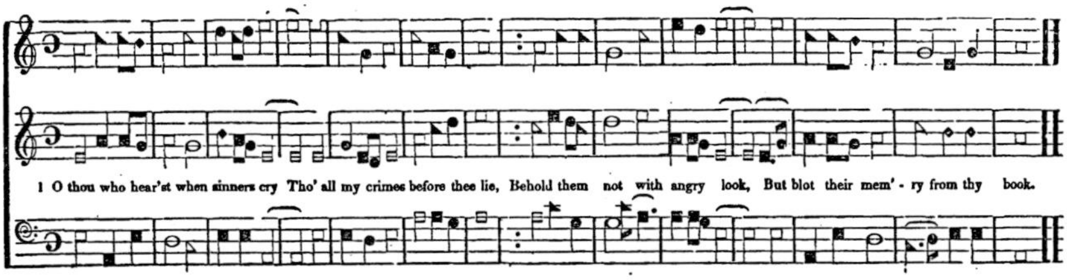
1 O thou who hear'st when sinners cry Tho' all my crimes before thee lie, Behold them not with angry look, But blot their mem' - ry from thy book.

RESTORATION. 8, 7.

Mercy, O thou Son of Da - vid! Thus blind Barti - meus pray'd: Others by thy grace are saved, O vouchsafe to me thine aid.
1
2

MARYSVILLE. L. M

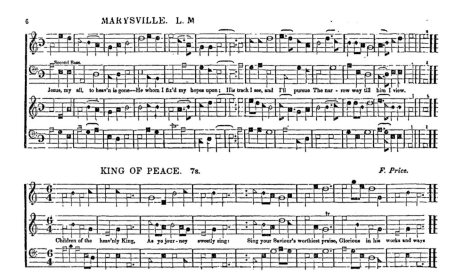

Second Bass.
Jesus, my all, to heav'n is gone—He whom I fix'd my hopes upon; His track I see, and I'll pursue The nar - row way till him I view.

KING OF PEACE. 7s.

F. Price.

Children of the heav'nly King, As ye jour - ney sweetly sing: Sing your Saviour's worthiest praise, Glorious in his works and ways

NINETY-THIRD PSALM. S. M.

Chapin. Baptist Harmony, p. 121.

1 Grace! 'tis a charm - ing sound: Har - mo - nious to the ear! Heav'n with the e - cho shall re sound, And all the earth shall hear.
2 Grace first con - trived the way To save re - bel - lious man; And all the steps that grace dis - play, Which drew the wondrous plan.

3 Grace first inscribed my name
In God's eternal book;
'Twas grace that gave me to the Lamb,
Who all my sorrows took.

4 Grace led my roving feet
To tread the heavenly road;
And new supplies each hour I meet,
While pressing on to God.

5 Grace taught my soul to pray,
And made my eyes o'erflow;
'Twas grace that kept me to this day,
And will not let me go.

6 Grace all the work shall crown,
Through everlasting days;
It lays in heaven the topmost stone,
And well deserves the praise

WEEPING SAVIOUR. S. M.

E. J. King.

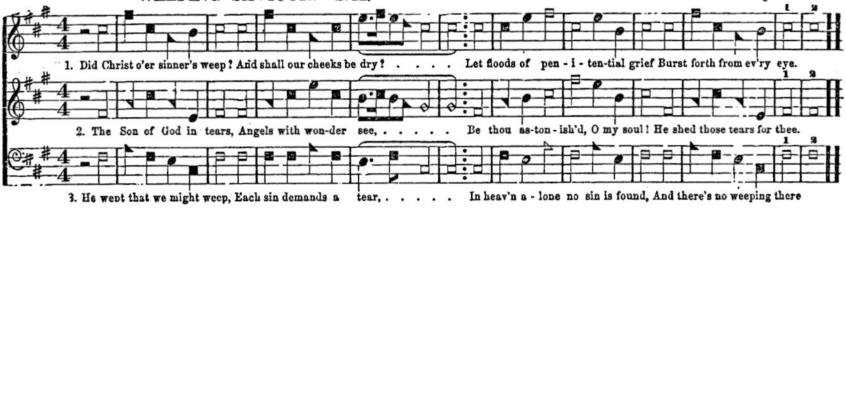
1. Did Christ o'er sinner's weep? And shall our cheeks be dry? . . . . . Let floods of pen - i - ten-tial grief Burst forth from ev'ry eye.
2. The Son of God in tears, Angels with won-der see, ... Be thou as-ton - ish'd, O my soul! He shed those tears for thee.
3. He went that we might weep, Each sin demands a tear, ... In heav'n a - lone no sin is found, And there's no weeping there

NEW BRITAIN. C. M.

Baptist Harmony, p. 123.

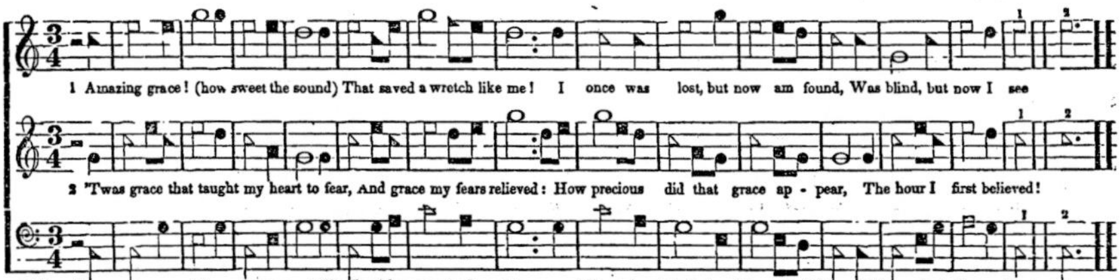
1 Amazing grace! (how sweet the sound) That saved a wretch like me! I once was lost, but now am found, Was blind, but now I see
2 'Twas grace that taught my heart to fear, And grace my fears relieved: How precious did that grace ap - pear, The hour I first believed!
1
2

3 Through many dangers, toils, and snares,
I have already come;
'Tis grace has brought me safe thus far,
And grace will lead me home.

4 The Lord has promised good to me,
His word my hope secures;
He will my shield and portion be,
As long as life endures.

5 Yes, when this flesh and heart shall fail,
And mortal life shall cease,
I shall possess, within the veil,
A life of joy and peace.

6 The earth shall soon dissolve like snow,
The sun forbear to shine;
But God, who call'd me here below,
Will be for ever mine.

COOKHAM. 7's.

Baptist Harmony, p. 329.

Lord I cannot let thee go, Till a blessing thou bestow; Do not turn a - way thy face, Mine's an urgent, pressing case.
1
2

THE CONVERTED THIEF. C. M. D *More.* Mercer's Cluster, p. 31.

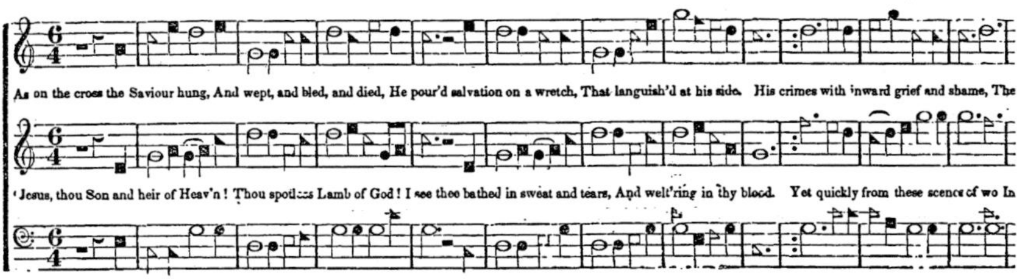
As on the cross the Saviour hung, And wept, and bled, and died, He pour'd salvation on a wretch, That languish'd at his side. His crimes with inward grief and shame, The
'Jesus, thou Son and heir of Heav'n! Thou spotless Lamb of God! I see thee bathed in sweat and tears, And welt'ring in thy blood. Yet quickly from these scenes of wo In

penitent confess'd; Then turn'd his dying eyes to Christ, And thus his prayer address'd:
triumph thou shalt rise; Burst thro' the gloomy shades of death, And shine above the skies

"Amid the glories of that world,
Dear Saviour, think on me,
And in the victories of thy death,
Let me a sharer be."
His prayer the dying Jesus hears,
And instantly replies,
To-day thy parting soul shall be
With me in Paradise.'

WEBSTER. S. M.

Come, we that love the Lord, And let our joys be known; Join in a song with sweet accord, And thus surround the throne

ORTONVILLE. C. M.

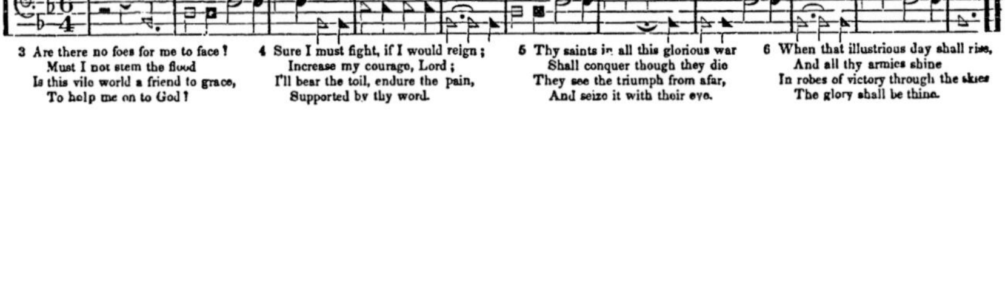
SLOW. NEW TREBLE.
1. Am I a sol-dier of the cross, A fol-low'r of the Lamb? And shall I fear to own his cause, Or blush to speak his name? Or blush to speak his name?
OLD TREBLE.
2. Must I be car-ried to the skies On flow'ry beds of ease, While others fought to win the prize, And sailed thro' bloody seas? And sailed thro' bloody seas?

3 Are there no foes for me to face?
Must I not stem the flood
Is this vile world a friend to grace,
To help me on to God?

4 Sure I must fight, if I would reign;
Increase my courage, Lord;
I'll bear the toil, endure the pain,
Supported by thy word.

5 Thy saints in all this glorious war
Shall conquer though they die
They see the triumph from afar,
And seize it with their eye.

6 When that illustrious day shall rise,
And all thy armies shine
In robes of victory through the skies
The glory shall be thine.

JERUSALEM. L. M.

Wm. Walker. Baptist Harmony, p. 70.

1 Je - sus my all to heav'n is gone, He whom I fix my hopes up - on;
His track I see, and I'll pur - sue The narrow way till him I view
Chorus.
2 The way the ho - ly prophets went; The road that leads from banishment;
The King's highway of ho - li - ness, I'll go, for all his paths are peace.
I'm on my journey home, to the new Jeru-
I'm on my journey home, to the new Jerusalem.
sa lem, :‖: So fare you well, :‖: :‖: I am going home.

3 This is the way I long have sought,
And mourn'd because I found it not;
My grief a burden long has been,
Because I was not saved from sin.

4 The more I strove against its power,
I felt its weight and guilt the more;
Till late I heard my Saviour say,
"Come hither, soul, I AM THE WAY."

5 Lo! glad I come, and thou, blest Lamb,
Shalt take me to thee, whose I am;
Nothing but sin have I to give,
Nothing but love shall I receive.

6 Then will I tell to sinners round,
What a dear Saviour I have found
I'll point to thy redeeming blood,
And say "Behold the way to God!"

SALEM C. M.

Dossey's Choice, p. 58.

1 How sweet the name of Jesus sounds, In a believer's ear; It soothes his sorrows, heals his wounds, And drives away his fear.
And drives away his fear. :‖: It soothes his sorrows, heals his wounds, And drives away his fear.
2 It makes the wounded spi - rit whole, And calms the troubled breast; 'Tis manna to the hungry soul, And to the weary rest
And to the weary rest. :‖: 'Tis manna to the hungry soul, And to the weary rest.

3 Dear name! the rock on which I build,
My shield and hiding-place;
My never-failing treasury, fill'd
With boundless stores of grace.

4 Jesus! my shepherd, husband, friend,
My prophet, priest, and king;
My Lord, my life, my way, my end,
Accept the praise I bring.

5 Weak is the effort of my heart,
And cold my warmest thought;
But when I see thee as thou art,
I'll praise thee as I ought.

6 Till then I would thy love proclaim
With every fleeting breath;
And may the music of thy name
Refresh my soul in death.

DUBLIN. C. M

Lord, what is man, poor fee-ble man! Born of the earth at first; His life a shadow, light and vain, Still hast'ning to the dust.

DEVOTION. L. M.

Sweet is the day of sacred rest, No mortal cares shall seize my breast.
O may my heart in tune be found, Like David's harp of solemn sound.
1
2

MINISTER'S FAREWELL C M

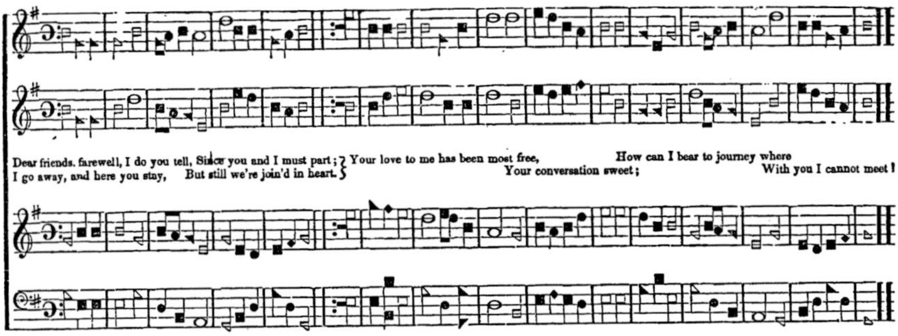
Dear friends, farewell, I do you tell, Since you and I must part; Your love to me has been most free, How can I bear to journey where
I go away, and here you stay, But still we're join'd in heart. Your conversation sweet; With you I cannot meet!

2 Yet do I find my heart inclined
To do my work below:
When Christ doth call, I trust I shall
Be ready then to go.
I leave you all, both great and small,
In Christ's encircling arms,
Who can you save from the cold grave,
And shield you from all harm.

3 I trust you'll pray, both night and day,
And keep your garments white,
For you and me, that we may be
The children of the light.
If you die first, anon you must,
The will of God be done
I hope the Lord will you reward,
With an immortal crown

4 If I'm call'd home whilst I am gone,
Indulge no tears for me;
I hope to sing and praise my King,
To all eternity.
Millions of years over the spheres
Shall pass in sweet repose,
While beauty bright unto my sight
Thy sacred sweets disclose.

5 I long to go, then farewell wo,
My soul will be at rest;
No more shall I complain or sigh,
But taste the heavenly feast.
O may we meet, and be complete,
And long together dwell,
And serve the Lord with one accord
And so, dear friends, farewell.

DAVIS. 11, 8.

Baptist Harmony, p. 460.

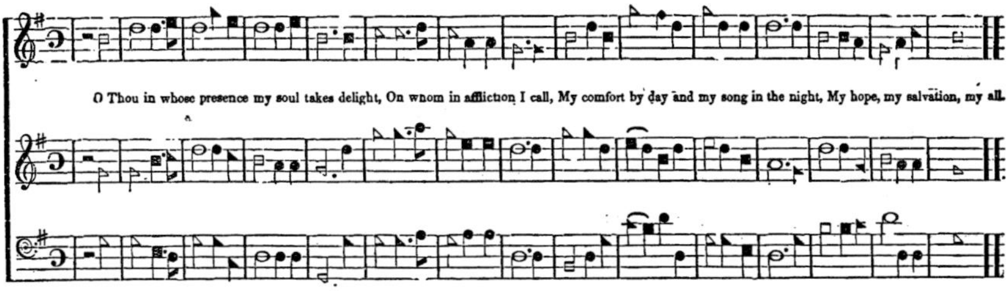
O Thou in whose presence my soul takes delight, On whom in affliction I call, My comfort by day and my song in the night, My hope, my salvation, my all.

2 Where dost thou at noontide resort with thy sheep,
To feed on the pasture of love ?
For why in the valley of death should I weep—
Alone in the wilderness rove !

3 O why should I wander an alien from thee,
Or cry in the desert for bread ?
My foes would rejoice when my sorrows they see,
And smile at the tears I have shed,

4 Ye daughters of Zion, declare, have you seen
The Star that on Israel shone ;
Say if in your tents my Beloved hath been
And where with his flock he hath gone.

5 This is my Beloved, his form is divine,
His vestments shed odours around ;
The locks on his head are as grapes on the vine,
When autumn with plenty is crown'd.

6 The roses of Sharon, the lilies that grow
In vales on the banks of the streams ;
His cheeks in the beauty of excellence blow,
His eye all invitingly beams.

7 His voice, as the sound of a dulcimer sweet,
Is heard through the shadow of death,
The cedars of Lebanon bow at his feet,
The air is perfumed with his breath.

8 His lips as a fountain of righteousness flow,
That waters the garden of grace,
From which their salvation the gentiles shall know
And bask in the smiles of his face.

9 Love sits on his eyelid and scatters delight,
Through all the bright mansions on high ;
Their faces the cherubim veil in his sight,
And tremble with fulness of joy.

10 He looks, and ten thousands of angels rejoice,
And myriads wait for his word ;
He speaks, and eternity, fill'd with his voice,
Re-echoes the praise of her Lord

STAR IN THE EAST 10, 11.

Baptist Harmony, p. 35

Hail the blest morn, see the great Mediator, Down from the regions of glory descend!
Shepherds, go worship the babe in the manger, Lo, for his guard the bright angels attend.
Chorus.
Brightest and best of the sons of the morning!
Dawn on our darkness, and lend us thine aid; Star in the east, the ho - ri - zon a - dorning, Guide where our infant Re - deemer was laid.

2 Cold on his cradle the dew-drops are shining;
Low lies his bed, with the beasts of the stall;
Angels adore him, in slumbers reclining,
Wise men and shepherds before him do fall.
Brightest and best, &c.

3 Say, shall we yield him, in costly devotion,
Odours of Eden, and offerings divine,
Gems from the mountain, and pearls from the ocean,
Myrrh from the forest, and gold from the mine?
Brightest and best, &c.

4 Vainly we offer each ample oblation,
Vainly with gold we his favour secure;
Richer by far is the heart's adoration:
Dearer to God are the prayers of the poor.
Brightest and best, &c.

MIDDLEBURY. 6, 6, 9

Methodist Hymn Book, p. 357

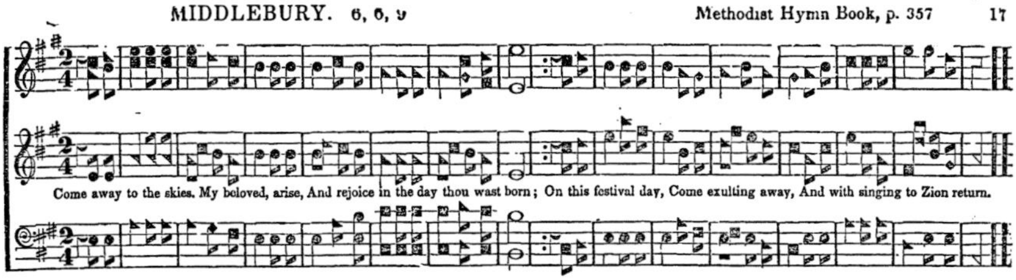
Come away to the skies, My beloved, arise, And rejoice in the day thou wast born; On this festival day, Come exulting away, And with singing to Zion return.

CONSOLATION. C. M.

Dean. Hymn 6. B. 2, Watts.

1 Once more, my soul, the ris - ing day Salutes thy waking eyes; Once more, my voice, thy tri - bute pay To him that rules the skies.
2 Night unto night his name re - peats, The day renews the sound, Wide as the heav'n on which he sits, To turn the sea - sons round.

3 'Tis he supports my mortal frame,
My tongue shall speak his praise;
My sins would rouse his wrath to flame,
And yet his wrath delays.

4 On a poor worm thy pow'r might tread,
And I could ne'er withstand,
Thy justice might have crush'd me dead,
But mercy held thine hand.

5 A thousand wretched souls are fled,
Since the last setting sun,
And yet thou length'nest out my thread,
And yet my moments run.

6 Dear God, let all my hours be thine,
Whilst I enjoy the light.
Then shall my sun in smiles decline,
And bring a pleasant night.

4

COMPLAINER 7. 6.

Wm. Walker

1 I am a great complainer, that bears the name of Christ; Come, all ye Zion mourners, and listen to my cries: I've many sore temptations, and sorrows to my
2 O Lord of life and glory, my sins to me reveal, And by thy love and power, my sin-sick soul be heal'd; I thought my warfare over, no trouble I should

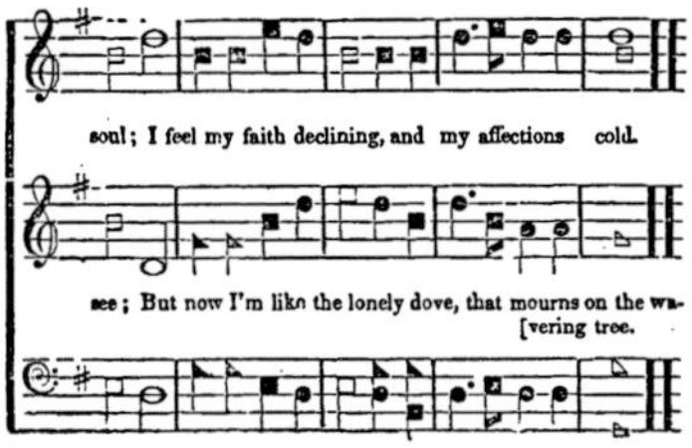
soul; I feel my faith declining, and my affections cold.
see; But now I'm like the lonely dove, that mourns on the wa-
[vering tree.

3 I wish it was with me now, as in the days of old,
When the glorious light of Jesus was flowing in my soul;
But now I am distressed, and no relief can find,
With a hard deceitful heart, and a wretched wandering mind.

4 It is great pride and passion, beset me on my way,
So I am fill'd with folly, and so neglect to pray;
While others run rejoicing, and seem to lose no time,
I am so weak I stumble, and so I'm left behind.

5 I read that peace and happiness meet Christians in their way,
That bear their cross with meekness, and don't neglect to pray
But I, a thousand objects beset me in my way
So I am fill'd with folly, and so neglect to pray.

HICKS' FAREWELL. C. M

Wm Walker.

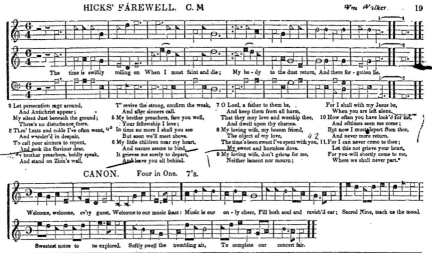

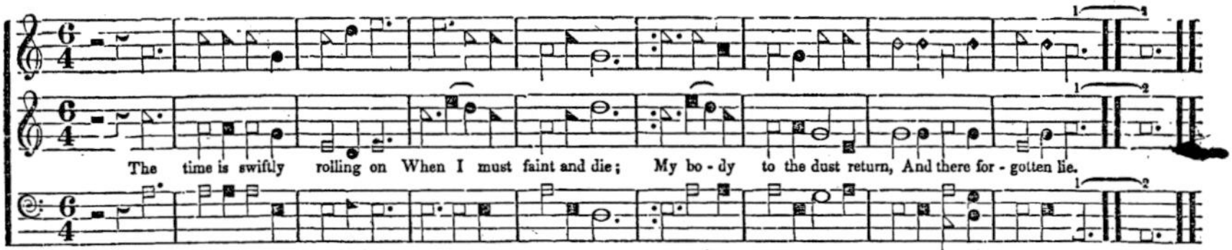

The time is swiftly rolling on When I must faint and die; My bo - dy to the dust return, And there for - gotten lie.

2 Let persecution rage around,
And Antichrist appear;
My silent dust beneath the ground;
There's no disturbance there.
3 Thro' heats and colds I've often went,
And wander'd in despair,
To call poor sinners to repent,
And seek the Saviour dear.
[illegible] brother preachers, boldly speak,
And stand on Zion's wall,
T' revive the strong, confirm the weak,
And after sinners call.
5 My brother preachers, fare you well,
Your fellowship I love;
In time no more I shall you see
But soon we'll meet above.
6 My little children near my heart,
And nature seems to bind,
It grieves me sorely to depart,
And leave you all behind.
7 O Lord, a father to them be,
And keep them from all harm,
That they may love and worship thee,
And dwell upon thy charms.
8 My loving wife, my bosom friend,
The object of my love,
The time's been sweet I've spent with you,
My sweet and harmless dove.
9 My loving wife, don't grieve for me,
Neither lament nor mourn;
For I shall with my Jesus be,
When you are left alone.
10 How often you have look'd for me,
And ofttimes seen me come;
But now I must depart from thee,
And never more return.
11 For I can never come to thee;
Let this not grieve your heart,
For you will shortly come to me,
Where we shall never part.*

CANON. Four in One. 7's.

Welcome, welcome, ev'ry guest, Welcome to our music feast: Music is our on - ly cheer, Fill both soul and ravish'd ear; Sacred Nine, teach us the mood.
Sweetest notes to be explored. Softly swell the trembling air, To complete our concert fair.

* This song was composed by the Rev. B. Hicks, (a Baptist minister of South Carolina,) and sent to his wife while he was confined in Tennessee by a fe[illegible] of which he afterwards recovered

THE FAMILY BIBLE. 12, 11.

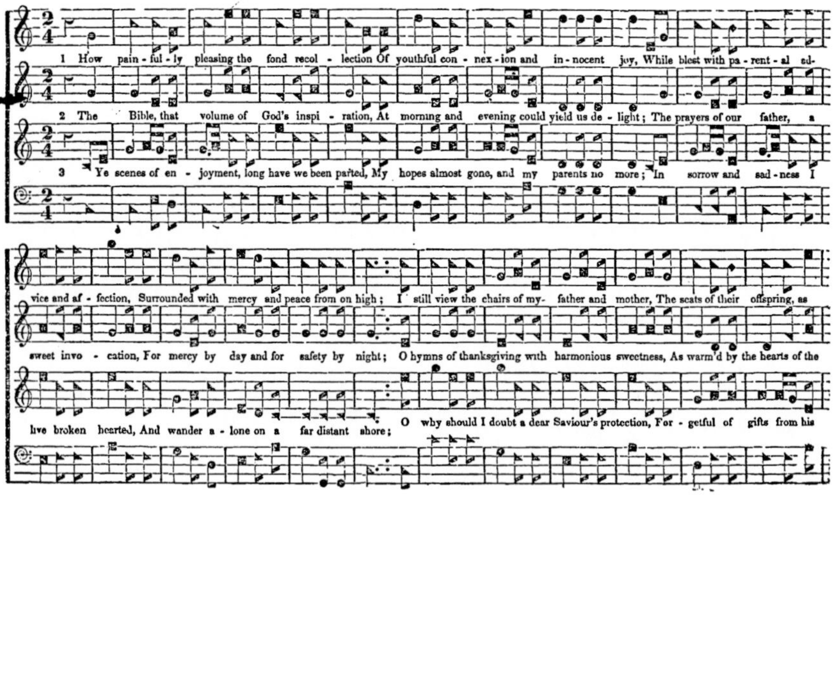
1 How pain - ful - ly pleasing the fond recol - lection Of youthful con - nex - ion and in - nocent joy, While blest with pa - rent - al ad-
2 The Bible, that volume of God's inspi - ration, At morning and evening could yield us de - light; The prayers of our father, a
3 Ye scenes of en - joyment, long have we been parted, My hopes almost gone, and my parents no more; In sorrow and sad - ness I
vice and af - fection, Surrounded with mercy and peace from on high; I still view the chairs of my father and mother, The seats of their offspring, as
sweet invo - cation, For mercy by day and for safety by night; O hymns of thanksgiving with harmonious sweetness, As warm'd by the hearts of the
live broken hearted, And wander a - lone on a far distant shore; O why should I doubt a dear Saviour's protection, For - getful of gifts from his

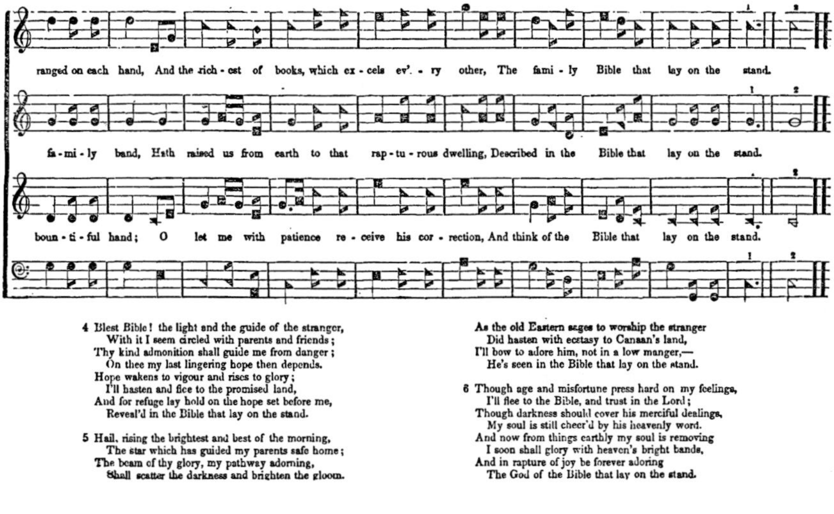
ranged on each hand, And the rich - est of books, which ex - cels ev'. - ry other, The fami - ly Bible that lay on the stand.
fa - mi - ly band, Hath raised us from earth to that rap - tu - rous dwelling, Described in the Bible that lay on the stand.
boun - ti - ful hand; O let me with patience re - ceive his cor - rection, And think of the Bible that lay on the stand.

4 Blest Bible! the light and the guide of the stranger,
With it I seem circled with parents and friends;
Thy kind admonition shall guide me from danger;
On thee my last lingering hope then depends.
Hope wakens to vigour and rises to glory;
I'll hasten and flee to the promised land,
And for refuge lay hold on the hope set before me,
Reveal'd in the Bible that lay on the stand.

5 Hail, rising the brightest and best of the morning,
The star which has guided my parents safe home;
The beam of thy glory, my pathway adorning,
Shall scatter the darkness and brighten the gloom.
As the old Eastern sages to worship the stranger
Did hasten with ecstasy to Canaan's land,
I'll bow to adore him, not in a low manger,—
He's seen in the Bible that lay on the stand.

6 Though age and misfortune press hard on my feelings,
I'll flee to the Bible, and trust in the Lord;
Though darkness should cover his merciful dealings,
My soul is still cheer'd by his heavenly word.
And now from things earthly my soul is removing
I soon shall glory with heaven's bright bands,
And in rapture of joy be forever adoring
The God of the Bible that lay on the stand.

OLD HUNDRED. L. M.

O come, loud anthems let us sing, Loud thanks to our Almighty King, For we our voices high should raise, When our salvation's Rock we praise.

DISTRESS. L. M.

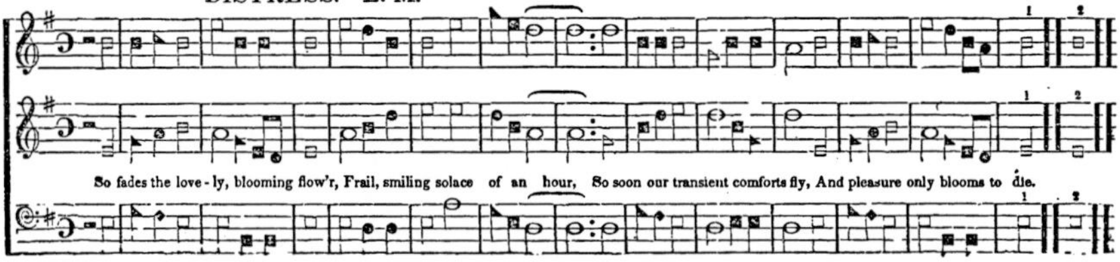
So fades the love - ly, blooming flow'r, Frail, smiling solace of an hour, So soon our transient comforts fly, And pleasure only blooms to die.

ALBION. S. M.

Boyd.

Come, ye that love the Lord, And let your joys be known; Join in a song with sweet accord, And thus surround the throne, And thus, &c.

CHARLESTOWN. 8, 7.

Mercy, O thou Son of David, Thus poor blind Bartimeus pray'd; Others by thy grace are saved, Now to me af - ford thine aid.

PROSPECT OF HEAVEN. 8, 7, 8, 8, 7.

A. Grambling. See Bap. Harm. p. 433

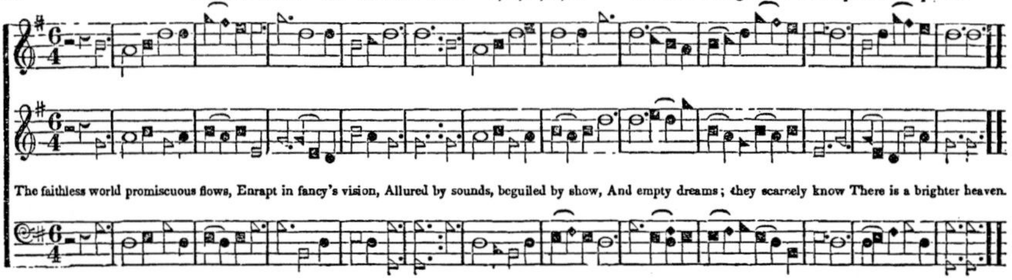
The faithless world promiscuous flows, Enrapt in fancy's vision, Allured by sounds, beguiled by show, And empty dreams; they scarcely know There is a brighter heaven.

MEAR. C. M.

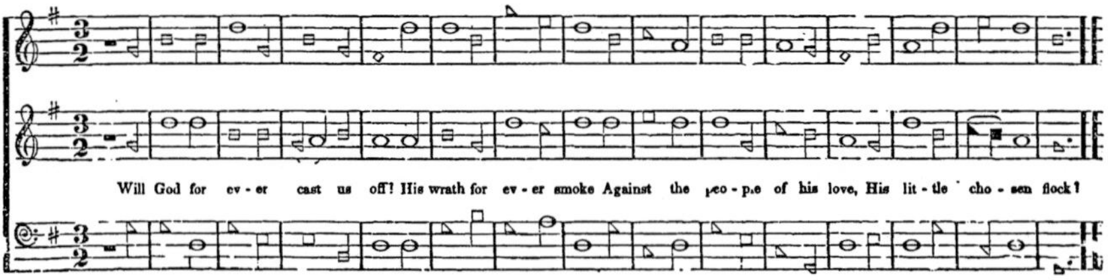
Will God for ev - er cast us off! His wrath for ev - er smoke Against the peo - ple of his love, His lit - tle cho - sen flock!

CRUCIFIXION. 7's, 8.

Baptist Harmony, p. 477

Saw ye my Saviour, :|: Saw ye my Saviour and God? O he died on Calvary, To atone for you and me, And to purchase our pardon with blood.

INDIAN'S FAREWELL. 6 lines 7's.

Wm. Walker.

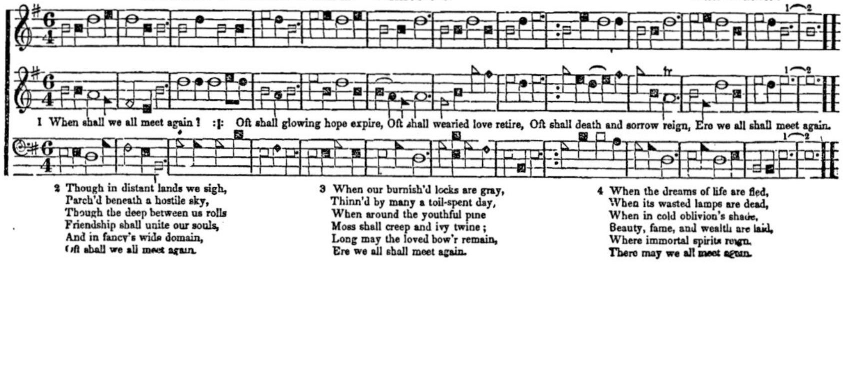
1 When shall we all meet again? :|: Oft shall glowing hope expire, Oft shall wearied love retire, Oft shall death and sorrow reign, Ere we all shall meet again.

2 Though in distant lands we sigh,
Parch'd beneath a hostile sky,
Though the deep between us rolls
Friendship shall unite our souls,
And in fancy's wide domain,
Oft shall we all meet again.

3 When our burnish'd locks are gray,
Thinn'd by many a toil-spent day,
When around the youthful pine
Moss shall creep and ivy twine;
Long may the loved bow'r remain,
Ere we all shall meet again.

4 When the dreams of life are fled,
When its wasted lamps are dead,
When in cold oblivion's shade,
Beauty, fame, and wealth are laid,
Where immortal spirits reign,
There may we all meet again.

THE CHRISTIAN. or CARNSVILLE. 7,7,7,6,7,7,7,6. Zion Songster, p. 78. *E. J. King*

Slow.
1. I love my bless-ed Sa-viour, I feel I'm in his fa-vour, And I am his for ev-er, If I but faith-ful prove;
2. Poor sin-ners may de-ride me, And un-be-liev-ers chide me, But no-thing shall di-vide me From Je-sus, my best friend.
3. The pleas-ing time is hast'-ning, My tott'ring frame is wast-ing While I'm en-gaged in prais-ing, Im-pell-ed by his love
And now I'm bound for Ca-naan, I feel my sins for-giv-en, And soon shall get to hea-ven, To sing re-deem-ing love.
Sup-port-ed by his pow-er, I long to see the hour That bids my spi-rit tow-er, And all my trou-bles end.
When yon-der shin-ing or-ders, Who sing on Ca-naan's bord-ers, Shall bear me to the Lord there To praise his name a-bove

AMERICA. S. M. *Whitmore.*

My soul, repeat his praise, Whose mercies are so great;
Whose anger is so slow to rise, So ready to a - bate.

NINETY-FIFTH. C. M. *Colton.*

When I can read my title clear, To mansions in the skies,
I'll bid farewell to ev'ry fear, and wipe my weeping eyes.

TENNESSEE. C. M.

Baptist Harmony, p. 227.

Afflictions, though they seem severe, Are oft in mercy sent,
They stopp'd the prodigal's career, And caused him to repent.
Although he no re - lent - ing felt Till he had spent his store, His stubborn heart be-

gan to melt When famine pinch'd him sore

3 What have I gain'd by sin, he said,
But hunger, shame, and fear!
My father's house abounds with bread,
Whilst I am starving here.

4 I'll go and tell him all I've done,
Fall down before his face,
Not worthy to be called his son,
I'll seek a servant's place.

5 He saw his son returning back,
He look'd, he ran, he smiled,
And threw his arms around the neck
Of his rebellious child.

6 Father, I've sinn'd, but O forgive.
And thus the father said;
Rejoice, my house! my son's alive,
For whom I mourn'd as dead.

7 Now let the fatted calf be slain,
Go spread the news abroad,
My son was dead, but lives again,
Was lost, but now is found.

8 'Tis thus the Lord himself reveals,
To call poor sinners home,
More than the father's love he feels,
And bids the sinner come

SOLEMN THOUGHT. 12, 9, 12, 12, 9. *F. Price.*

Re - member, sinful youth, you must die, you must die, Re - member, sinful youth, you must die; Re member, sinful
youth, who hato the way of truth. And in your pleasures boast, you must die, you must die; And in your pleasures boast, you must die.

SEPARATION. C. M.

Our cheerful voices let us raise, And sing a part - ing song; Although I'm with you now, my friends, I can't be with you long
For I must go and leave you all, It fills my heart with pain; Although we part, perhaps, in tears, I hope we'll meet again.

IDUMEA S. M

Davison. Meth. Hymn Book. p. 231

And am I born to die? To lay this bo-dy down? And must my trem-bling spi-rit fly, In-to a world un-known?

SUFFIELD. C M.

Teach me the measure of my days, Thou Maker of my frame, I would sur-vey life's nar-row space, And learn how frail I am.

THE MIDNIGHT CRY. 7, 6, 7, 6, 7, 6, 7, 7

Baptist Harmony, p. 483

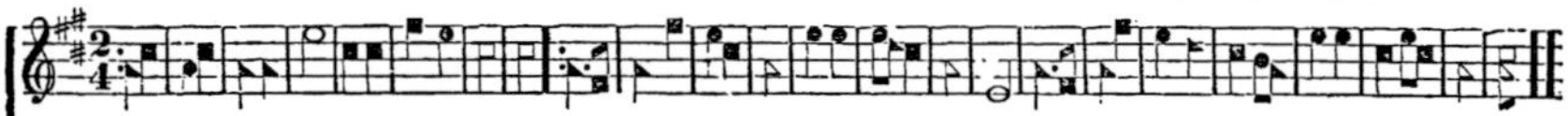

1 When the midnight cry began, O what lamentation,
Thousands sleeping in their sins, Neglecting their salvation. } Lo, the bridegroom is at hand,
Who will kindly treat him? Surely all the waiting bend
Will now go forth to meet him.

2 Some, indeed, did wait awhile, And shone without a rival;
But they spent their seeming oil Long since the last revival. } Many souls who thought they'd light,
O, when the scene was closed, Now against the Bridegroom fight,
And so they stand opposed.

3 While the wise are passing by,
With all their lamps prepared,
Give us of your oil, they cry,
If any can be spared.
Others trimm'd their former snuff,
O, is it not amazing!
Those conclude they've light enough,
And think their lamps are blazing.

4 Foolish virgins! do you think
Our Bridegroom's a deceiver?
Then may you pass your lives away,
And think to sleep for ever;
But we by faith do see his face,
On whom we have believed;
If there's deception in the case,
'Tis you that are deceived.

5 And now the door is open wide,
And Christians are invited,
And virgins wise compass the bride,
March to the place appointed.
Who do you think is now a guest?
Yea, listen, carnal lovers,
'Tis those in wedding garments dress'd;
They cease from sin for ever.

6 The door is shut, and they within,
They're freed from every danger;
They reign with Christ, for sinners slain,
Who once lay in a manger;
They join with saints and angels too
In songs of love and favour;
Glory, honour, praise and power,
To God and Lamb for ever.

7 The foolish virgins are without;
The sentence, Go ye cursed—
For want of oil they're out—away
From Christ they then are forced.
No more on earth with saints to join
In sharing of my favour;
Although you did my children blind,
Mourn with the damn'd for ever.

8 Virgins wise, I pray draw near,
And listen to your Saviour;
He is your friend, you need not fear,
O, why not seek his favour?
He speaks to you in whispers sweet,
In words of consolation:
By grace in him you stand complete,
He is your great salvation.

9 Dying sinners, will you come,
The Saviour now invites you;
His bleeding wounds proclaim there's [room,
Let nothing then affright you—
Room for you, and room for me,
And room for coming sinners:
Salvation pours a living stream
For you and all believers.

10 When earth and sea shall be no more,
And all their glory perish,
When sun and moon shall cease to shine,
And stars at midnight languish;
When Gabriel's trump shall sound aloud,
To call the slumb'ring nations,
Then, Christians, we shall see our God
The God of our salvation.

CONFIDENCE. 10, 10, 11, 11.

Mercer's Cluster, p. 405

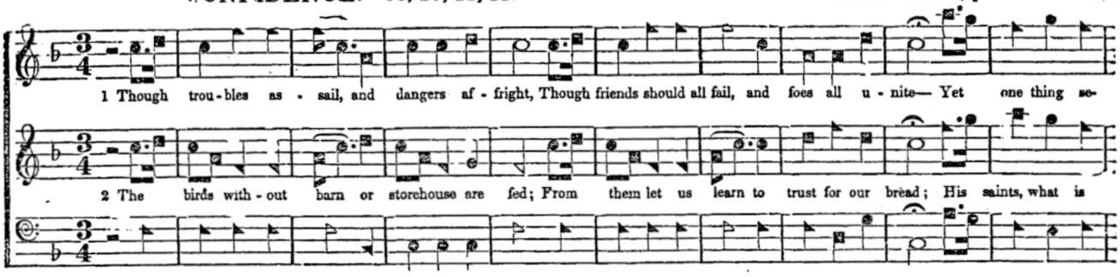
1 Though trou-bles as - sail, and dangers af - fright, Though friends should all fail, and foes all u - nite— Yet one thing se-
2 The birds with-out barn or storehouse are fed; From them let us learn to trust for our bread; His saints, what is

cures us, what - ev - er be - tide, The Scripture as - sures us the Lord will provide.
fi - ting shall ne'er be de - nied, So long as 'tis written, the Lord will pro - vide.

3 We may, like the ships, by tempests be toss'd
On perilous deeps, but cannot be lost:
Though Satan enrages the wind and the tide,
The promise engages the Lord will provide

4 His call we obey, like Abram of old,
Not knowing our way, but faith makes us bold;
For though we are strangers, we have a good guide,
And trust, in all dangers, the Lord will provide.

5 When Satan appears to stop up our path,
And fill us with fears, we triumph by faith;
He cannot take from us, though oft he has tried,
This heart-cheering promise, the Lord will provide

6 He tells us we're weak, our hope is in vain;
The good that we seek we ne'er shall obtain;
But when such suggestions our spirits have plied,
This answers all questions, the Lord will provide.

7 No strength of our own, or goodness we claim;
Yet since we have known the Saviour's great name,
In this our strong tow'r for safety we hide;
The Lord is our pow'r, the Lord will provide.

8 When life sinks apace, and death is in view,
This word of his grace shall comfort us through:
No fearing or doubting with Christ on our side,
We hope to die shouting, the Lord will provide

VERNON. L. M

Chapin. Methodist Hymn Book, p. 77.

Come, O thou travel - ler unknown, Whom still I hold, but cannot see,
My company before is gone, And I am left alone with thee;
With thee all night I mean to stay, And wrestle till the break of day.

2 I need not tell thee who I am;
My misery and sin declare;
Thyself hast call'd me by my name,
Look on thy hands and read it there.
But who, I ask thee, who art thou?
Tell me thy name, and tell me now.

3 In vain thou strugglest to get free,
I never will unloose my hold;
Art thou the man who died for me?
The secret of thy love unfold:
Wrestling, I will not let thee go,
Till I thy name, thy nature know.

4 Wilt thou not yet to me reveal
Thy new, unutterable name?
Tell me, I still beseech thee, tell;
To know it now resolved I am:
Wrestling, I will not let thee go,
Till I thy name, thy nature know.

5 What though my shrinking flesh complain,
And murmur to contend so long,
I rise superior to my pain;
When I am weak, then I am strong!
And when my all of strength shall fail,
I shall with the God-man prevail.

IMANDRA NEW. 11's.

Dover Selection, p. 196.

Farewell, my dear brethren, the time is at hand,
When we must be parted from this social band:
Our several engagements now call us away,
Our parting is needful, and we must obey.

CROSS OF CHRIST. C. M. D.

L. P. Breedlove.

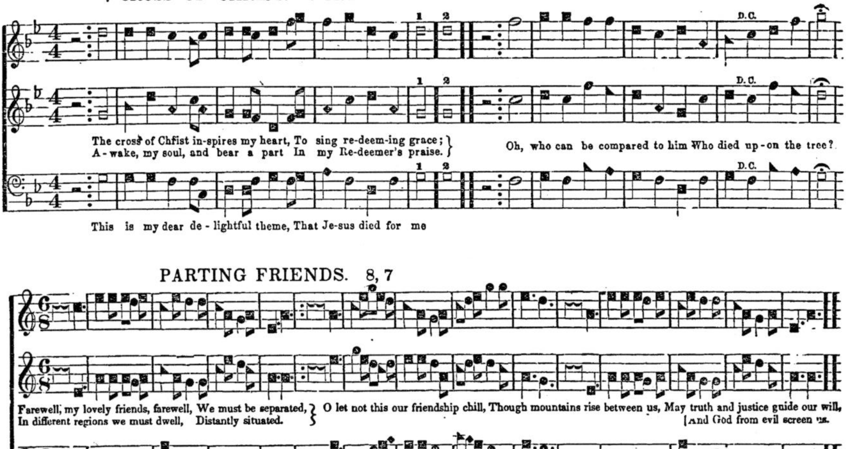
1 2
D.C.
The cross of Christ in-spires my heart, To sing re-deem-ing grace;
A-wake, my soul, and bear a part In my Re-deemer's praise.
Oh, who can be compared to him Who died up-on the tree?
This is my dear de-lightful theme, That Je-sus died for me

PARTING FRIENDS. 8, 7

Farewell, my lovely friends, farewell, We must be separated,
In different regions we must dwell, Distantly situated.
O let not this our friendship chill, Though mountains rise between us, May truth and justice guide our will,
And God from evil screen us.

THE SOLDIER'S RETURN. 8. 7

1 Bright scenes of glory strike my sense, And all my pas - sions cap - ture ; } I live in pleasures deep and full, In
E - ternal beauties round me shine, In - fusing warm - est rap - ture. }
swell - ng waves of glo - ry I feel my Saviour in my soul, And groan to tell my sto ry
1 2

I find myself placed in a state of probation, Which God has commanded us well to improve,
And I am resolved to regard all his precepts, And on in the way of obedience to move.
I know I must go through great tribulation,
And many sore conflicts on ev-e-ry hand; But grace will support and comfort my spi-rit, And I shall be able for ever to stand.
1
2

2 I'm call'd to contend with the powers of darkness,
And many sore conflicts I have to pass through;
O Jesus, be with me in every battle,
And help me my enemies all to subdue;
If thou, gracious Lord, will only be with me,
To aid and direct me, then all will be right;
Apollyon, with all his powerful forces,
In thy name and thy strength I shall soon put to flight.

3 And when I must cross the cold stream of Jordan,
I'll bid all my sorrows a final adieu,
And hasten away to the land of sweet Canaan,
Where, Christians, I hope I shall there meet with you.
That rest into which my soul shall then enter,
Is perfectly glorious, and never shall end—
A rest of exemption from warfare and labour,
A rest in the bosom of Jesus, my friend.

4 And more than exemption from fighting and hardship
My gracious Redeemer will grant unto me;
A portion of bliss he has promised to give me,
And true to that promise he surely will be.
Yes, I shall receive and always inherit
A happy reception and truly divine.
For which all the praises and glory, my Saviour
Are due unto thee, and shall ever be thine.

RESIGNATION. C. M.

My Shep-herd will sup-ply my need; Je - ho - vah is his name;
In pas - tures fresh he makes me feed, Be - side the liv - ing stream.
He brings my wand'-ring spi - rit

back, When I for - sake his ways, And leads me, for his mer - cy's sake, In paths of truth and grace.

2. When I walk thro' the shades of death
   Thy presence is my stay;
   One word of thy supporting breath
   Drives all my fears away.
   Thy hand, in sight of all my foes,
   Doth still my table spread;
   My cup with blessings overflows,
   Thine oil anoints my head.

3. The sure provisions of my God
   Attend me all my days;
   O may thy house be mine abode,
   And all my work be praise!
   There would I find a settled rest,
   (While others go and come,)
   No more a stranger, nor a guest;
   But like a child at home.

BOZRAH 8 lines 7's

Who is this that comes from far, With his garments dipp'd in blood,
Strong, triumphant traveller— Is he man, or is he God?
I that reign in righteousness,
Son of God and man I am;
Mighty to redeem your race,
Jesus is your Saviour's name.

UNION. 8's.

Billings.

1 2
From whence does this union arise, That hatred is conquer'd by love? It fastens our souls with such ties, That distance and time can't remove.

2 It cannot in Eden be found,
Nor yet in Paradise lost;
grows on Immanuel's ground,
And Jesus' dear blood it did cost.

3 My friends once so dear unto me,
Our souls so united in love:
Where Jesus is gone we shall be
In yonder blest mansions above.

4 With Jesus we ever shall reign,
And all his bright glory shall see,
Singing hallelujahs, Amen,
Amen! even so let it be.

DETROIT. C. M

Bradshaw. Baptist Harmony, p. 139

1 Do not I love thee, O my Lord? Behold my heart, and see: And turn each cursed idol out, That dares to rival thee.
2 Do not I love thee from my soul? Then let me nothing love; Dead be my heart to every joy, When Jesus cannot move.
3 Is not thy name melodious still, To mine attentive ear? Doth not each pulse with pleasure bound, My Saviour's voice to hear?

4 Hast thou a lamb in all thy flock,
I would disdain to feed?
Hast thou a foe before whose face
I fear thy cause to plead?

5 Would not my ardent spirit vie,
With angels round thy throne,
To execute thy sacred will,
And make thy glory known?

6 Would not my heart pour forth its blood
In honour of thy name,
And challenge the cold hand of death
To damp th' immortal flame!

7 Thou know'st I love thee, dearest Lord ·
But, O! I long to soar,
Far from the sphere of mortal joys,
And learn to love thee more.

HAPPINESS. C. M

No more beneath th' op - pressive hand Of ty - ran - ny we mourn, Be - hold, a smil - ing, hap - py land, That freedom calls her own.

THE SPIRITUAL SAILOR. 7, 6. *I. Neighbours.* Dover Selection, p. 133.

1 The people called Christians Have many things to tell About the land of Canaan, Where saints and angels dwell; But here a dismal ocean, Enclosing them a
2 Many have been impatient To work their passage through, And with united wisdom Have tied what they could do; But vessels built by human skill Have never sailed

1 2
round, With its tides, still divides Them from Canaan's happy ground.
far, Till we found them aground On some dreadful, sandy bar.

3 The everlasting gospel
  Hath launch'd the deep at last
Behold the sails expanded
  Around the tow'ring mast!
Along the deck in order,
  The joyful sailors stand,
Crying, "Ho!—here we go
  To Immanuel's happy land

4 We're now on the wide ocean
  We bid the world farewell!
And though where we shall anchor
  No human tongue can tell;
About our future destiny
  There need be no debate,
While we ride on the tide,
  With our Captain and his Mate.

5 To those who are spectators
  What anguish must ensue,
To hear their old companions
  Bid them a last adieu!
The pleasures of your paradise
  No more our hearts invite;
We will sail—you may rail,
  We shall soon be out of sight.

6 The passengers united
  In order, peace, and love;—
The wind is in our favour,
  How swiftly do we move!
Though tempests may assail us,
  And raging billows roar,
We will sweep through the deep,
  Till we reach fair Canaan's shore.

JEFFERSON. 8. 7.

Glorious things of thee are spoken, Zi - on, ci - ty of our God! With sal - va - tion's wall sur - round - ed,
He whose word can ne'er be bro - ken, Form'd thee for his own a - bode.
Thou mayst smile at all thy foes; On the Rock of a - ges found - ed, Who can shake thy sure re - pose!

6
4
Hark ! don't you hear the turtle dove, The token of redeeming love ?
From hill to hill we hear the sound, The neighb'ring valleys echo round.
O Zion, hear the turtle dove, The token of your Saviour's love ! She comes the

desert land to cheer, And welcome in the jubil - year.

2 The winter's past, the rain is o'er,
We fcel the chilling winds no more;
The spring is come; how sweet the view,
All things appear divinely new.
On Zion's mount the watchmen cry,
" The resurrection's drawing nigh :"
Behold, the nations from abroad,
Are flocking to the mount of God.

3 The trumpet sounds, bota far and nigh;
O sinners, turn! why will ye die?
How can you spurn the gospel charms?
Enlist with Christ, gird on your arms.
These are the days that were foretold,
In ancient times, by prophets old:
They long'd to see this glorious light,
But all have died without the sight.

4 The latter days on us have come,
And fugitives ae flocking home;
Bchold them crowd the gospel road,
All pressing to the mount of God.
O yes! and I will join that band,
Now here's my heart, and here's my hand
With Satan's band no more I'll be,
But fight for Christ and liberty.

5 His banner soon will be unfurl'd,
And he will come to judge the world;
On Zion's mountain we shall stand,
In Canaan's fair, celestial land.
When sun and moon shall darken'd be,
And flames consume the land and sea,
When worlds on worlds together blaze,
We'll shout, and loud hosannas raise.

MORALITY. 10, 11, 11

While beauty and youth are in their full prime, And folly and fashion affect our whole time; O let not the phantom our wishes engage, Let us live so in youth that we

blush not in age.

2 The vain and the young may attend us a while,
But let not their flatt'ry our prudence beguile;
Let us covet those charms that shall never decay
Nor listen to all that deceivers can say.

3 I sigh not for beauty, nor languish for wealth,
But grant me, kind Providence, virtue and health;
Then richer than kings, and far happier than they,
My days shall pass swiftly and sweetly away.

4 For when age steals on me, and youth is no more,
And the moralist time shakes his glass at my door,
What pleasure in beauty or wealth can I find?
My beauty, my wealth, is a sweet peace of mind.

5 That peace! I'll preserve it as pure as 'twas given
Shall last in my bosom an earnest of heaven;
For virtue and wisdom can warm the cold scene,
And sixty can flourish as gay as sixteen.

6 And when I the burden of life shall have borne,
And death with his sickle shall cut the ripe corn,
Reascend to my God without murmur or sigh,
I'll bless the kind summons, and lie down and die.

CHRISTIAN SOLDIER. C. M. *F. Price.* Dover Selection, p. 135.

1 Am I a soldier of the cross, A follower of the Lamb,
And shall I fear to own his cause, Or blush to speak his name?
2 Must I be car - ried to the skies On flow'ry beds of ease, While

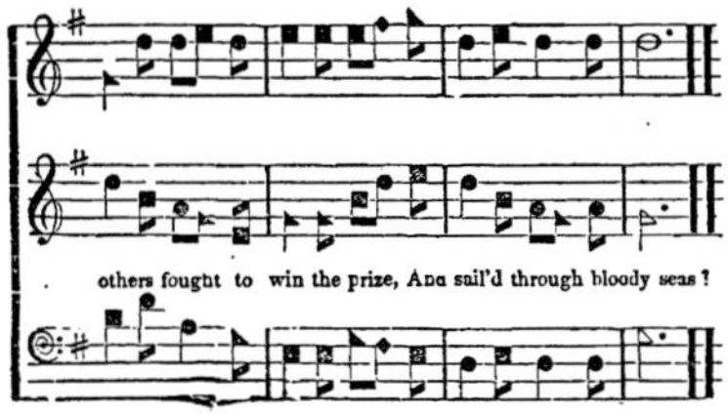
others fought to win the prize, And sail'd through bloody seas?

3 Are there no foes for me to face?
Must I not stem the flood?
Is this vile world a friend to grace,
To help me on to God?

4 Sure I must fight if I would reign;—
Increase my courage, Lord;
I'll bear the toil, endure the pain,
Supported by thy word.

5 Thy saints, in all this glorious war,
Shall conquer though they die;
They see the triumph from afar,
And seize it with their eye.

6 When that illustrious day shall rise,
And all thine armies shine
In robes of vict'ry through the skies,
The glory shall be thine

EVENING SHADE. S. M.

Baptist Harmony, p. 573.

Th. day is past and gone, The evening shades appear; O may we all remember well, O

may we all re - member well, The night of death is near.

2 We lay our garments by,
  Upon our beds to rest;
So death will soon disrobe us all,
  Of what we here possess.

3 Lord, keep us safe this night,
  Secure from all our fears:
May angels guard us while we sleep,
  Till morning light appears.

4 And when we early rise,
  And view th' unwearied sun,
May we set out to win the prize,
  And after glory run.

5 And when our days are past,
  And we from time remove,
O may we in thy bosom rest,
  The bosom of thy love.

Rise, my soul, and   stretch thy wings, Thy better   por - tion trace; Rise from transi -   to - ry things, To heav'n, thy na - tive place

WINDHAM. L. M.

Read. Hymn 158, Book 2, Watts.

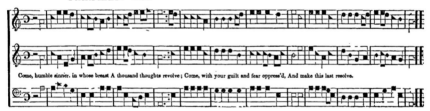

Broad is the road that leads to death, And thousands walk together there; But wisdom shows a narrow path, With here and there a tra - veller.

FAIRFIELD. C. M.

Come, humble sinner, in whose breast A thousand thoughts revolve; Come, with your guilt and fear oppress'd, And make this last resolve.

How lost was my condition, Till Jesus made me whole; There is but one Physician Can cure a sin-sick soul. Next door to death he found me, And snatch'd me from the

grave, To tell to all around me, His wondrous pow'r to save.
6

2 The worst of all diseases
Is light compared with sin;
On every part it seizes,
But rages most within:
'Tis palsy, plague, and fever,
And madness, all combin'd;
And none but a believer
The least relief can find.

3 From men great skill professing,
I thought a cure to gain;
But this proved more distressing,
And added to my pain;
Some said that nothing ail'd me,
Some gave me up for lost;
Thus every refuge fail'd me,
And all my hopes were cross'd.

4 At length this great Physician
(How matchless is his grace.)
Accepted my petition,
And undertook my case;
First gave me sight to view him,
For sin my eyes had seal'd;
Then bid me look unto him—
I look'd, and I was heal'd.

5 A dying, risen Jesus.
Seen by the eye of faith,
At once from anguish frees us,
And saves the soul from death;
Come, then, to this Physician,
His help he'll freely give;
He makes no hard condition,
'Tis only Look and live.

CAPTAIN KIDD. 6, 6, 6, 3, 6, 6, 6, 6, 6, 3.

Mercer's Cluster, p.

Through all the world below, God is seen all around; Search hills and valleys through, There he's found. The growing of the corn, The lily and the thorn, The

pleasant and forlorn, All declare God is there, In the meadows drest in green, There he's [seen.

2 See springs of water rise,
Fountains flow, rivers run;
The mist below the skies
Hides the sun;
Then down the rain doth pour
The ocean it doth roar,
And dash against the shore,
All to praise, in their lays,
That God that ne'er declines
His designs.

3 The sun, to my surprise,
Speaks of God as he flies;
The comets in their blaze
Give him praise;
The shining of the stars.
The moon as it appears,
His sacred name declares;
See them shine, all divine!
The shades in silence prove
God's above.

4 Then let my station be
Here on earth, as I see
The sacred One in Three
All agree;
Through all the world is made,
The forest and the glade;
Nor let me be afraid,
Though I dwell on the hill,
Since nature's works declare
God is there.

THE PROMISED LAND. C. M. *Miss M. Durham* Meth. H. B. p. 471

Chorus.
Tenor.
On Jordan's stormy banks I stand, And cast a wish - ful eye, To Canaan's fair and happy land, Where my possessions lie. I am
bound for the pro - mised land, I'm bound for the pro - mised land, O, who will come and go with me? I am bound for the promised land

BABEL'S STREAMS. C. M.

By Ba - bel's streams we sat and wept, While Zi - on we thought on; A - midst thereof we hung our harps, The willow trees up - on.
With all the pow'r and skill I have, I'll gently touch each string; If I can reach the charming sound, I'll tune my harp a - gain.

MUTUAL LOVE. 7, 6

William Walker

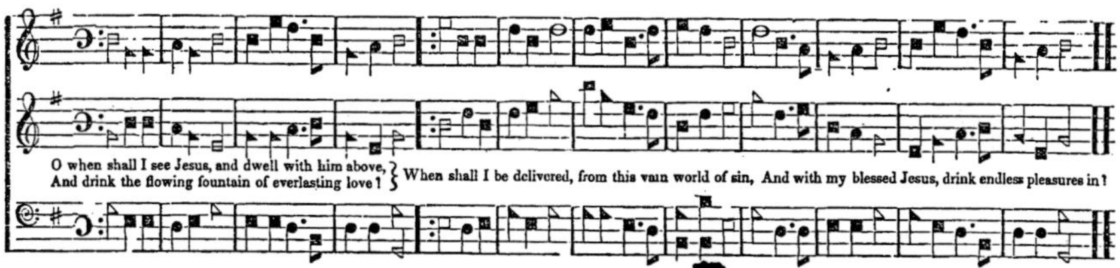
O when shall I see Jesus, and dwell with him above,
And drink the flowing fountain of everlasting love?
When shall I be delivered, from this vain world of sin, And with my blessed Jesus, drink endless pleasures in?

SALEM. L. M.

Methodist Hymn Book, p. 455.

He dies, the Friend of sinners dies! Lo, Salem's daughters weep around; A solemn darkness veils the skies, A sudden trembling shakes the ground.

EXHILARATION. L. M.

Dr. T. W. Carter.

Chorus.
Oh! may I wor - thy prove to see The saints in full pros - per - i - ty: Then my trou-bles will be o - ver.
To see the bride, the glitt'ring bride, Close seat-ed by her Sa-viour's side: Then my trou-bles will be o - ver.
I nev - er shall for - get the day when
Jesus wash'd my sins a-way: And then my troubles will be o - ver, Will be o - - ver, Will be o - ver, And re - joic - ing, And then my trou-bles will be o - ver.

1 O, once I had a glorious view Of my redeeming Lord;
He said, I'll be a God to you, And I believed his word.
But now I have a deeper stroke Than all my groanings are; My
2 O what im - mortal joys I felt, On that ce - les - tial day,
When my hard heart began to melt, By love dissolved away!
But my complaint is bitter now, For all my joys are gone; I've

God has me of late forsook,— He's gone, I know not where.
stray'd!—I'm left!—I know not how · The light's from the withdrawn.

3 Once I could joy the saints to meet,
To me they were most dear;
I then could stoop to wash their feet,
And shed a joyful tea
But now I meet them as the rest,
And with them joyless stay;
My conversation's spiritless,
Or else I've naught to say.

4 I once could mourn o'er dying men,
And long'd their souls to win:
I travail'd for their poor children,
And warn'd them of their sin:
But now my heart's so careless grown,
Although they're drown'd in vice,
My bowels o'er them cease to yearn—
My tears have left mine eyes

5 I forward go in duty's way,
But can't perceive him there;
Then backwards on the road I stray,
But cannot find him there:
On the left hand, where he doth work,
Among the wicked crew,
And on the right, I find him not,
Among the favour'd few.

6 What shall I do?—shall I lie down,
And sink in deep despair?
Will he for ever wear a frown,
Nor hear my feeble pray'r?
No: he will put his strength in me,
He knows the way I've stroll'd
And when I'm tried sufficiently,
I shall come forth as gold.

REDEEMING GRACE. 7. 6

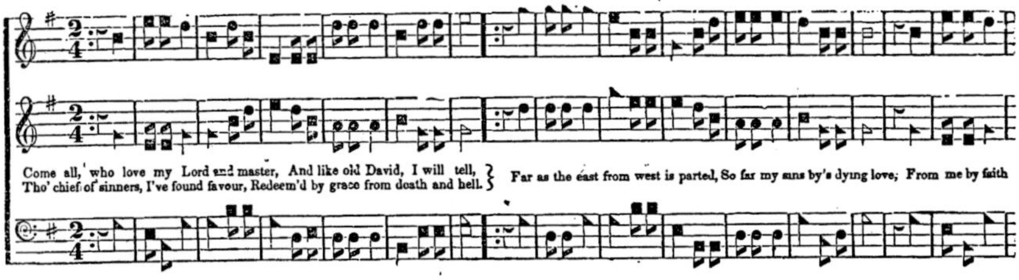
Come all, who love my Lord and master, And like old David, I will tell,
Tho' chief of sinners, I've found favour, Redeem'd by grace from death and hell.
Far as the east from west is parted, So far my sins by's dying love; From me by faith

are se - pa - rated, Blest antepast of joys a - bove.

2 I late estranged from Jesus wander'd,
An thought each dang'rous poison good,
But h in mercy long pursued me,
Wi cries of his redeeming blood.
Thoug a like Bartimeus I was blinde,
In nature's darkest night conceal'd,
But Jesus' love removed my blindness,
And he his pardoning grace reveal'd.

3 Now I will praise him, he spares me,
And with his people sing aloud,
Though opposed, and sinners mock me,
In rapturous songs I'll praise my God.
By faith I view the heavenly concert,
They sing high strains of Jesus' love
O! with desire my soul is longing,
And fain would be with Christ above.

4 That blessed day is fast approaching,
When Christ in glorious clouds will come,
With sounding trumps and shouts of angels,
To call each faithful spirit home.
There's Abraham, Isaac, holy prophets,
And all the saints at God's right hand,
There hosts of angels join in concert,
Shout as they reach the promised land.

THE TRUMPET. 12's

J. Wilh

Treble by Wm. Walker.
The chariot! the chariot! its wheels roll in fire, As the Lord cometh down in the pomp of his ire! Lo! self-moving it drives on its pathway of

cloud, And the heav'ns with the burden of Godhead are bow'd.

2 The glory! the glory! around him are pour'd
Mighty hosts of the angels that wait on the Lord;
And the glorified saints and the martyrs are there,
And there all who the palm wreaths of victory wear.

3 The trumpet! the trumpet! the dead have all heard,
Lo! the depths of the stone-cover'd charnel are stirr'd;
From the sea, from the earth, from the south, from the north,
And the vast generations of man are come forth.

4 The judgment! the judgment! the thrones are all set,
Where the Lamb and the white-vested elders are met;
There all flesh is at once in the sight of the Lord,
And the doom of eternity hangs on his word.

5 O mercy! O mercy! look down from above.
Great Creator, on us, thy sad children, with love;
When beneath to their darkness the wicked are driv'n,
May our justified souls find a welcome in heav'n.

CONSOLATION NEW. – 8, 8, 6

Come on, my partners in dis - tress, My comrades through the wilderness, Who still your bo - dies feel; Awhile forget your
griefs and fears, And look beyond this vale of tears, To that ce - les - tial hill. To that ce - les - tial hill.

SWEET HARMONY. 10's

Wm. Walker. Mercer's Cluster, p. 236

O tell me no more of this world's vain store! The time for such trifles with me is now o'er; A country I've found where true joys abound. To

dwell I'm de - ter - min'd on that happy ground.

2 No mortal doth know what Christ will bestow,
What life, strength and comfort! go after him, go!
Lo, onward I move, to see Christ above,
None guesses how wondrous my journey will prove.

3 Great spoils I shall win, from death, hell, and sin;
Midst outward affliction shall feel Christ within;
And still, which is best, I in his dear breast,
As at the beginning, find pardon and rest.

4 When I am to die, receive me, I'll cry,
For Jesus has lov'd me, I cannot tell why;
But this I do find, we two are so join'd,
He'll not live in glory and leave me behind.

5 This blessing is mine, through favour divine,
And O, my dear Jesus, the praise shall be thine:
In heaven we'll meet in harmony sweet,
And, glory to Jesus! we'll then be complete.

THE ROCK. 11s.

Arranged by Wm. Houser

1. In sea-sons of grief to my God I'll re-pair, When my heart is o'er-whelm'd in sor-row and care; From the ends of the earth unto Thee will I
2. When Sa-tan, my foe, comes in like a flood, To drive my poor soul from the fountain of good, I'll pray to the Sa-viour who kind-ly did
cry, "Lead me to the Rock that is high-er than I!" High-er than I, High-er than I: Lead me to the Rock that is high-er than I!
die: "Lead me to the Rock that is high-er than I!" High-er than I, High-er than I: Lead me to the Rock that is high-er than I!

3. And when I have ended my pilgrimage here,
In Jesus' pure righteousness let me appear:
From the swellings of Jordan to thee will I cry:
"Lead me to the Rock that is higher than I!"

4. And when the last trumpet shall sound through the skies,
And the dead from the dust of the earth shall arise,
With millions I'll join, far above yonder sky,
To praise the Great Rock that is higher than I.

1 Brethren, don't you hear the sound? Men in order listing round, Bounty's offer'd—joy and peace;
The martial trumpet now is blowing! And soldiers to the standard flowing. To ev'ry
2 They who long in sin have lain, Are all released from Satan's chain, The sick and sore, the blind and lame.
And felt the hand of dire oppression, And are endow'd with long possession. The mala
3 The battle is not to the strong, None so aged or so young, Those who cannot fight nor fly,
The burden's on our Captain's shoulder; But may enlist, and be a soldier: Beneath his

soldier this is giv'n—When from toils of war they cease, A mansion bright prepared in heav'n.
dies of all are healed, Outlaw'd rebels, too, may claim, And find a pardon freely sealed.
banner find protection; None who on his arm rely Shall be reduced to base subjection.

4 You need not fear;—the cause is good;
Come! who will to the crown aspire?
In this cause the martyrs bled,
Or shouted vict'ry in the fire;
In this cause let's follow on,
And soon we'll tell the pleasing story,
How by faith we gain'd the crown,
And fought our way to life and glory.

5 The battle, brethren, is begun,
Behold the armies now in motion!
Some, by faith, behold the crown,
And almost grasp their future portion.
Hark! the victory's sounding loud!
Immanuel's chariot wheels are rumbling
Mourners weeping through the crowd,
And Satan's kingdom down is tumbling

LOUISIANA. 8, 7

William Walker.

Come, little children, now we may Partake a lit - tle morsel,
For little songs and little ways Adorn'd a great a - postle;
A lit - tle drop of Jesus' blood Can make a feast of u - nion; It

is by little steps we move In - to a fu. communion.

2 A little faith does mighty deeds,
Quite past all my recounting;
Faith, like a little mustard seed,
Can move a lofty mountain.
A little charity and zeal,
A little tribulation,
A little patience makes us feel
Great peace and consolation.

3 A little cross with cheerfulness,
A little self-denial,
Will serve to make our troubles less,
And bear the greatest trial.
The Spirit like a little dove
On Jesus once descended;
To show his meekness and his love
The emblem was intended.

4 The title of the little Lamb
Unto our Lord was given;
Such was our Saviour's little name,
The Lord of earth and heaven.
A little voice that's small and still
Can rule the whole creation;
A little stone the earth shall fill,
And humble every nation.

5 A little zeal supplies the soul,
It doth the heart inspire;
A little spark lights up the whole,
And sets the crowd on fire.
A little union serves to hold
The good and tender-hearted;
It's stronger than a chain of gold
And never can be parted.

6 Come, let us labour here below,
And who can be the straitest;
For in God's kingdom, all must know
The least shall be the greatest.
O give us, Lord, a little drop
Of heavenly love and union
O may we never, never stop
Short of a full communion.

LAND OF PLEASURE. 7, 8. *Davison & Walker.* Dover Selection, p. 94.

There is a land of pleasure, Where streams of joy for ever roll,
'Tis there I have my tieasure, And there I long to rest my soul.
Long darkness dwelt around me,
With scarcely once a cheering ray,
But since my Saviour found

me, A lamp has shone along my way.

2 My way is full of danger,
But 'tis the path that leads to God;
And like a faithful soldier,
I'll march along the heavenly road;
Now I must gird my sword on,
My breastplate, helmet, and my shield,
And fight the hosts of Satan
Until I reach the heavenly field.

3 I'm on the way to Zion,
Still guarded by my Saviour's hand;
O, come along, dear sinners,
And view Emmanuel's happy land:
To all that stay behind me,
I oid a long, a sad farewell!
O come! or you'll repent it,
When you shall reach the gates of hell.

4 The vale of tears surrounds me,
And Jordan's current rolls before;
O! how I stand and tremble,
To hear the dismal waters roar!
Whose hand shall then support me,
And keep my soul from sinking there
Fiom sinking down to darkness,
And to the regions of despair!

5 This stream shall not affright me,
Although it take me to the grave;
If Jesus stand beside me,
I'll safely ride on Jordan's wave:
His word can calm the ocean,
His lamp can cheer the gloomy vale:
O may this friend be with me,
When through the gates of death I sail!

6 Come, then, thou king of terrors,
Thy fatal dart may lay me low;
But soon I'll reach those regions
Where everlasting pleasures flow:
O sinners, I must leave you,
And join that bless'd immortal band,
No more to stand beside you,
Till at the judgment-bar we stand.

7 Soon the archangel's trumpet
Shall shake the globe from pole to pole,
And all the wheels of nature
Shall in a moment cease to roll:
Then we shall see the Saviour,
With shining ranks of angels come,
To execute his vengeance,
And take bis iansom'd people home

OLNEY. 8, 7

Chapin.

Come, thou fount of ev' - ry bless - ing, Tune my heart to sing thy grace;
Streams of mercy never ceas - ing, Call for songs of loud - est praise.
Teach me some me - lo - dious sonnet,
Sung by flaming tongues a bove. Praise the mount, O fix me on it, Mount of thy un - changing love.

THE WATCHMAN'S CALL. L. M.

Wm Walker

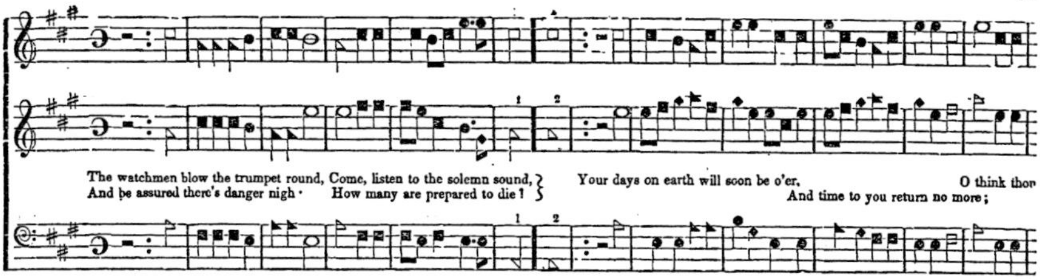
1
2
The watchmen blow the trumpet round, Come, listen to the solemn sound,
And be assured there's danger nigh · How many are prepared to die?
Your days on earth will soon be o'er,
And time to you return no more;
O think thou

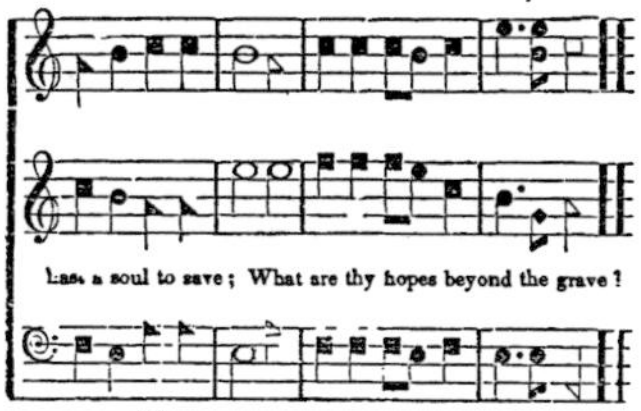
hast a soul to save; What are thy hopes beyond the grave?

7

2 Come, old and young; come, rich and poor;
You'll all be call'd to stand before
The God that made the earth and sea,
And there proclaim his majesty.
Will you remain quite unconcern'd,
While for your souls the watchmen mourn?
They weep to think how you will stand
With frightful ghosts at God's left hand.

3 O mortals! view the dream of life,
And see how thousands end the strife,
Who, though convinced, do still delay,
Till death ensues and drags away;
Will you for fancied earthly toys
Deprive yourselves of heav'nly joys?
And will the calls you have to-day
Be slighted still and pass away?

4 The trying scene will shortly come,
When you must hear your certain doom;
And if you then go unprepared,
You'll bear in mind the truths you've heard,
Your sparkling eyes will then roll round,
While death will bring you to the ground
The coffin, grave, and winding sheet,
Will hold your lifeless frame complete.

5 Your friends will then pass by your tomb,
And view the grass around it grown,
And heave a sigh to think you're gone
To the land where there's no return.
O mortals! now improve your time,
And while the gospel sun doth shine
Fly swift to Christ, he is your friend,
And then in heav'n your souls will end.

PLEASANT HILL. C. M.

Baptist Harmony, p. 273.

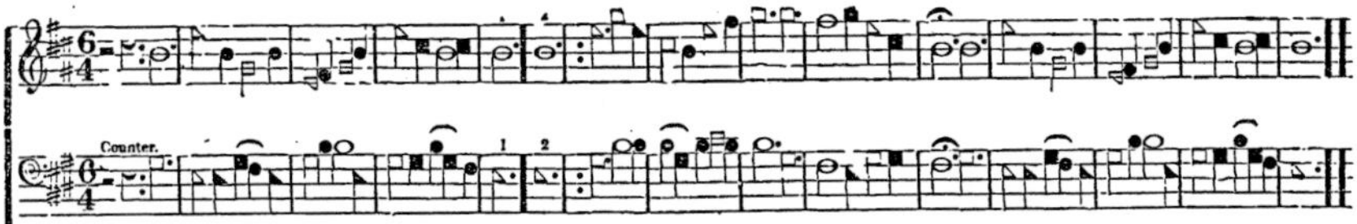

1 Religion is the chief concern Of mortals here below; May I its great importance learn, Its sovereign virtues know.

2 More needful this than glittering wealth, Or aught the world bestows; Nor reputation, food, or health, Can give us such repose.

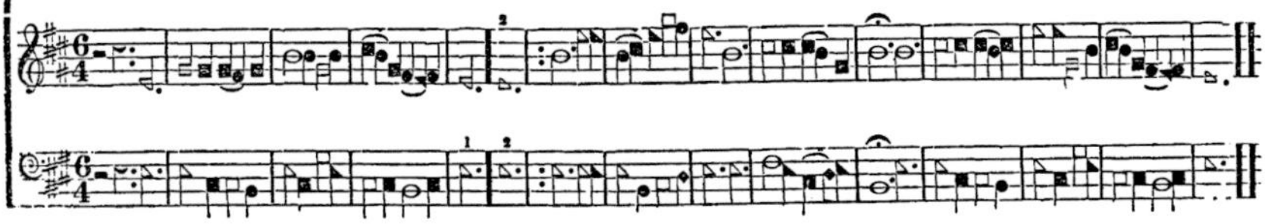

3 Religion should our thoughts engage
Amidst our youthful bloom;
'Twill fit us for declining age,
And for the awful tomb.

4 O, may my heart, by [illegible]
Be my Redeemer's thron
And be my stubborn will subdued,
His government to own

5 Let deep repentance, faith, and love
Be join'd with godly fear;
And all my conversation prove
My heart to be sincere.

6 Preserve me from the snares of sin
Through my remaining days,
And in me let each virtue shine
To my Redeemer's praise.

7 Let lively hope my soul inspire,
Let warm affections rise;
And may I wait, with strong desire
To mount above the skies.

Dismiss us with thy blessing, Lord, Help us to feed upon thy word;
All that has been amiss forgive, And let thy truth within us live.
Though we are guilty, thou art good, Wash all our works in Jesus' blood;
Give every fet - ter'd soul release, And bid us all depart in peace. Give every fetter'd soul release, And bid us all depart in peace.

LIBERTY. C. M

No more beneath th' oppressive hand Of tyran - ny we mourn, Be - hold the smiling, happy land, Be - hold the smiling, happy land, That
free - dom calls her own.
That free - dom calls her own.

How firm a foun - da - tion, ye saints of the Lord, Is laid for your faith in his ex - cel - lent word; What
more can he say, than to you he hath said, You who un - to Je - sus for refuge have fled!

BOWER OF PRAYER. 11s.

Richerson & Walker.

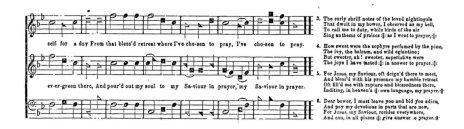

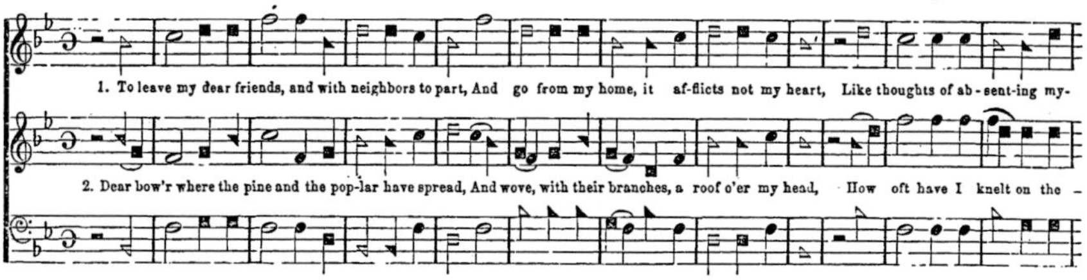
1. To leave my dear friends, and with neighbors to part, And go from my home, it af-flicts not my heart, Like thoughts of ab - sent-ing my-
2. Dear bow'r where the pine and the pop-lar have spread, And wove, with their branches, a roof o'er my head, How oft have I knelt on the -

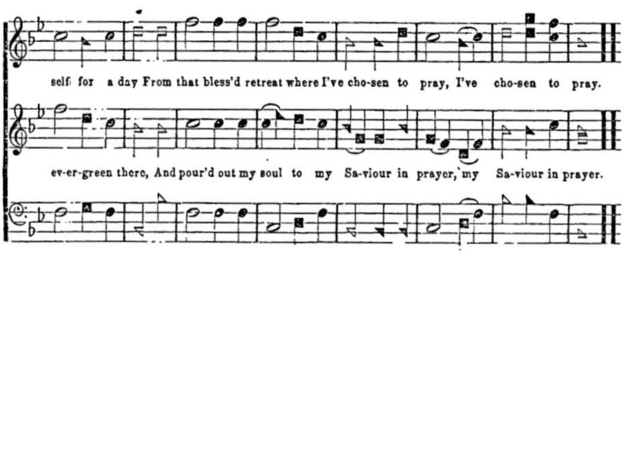
self for a day From that bless'd retreat where I've cho-sen to pray, I've cho-sen to pray.
ev-er-green there, And pour'd out my soul to my Sa-viour in prayer, my Sa-viour in prayer.

3. The early shrill notes of the loved nightingale
That dwelt in my bower, I observed as my bell,
To call me to duty, while birds of the air
Sing anthems of praises :‖: as I went to prayer,:‖:

4. How sweet were the zephyrs perfumed by the pine,
The ivy, the balsam, and wild eglantine;
But sweeter, ah! sweeter, superlative were
The joys I have tasted :‖: in answer to prayer.:‖:

5. For Jesus, my Saviour, oft deign'd there to meet,
And bless'd with his presence my humble retreat
Oft fill'd me with rapture and blessedness there,
Inditing, in heaven's :‖: own language, my prayer.:‖:

6. Dear bower, I must leave you and bid you adieu,
And pay my devotions in parts that are new,
For Jesus, my Saviour, resides everywhere,
And can, in all places :‖: give answer to prayer.:‖:

GREEN FIELDS. 8's.

Baptist Harmony, p. 193

Counter.
How tedious and tasteless the hours, When Jesus no longer I see;
Sweet prospects, sweet birds, and sweet flow'rs, Have all lost their sweetness to me.
The midsummer sun shines but dim, The fields strive in vain to look gay, But

when I am happy in him, December's as pleasant as May.

2 His name yields the richest perfume,
And sweeter than music his voice;
His presence disperses my gloom,
And makes all within me rejoice;
I should, were he always thus nigh,
Have nothing to wish or to fear;
No mortal so happy as I,
My summer would last all the year.

3 Content with beholding his face,
My all to his pleasure resign'd;
No changes of season or place,
Would make any change in my mind
While bless'd with a sense of his love,
A palace a toy would appear,
And prisons would palaces prove,
If Jesus would dwell with me there.

4 Dear Lord, if indeed I am thine,
If thou art my sun and my song,
Say, why do I languish and pine,
And why are my winters so long!
O, drive these dark clouds from my sky
Thy soul-cheering presence restore·
Or take me unto thee on high,
Where winter and clouds are no more

GEORGIA. C. M.

Return, O God of love, re - turn, Earth is a tire - some place; How long shall we, thy children, mourn Our absence from thy face?

INVOCATION. 7, 6, 7, 6, 7, 7, 7, 6.

Rise, my soul, and stretch thy wings, Thy better portion trace, Sun, and moon, and stars decay, Rise, my soul, and haste away,
Rise from tran-itory things. To heav'n, thy native place. Time shall soon this earth remove, To seats prepared above.

When in death I shall calm reoline, O bear my heart to my mistress dear;
Tell her it lived upon smiles and wine Of the brightest hue, while it linger'd here.
Bid her not shed one tear of sorrow, To sul - ly a
heart so bril - liant and light; But balmy drops of the red grape borrow, To bathe the re - lic from morn to night.

THE CHRISTIAN'S HOPE. 8, 8, 8, 6, 8, 8, 8, 6.

Wm Walker . Dover Sel. p. 173

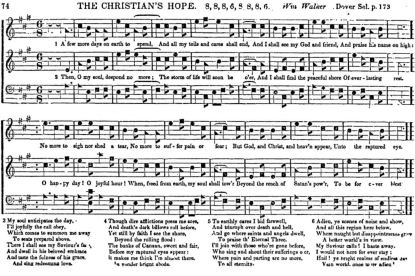

1 A few more days on earth to spend, And all my toils and cares shall end, And I shall see my God and friend, And praise his name on high:
2 Then, O my soul, despond no more; The storm of life will soon be o'er, And I shall find the peaceful shore Of ever-lasting rest.
No more to sigh nor shed a tear, No more to suf-fer pain or fear; But God, and Christ, and heav'n appear, Unto the raptured eye.
O hap-py day! O joyful hour! When, freed from earth, my soul shall tow'r Beyond the reach of Satan's pow'r, To be for e-ver blest

3 My soul anticipates the day,
I'll joyfully the call obey,
Which comes to summon me away
To seats prepared above.
There I shall see my Saviour's fa ,
And dwell in his beloved embrace
And taste the fulness of his grace,
And sing redeeming love.

4 Though dire afflictions press me sore,
And death's dark billows roll before,
Yet still by faith I see the shore,
Beyond the rolling flood:
The banks of Canaan, sweet and fair,
Before my raptured eyes appear:
It makes me think I'm almost there.
In yonder bright abode.

5 To earthly cares I bid farewell,
And triumph over death and hell,
And go where saints and angels dwell,
To praise th' Eternal Three.
I'll join with those who're gone before,
Who sing and shout their sufferings o'er,
Where pain and parting are no more,
To all eternity.

6 Adieu, ye scenes of noise and show,
And all this region here below,
Where naught but disappointments grow
A better world's in view.
My Saviour calls! I haste away.
I would not here for ever stay;
Hail! ye bright realms of endless day
Vain world, once more adieu!

MILLENNIUM. 12, 12, 12, 13 *Wm. Walker.* Zion Songster, p. 53

Slow.
The time is soon com-ing, By the pro-phets fore-told, When Zi-on in pu-ri-ty, The world shall be-hold.
When Je-sus' pure tes ti-mo-ny will gain the day, De-no-mi-nations, sel-fish-ness, will va-nish a-way.

NEW ORLEANS. C. M

Boyd.

Why do we mourn de - part - ing friends? Or shake at death's a - larms? 'Tis but the voice that Je - sus sends, To
call them to his arms. Are we not tending upwards too, As fast as time can move? Nor should we wish the hours more slow, To keep us from our love.

LENOX. P. M

Edson. Baptist Harmony, p. 356.

Blow ye the trumpet, blow, The glad - ly solemn sound, Let all the nations know, To earth's remotest bounds.
The year of jubi - lee is come, The year of jubi - lee is come; Re - turn, ye ran - som'd sin - ners, home.

THE BABE OF BETHLEHEM. 8, 7

Wm. Walker.

Ye nations all, on you I call,
Come, hear this declaration,
And don't refuse this glorious news
Of Jesus and salvation.
To royal Jews came first the news
Of

Christ the great Messiah,
As was foretold by prophets old,
Isai - ah, Jeremiah.

2 To Abraham the promise came, and to his seed for ever,
A light to shine in Isaac's line, by Scripture we discover;
Hail, promised morn! the Saviour's born, the glorious Mediator—
God's blessed Word made flesh and blood, assumed the human nature.

3 His parents poor in earthly store, to entertain the stranger
They found no bed to lay his head, but in the ox's manger:
No royal things, as used by kings, were seen by those that found him,
But in the hay the stranger lay, with swaddling bands around him

4 On the same night a glorious light to shepherds there appeared,
Bright angels came in shining flame, they saw and greatly feared
The angels said, "Be not afraid, although we much alarm you,
We do appear good news to bear, as now we will inform you.

5 "The city's name is Bethlehem, in which God hath appointed,
This glorious morn a Saviour's born, for him God hath anointed;
By this you'll know, if you will go, to see this little stranger,
His lovely charms in Mary's arms, both lying in a manger."

6 When this was said, straightway was made a glorious sound from heaven
Each flaming tongue an anthem sung, "To men a Saviour's given,
In Jesus' name, the glorious theme, we elevate our voices,
At Jesus' birth be peace on earth, meanwhile all heaven rejoices.'

7 Then with delight they took their flight, and wing'd their way to glory,
The shepherds gazed and were amazed, to hear the pleasing story;
To Bethlehem they quickly came, the glorious news to carry,
And in the stall they found them all, Joseph, the Babe, and Mary

8 The shepherds then return'd again to their own habitation,
With joy of heart they did depart, now they have found salvation
Glory, they cry, to God on high, who sent his Son to save us
This glorious morn the Saviour's born, his name it is Christ Jesus

THE TRAVELLER. 7, 6.

J. C. Lowry

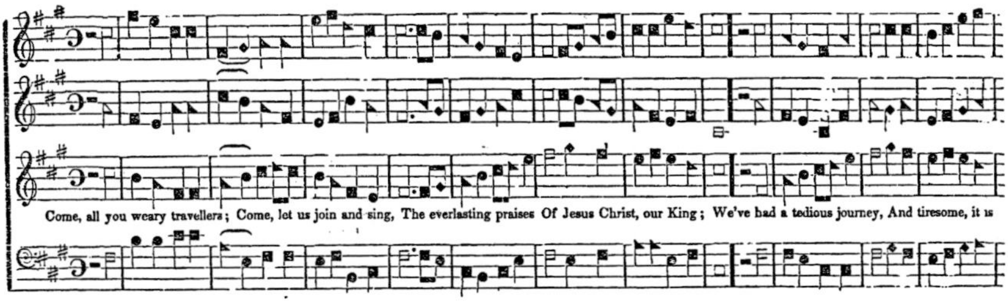
Come, all you weary travellers; Come, let us join and sing, The everlasting praises Of Jesus Christ, our King; We've had a tedious journey, And tiresome, it is

true; But see how many dangers The Lord has brought us through.

2 At first when Jesus found us,
He call'd us unto him,
And pointed out the danger
Of falling into sin;
The world, the flesh, and Satan,
Will prove a fatal snare,
Unless we do resist them,
By faith and fervent prayer.

3 But by our disobedience,
With sorrow we confess,
We've had too long to wander
In a dark wilderness
Where we might soon have fainted,
In that enchanted ground,
But Jesus interposed,
And pleasant fruits were found.

4 Gracious foretastes of heaven
Give life, and health, and peace,
Revive our drooping spirits,
And faith and love increase;
Confessing Christ, our master,
Obeying his command,
We hasten on our journey,
Unto the promised land

PISGAH. C. M

Lowry. Baptist Harmony, p. 250.

Second Treble.
Je - sus, thou art the sinner's friend, As such I look to thee; Now in the bowels of thy love, O Lord, remember me.
Soft.
O Lord, &c.
O Lord, &c.
Now in, &c.
1
2

1 Come, Christians, be valiant, our Jesus is near us,   Through grace and the Spirit we'll glory inherit,
    We'll conquer the powers of darkness and sin;   And peace, like a river, give comfort within.

2 We have trials, and cares, and hardships, and losses,   We'll soon end in pleasures and glory for ever,
    But heaven will pay us for all that we bear;   And bright crowns of glory for ever we'll wear.

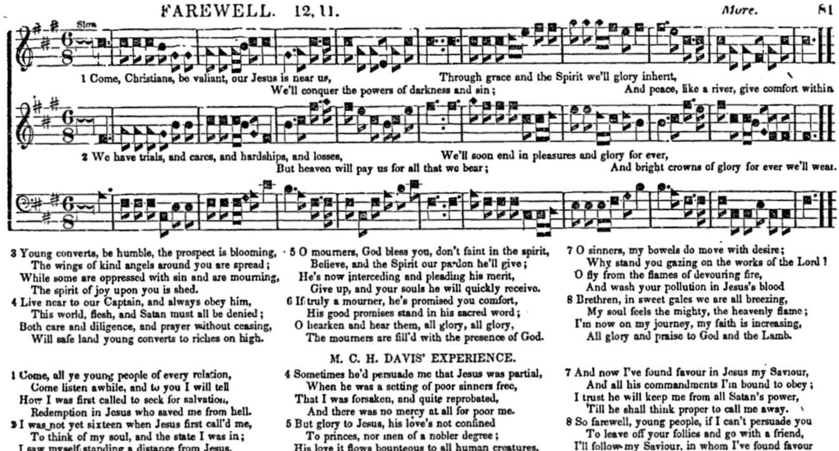

3 Young converts, be humble, the prospect is blooming,
    The wings of kind angels around you are spread;
While some are oppressed with sin and are mourning,
    The spirit of joy upon you is shed.
4 Live near to our Captain, and always obey him,
    This world, flesh, and Satan must all be denied;
Both care and diligence, and prayer without ceasing,
    Will safe land young converts to riches on high.

1 Come, all ye young people of every relation,
    Come listen awhile, and to you I will tell
How I was first called to seek for salvation,
    Redemption in Jesus who saved me from hell.
2 I was not yet sixteen when Jesus first call'd me,
    To think of my soul, and the state I was in;
I saw myself standing a distance from Jesus,
    Between me and him was a mountain of sin.
3 The devil perceived that I was convinced,
    He strove to persuade me that I was too young,
That I would get weary before my ascension,
    And wish that I had not so early begun.
    8

5 O mourners, God bless you, don't faint in the spirit,
    Believe, and the Spirit our pardon he'll give;
He's now interceding and pleading his merit,
    Give up, and your souls he will quickly receive.
6 If truly a mourner, he's promised you comfort,
    His good promises stand in his sacred word;
O hearken and hear them, all glory, all glory,
    The mourners are fill'd with the presence of God.

M. C. H. DAVIS' EXPERIENCE.

4 Sometimes he'd persuade me that Jesus was partial,
    When he was a setting of poor sinners free,
That I was forsaken, and quite reprobated,
    And there was no mercy at all for poor me.
5 But glory to Jesus, his love's not confined
    To princes, nor men of a nobler degree;
His love it flows bounteous to all human creatures,
    He died for poor sinners, when nail'd to the tree.
6 And when I was groaning in sad lamentation,
    My soul overwhelm'd in sorrow and in sin,
He drew near me in mercy, and look'd on me with pity,
    He pardon'd my sins, and he gave me relief.

7 O sinners, my bowels do move with desire;
    Why stand you gazing on the works of the Lord !
O fly from the flames of devouring fire,
    And wash your pollution in Jesus's blood.
8 Brethren, in sweet gales we are all breezing,
    My soul feels the mighty, the heavenly flame ;
I'm now on my journey, my faith is increasing,
    All glory and praise to God and the Lamb.

7 And now I've found favour in Jesus my Saviour,
    And all his commandments I'm bound to obey ;
I trust he will keep me from all Satan's power,
    Till he shall think proper to call me away.
8 So farewell, young people, if I can't persuade you
    To leave off your follies and go with a friend,
I'll follow my Saviour, in whom I've found favour
    My days to his glory I'm bound for to spend.

THE ROMISH LADY. 7, 6.

There was a Romish lady brought up in popery, Her mother always taught her the priest she must obey ; O pardon me, dear mother, I humbly pray thee now

For unto these false idols I can no longer bow.

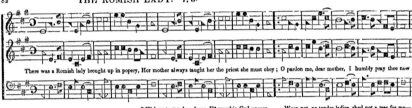

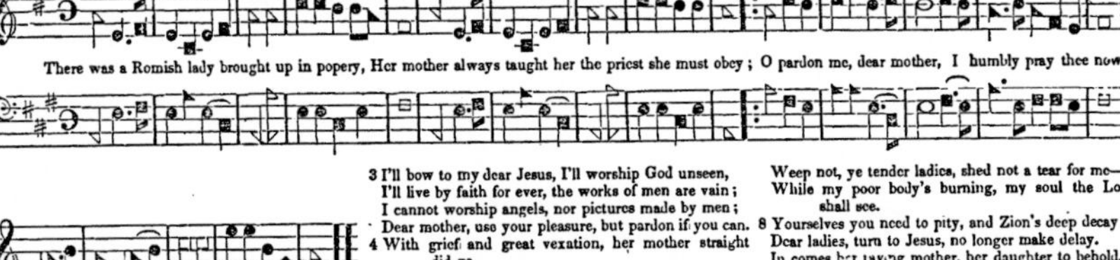

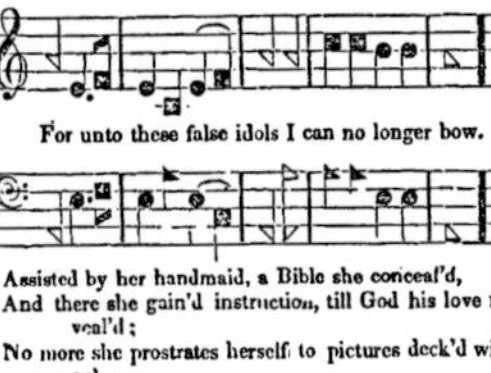

2 Assisted by her handmaid, a Bible she conceal'd,
And there she gain'd instruction, till God his love reveal'd ;
No more she prostrates herself to pictures deck'd with
gold,
But soon she was betray'd, and her Bible from her
do

3 I'll bow to my dear Jesus, I'll worship God unseen,
I'll live by faith for ever, the works of men are vain ;
I cannot worship angels, nor pictures made by men ;
Dear mother, use your pleasure, but pardon if you can.
4 With grief and great vexation, her mother straight
did go
T" inform the Roman clergy the cause of all her wo :
The priests were soon-assembled, and for the maid did
call,
And forced her in the dungeon, to fright her soul withal.
5 The more they strove to fright her, the more she did
endure,
Although her age was tender, her faith was strong and
sure.
The chains of gold so costly they from this lady took,
And she with all her spirits, the pride of life forsook.
6 Before the pope they brought her, in hopes of her
return,
And there she was condemned in horrid flames to
burn.
Before the place of torment they brought her speedily,
With lifted hands to heaven, she then agreed to die.
7 There being many ladies assembled at the place,
She raised her eyes to heaven, and begg'd supplying
grace

Weep not, ye tender ladies, shed not a tear for me—
While my poor body's burning, my soul the Lord
shall see.
8 Yourselves you need to pity, and Zion's deep decay ;
Dear ladies, turn to Jesus, no longer make delay.
In comes her raving mother, her daughter to behold,
And in her hand she brought her pictures deck'd with
gold.
9 O take from me these idols, remove them from my
sight ;
Restore to me my Bible, wherein I take delight.
Alas, my aged mother, why on my ruin bent !
'Twas you that did betray me, but I am innocent.
10 Tormentors, use your pleasure, and do as you think
best—
I hope my blessed Jesus will take my soul to rest.
Soon as these words were spoken, up steps the man
of death,
11 Instead of golden bracelets, with chains they bound
her fast ;
She cried, "My God give power now must I die at
last !
With Jesus and his angels for ever I shall dwell,
God pardon priest and people, and so I bid farewell"

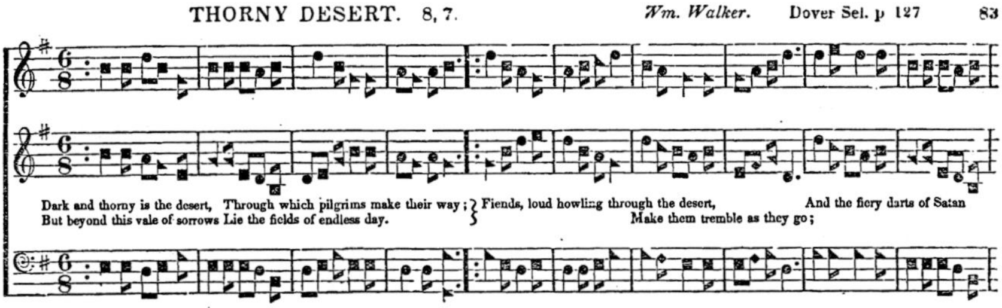
Dark and thorny is the desert, Through which pilgrims make their way;
But beyond this vale of sorrows Lie the fields of endless day.
Fiends, loud howling through the desert,
Make them tremble as they go;
And the fiery darts of Satan

Often bring their courage low.

2 O, young soldiers, are you weary
Of the troubles of the way?
Does your strength begin to fail you,
And your vigour to decay?
Jesus, Jesus, will go with you,
He will lead you to his throne;
He who dyed his garments for you,
And the wine-press trod alone.

3 He whose thunder shakes creation,
He who bids the planets roll;
He who rides upon the tempest,
And whose sceptre sways the whole.
Round him are ten thousand angels,
Ready to obey command;
They are always hovering round you,
Till you reach the heav'nly land.

4 There, on flowery hills of pleasure,
In the fields of endless rest,
Love, and joy, and peace shall ever
Reign and triumph in your breas
Who can paint those scenes of glory,
Where the ransom'd dwell on high?
Where the golden harps for ever
Sound redemption through the sky?

5 Millions there of flaming seraphs
Fly across the heavenly Plain;
There they sing immortal praises—
Glory! glory! is their strain:
But methinks a sweeter concert
Makes the heavenly arches ring.
And a song is heard in Zion
Which the angels cannot sing.

6 See the heavenly host, in rapture,
Gaze upon this shining band;
Wondering at their costly garments,
And the laurels in their hand!
There, upon the golden pavement,
See the ransom'd march along,
While the splendid courts of glory
Sweetly echo to their song.

7 O their crowns, how bright they sparkle!
Such as monarchs never wear;
They are gone to heav'nly pastures—
Jesus is their Shepherd there.
Hail, ye happy, happy spirits!
Welcome to the blissful plain!—
Glory, honour, and salvation!
Reign, sweet Shepherd, ever reign

SALVATION. C. M.

B

Come, humble sinner, in whose breast A thousand thoughts revolve, } I'll go to Jesus, though my sin I know his courts, I'll enter in,
Come, with your guilt and fear opprest, And make this last resolve : } Hath like a mountain rose ; Whatever may oppose.

DAY OF JUDGMENT. 11, 11, 6, 6, 7, 6.

Mercer's Cluster, p. 495.

The day of the Lord—the day of sal - vation, } Is swiftly coming on ; It surely will appear ; And you and I must meet it With ecstasy or fear
The day of his wrath and dire indig - nation, }

THE SUFFERINGS OF CHRIST. 8s.

Wm. Walker.

A sto-ry most love-ly I'll tell, Of Je-sus (O wond'rous sur-prise!)
He suffer'd the tor-ments of hell, That sin-ners, vile sin-ners might rise;)

Ho left his ex-alt-ed a-bode, When

man by trans-gress-ion was lost; Ap-peas-ing the wrath of a God, He shed forth his blood as the cost.

5. They loaded the Lamb with the cross,
   And drove him up Calvary's hill;
Come, mourners, a moment, and pause,
   All nature look'd solemn and still!
They rushed the nails through his hands,
   Transfixed and tortured his feet;
O brethren, see passive he stands;
   To look at the sight it is great!

6. He cried, My Father, my God.
   Forsaken! thou'st left me in pain!
The cross was all colour'd with blood,
   The temple-rail bursted in twain:
He groaned his last and he died,
   The sun it refused to shine:
They rushed the spear in his side;
   This lovely Redeemer is mine.

7. He fought the hard battle, and won
   The vict'ry, and gives it most free:
O Christians! look forward and run,
   In hopes that his kingdom you'll see;
When he in the clouds shall appear,
   With angels all at his command,
And thousands of Christians be there,
   All singing with harps in a band.

8. How pleasant and happy the view!
   Enjoying such beams of delight!
His beauty to Christians he'll show,
   O Jesus, I long for the sight!
I long to mount up in the skies,
   In Paradise make my abode,
And sing of salvation on high,
   And rest with a peaceful God.

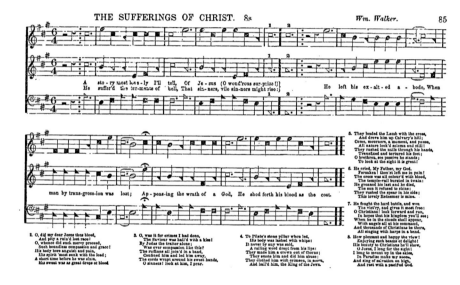

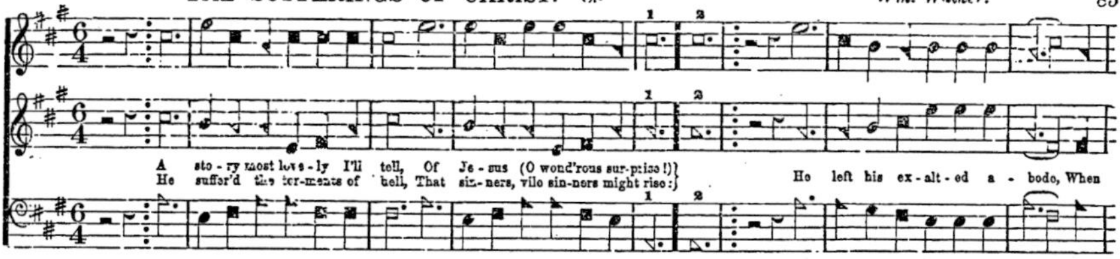

2. O, did my dear Jesus thus bleed,
   And pity a ruin'd lost race!
O, whence did such mercy proceed,
   Such boundless compassion and grace!
His body bore anguish and pain,
   His spirit 'most sunk with the load;
A short time before he was slain,
   His sweat was as great drops ot blood.

3. O, was it for crimes I had done,
   The Saviour was hail'd with a kiss!
By Judas the traitor alone;
   Was ever compassion like this?
The ruffians all join'd in a band,
   Confined him and led him away,
The cords wrapt around his sweet hands,
   O sinners! look at him, I pray.

4. To Pilate's stone pillar when led,
   His body was lashed with whips:
It never by any was said,
   A railing word dropt from his lips:
They made him a crown out of thorns;
   They smote him and did him abuse;
They clothed him with crimson, in scorn,
   And hail'd him, the King of the Jews.

ISLES OF THE SOUTH.* 11s.

Wm. Houser.

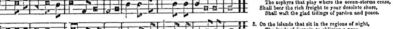

1. Wake, Isles of the South! your re - demp-tion is near, No lon - ger re - pose in the bord-ers of gloom; The strength of his cho - sen in love shall ap- pear, And

light shall a - rise on the verge of the tomb, And light shall a - rise on the verge of the tomb.

2. The billows that girt you, the wild waves that roar,
   The zephyrs that play where the ocean-storms cease,
Shall bear the rich freight to your desolate shore,
   Shall waft the glad tidings of pardon and peace.

3. On the islands that sit in the regions of night,
   The lands of despair, to oblivion a prey,
The morning will open with healing and light,
   The glad Star of Bethlehem brighten to day.

4. The altar and idol in dust overthrown,
   The incense forbade that was hallow'd with blood;
The priest of Melchizedek there shall atone,
   And the shrine of Atöol be sacred to God.

5. The heathen will hasten to welcome the time,
   The day-spring, the prophet in vision once saw,
When the beams of Messiah will 'lumine each clime,
   And the isles of the ocean shall wait for his law.

* The words of this piece were "composed by Wm. B. Tappan, Esq., and sung on the wharf at New Haven, at the embarkation of the missionaries for the Sandwich Islands, in 1822." O what hath God wrought in those islands since that time! "The parched ground has become a pool"—"The shrines of Atöol" have, indeed, become "sacred to God." The largest church on earth is there; those poor heathens have been given to Jesus for his "inheritance"—those "uttermost parts of the earth, for his possession!" "Alleluia! the Lord God Omnipotent reigneth!"—W. H.

Hail! ye sighing sons of sorrow, Learn from me your certain doom;
Learn from me your fate to-morrow, Dead—per - haps laid in your tomb!
See all nature fading, dying! Si - lent all things seem to pine;

Life from vege - tation fly - ing, Brings to mind "the mould'ring vine."

2 See! in yonder forest standing,
Lofty cedars, how they nod!
Scenes of nature how surprising,
Read in nature nature's God.
Whilst the annual frosts are cropping,
Leaves and tendrils from the trees,
So our friends are early drooping,
We are like to one of these.

3 Hollow winds about me roaring,
Noisy waters round me rise;
Whilst I sit my fate deploring,
Tears fast streaming from my eyes
What to me is autumn's treasure
Since I know no earthly joy,
Long I've lost all youthful pleasure,
Time must youth and health destroy

EXULTATION. 6, 6, 9

Humphreys

Come away to the skies, My beloved, arise, And rejoice in the day thou wast born: On this fes - ti - val day, Come exult - ing away,

And with singing to Zi - on return.

2 We have laid up our love And our treasure above,
Though our bodies continue below,
The redeem'd of the Lord Will remember his word,
And with singing to paradise go.

3 Now with singing and praise, Let us spend all the days,
By our heavenly Father bestow'd,
While his grace we receive From his bounty, and live
To the honour and glory of God.

4 For the glory we were First created to share,
Both the nature and kingdom divine!
Now created again That our souls may remain,
Throughout time and eternity thine.

5 We with thanks do approve, The design of that love
Which hath join'd us to Jesus's name;
So united in heart, Let us never more part,
Till we meet at the feast of the Lamb.

6 There, O! there at his feet, We shall all likewise meet,
And be parted in body no more;
We shall sing to our lyres, With the heavenly choirs,
And our Saviour in glory adore.

7 Hallelujah we sing, To our Father and King,
And his rapturous praises repeat;
To the Lamb that was slain, Hallelujah again,
Sing, all heaven and fall at his feet.

DOVE OF PEACE. C. M.

Treble by Wm. Houser.

1. O tell me where the Dove has flown To build her dow-ny nest, And I will rove this world all o'er, To win her to my breast, To win her to my breast.
2. I sought her in the groves of love, I knew her ten-der heart; But she had flown—the Dove of Peace Had felt a trai-tor's dart, Had felt a trai-tor's dart.

3 I sought her on the flow'ry lawn,
Where pleasure holds her train;
But fancy flies from flower to flower,
So there I sought in vain,
So there I sought in vain.

4. 'Twas on Ambition's craggy hill,
The Bird of Peace might stray;
I sought her there, tho' vainly still,
She never flew that way,
She never flew that way.

5. Faith smiled, and shed a silent tear,
To see my search around,
Then whisper'd, "I will tell you where
The Dove may yet be found,
The Dove may yet be found.

6. "By meek Religion's humble cot,
She builds her downy nest;
Go, seek that sweet secluded spot,
And win her to your breast,
And win her to your breast."

HAPPY LAND. 6,4,6,4,6,7,6,4.

Leonard P. Breedlove.

Cheerful and animating.

1. There is a hap-py land, Far, far a-way; Where saints in glo-ry stand, Bright, bright as day. O how they sweet-ly sing, Wor-thy is our Sa-viour King; Loud, let his prai-ses ring, Praise, praise for aye.
2. Come to the hap-py land, Come, come a-way! Why will you doubting stand? Why yet de-lay? O we shall hap-py be, When from sin and sor-row free, Lord, we shall live with thee, Blest, blest for aye.
3. Bright, in that hap-py land, Beams ev'-ry eye; Kept by a father's hand, Love can-not die. Then shall his king-dom come, Saints shall share a glo-rious home, And bright a-bove the sun, We'll reign for aye

GARDEN HYMN. 8, 8, 6

The Lord in - to his garden comes, The spices yield a rich perfume, The lilies grow and thrive, The lilies grow and thrive; Re-
freshing showers of grace divine, From Je - sus flow to eve - ry vine, And make the dead re - vive, And make the dead re - vive.

CHEERFUL. 11s

O how I have long'd for the com-ing of God, And sought him by pray-ing, and searching his word; With
watching and fast-ing my soul was op-prest, Nor would I give o-ver, till Je-sus had bless'd.
1
2

FIDUCIA. C. M.

Robison.

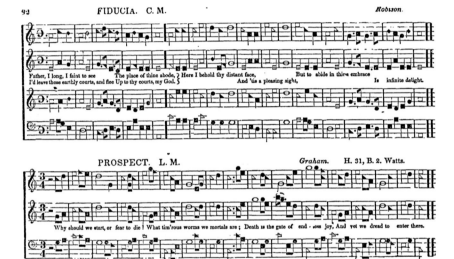

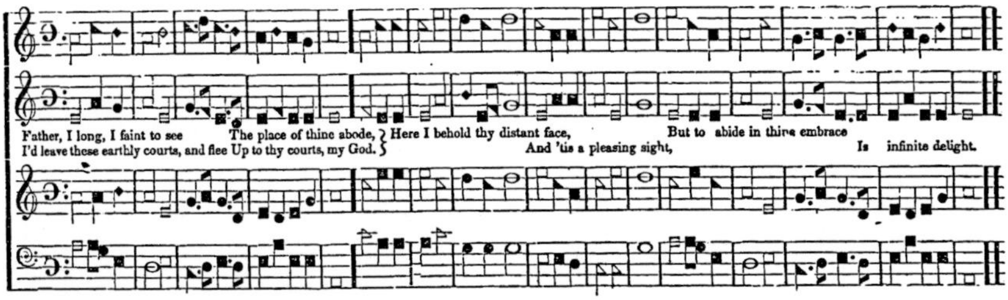
Father, I long, I faint to see The place of thine abode, Here I behold thy distant face, But to abide in thine embrace
I'd leave these earthly courts, and flee Up to thy courts, my God. And 'tis a pleasing sight, Is infinite delight.

PROSPECT. L. M.

Graham. H. 31, B. 2. Watts.

Why should we start, or fear to die! What tim'rous worms we mortals are; Death is the gate of end - less joy, And yet we dread to enter there.

1 2
And if you meet with trou - bles And tri - als on the way,
Then cast your care on Je - sus, And don't for - get to pray.
Gird on the heav'n - ly
ar mour Of faith, and hope, and love; And when the com - bat's end - ed, He'll take you up a - bove.

WARRENTON. 8, 7

Chorus.
Come, thou fount of every blessing, Tune my heart to sing thy grace;
Streams of mercy never ceasing Call for songs of loudest praise.
I am bound for the kingdom, Will you go to glory with me? Hallelujah, praise the Lord.

WAR DEPARTMENT. 11's.

Mercer's Cluster, p. 125.

No more shall the sound of the war-whoop be heard
The ambush and slaughter no longer be fear'd.
The tomahawk buried, shall rest in the ground,
And peace and good-will to the nations around.

CHRISTIAN SOLDIER. 7, 8, 7, 8, 7, 8, 7, 8, 7, 7, 8, 8.

Dover Sel p. 134.

Soldiers, go, but not to claim Mouldering spoils of earthborn treasure,
Not to build a vaunting name, Not to dwell in tents of pleasure,
Dream not that the way is smooth,
Hope not that the thorns are roses,
Turn no wishful eye of youth,
Where the
sunny beam re poses. Thou hast sterner work to do, Hast to cut thy passage through; Cle e behind the gulfs are burning: Forward then, there's no returning.

MISSION. L. M.

A. Grambling Baptist Harmony, p. 266.

1 Young people all, attention give, While I address you in God's name; } I've sought for bliss in glitt'ring toys, But never
You who in sin and folly live, Come hear the counsel of a friend. } And ranged the luring scenes of vice;

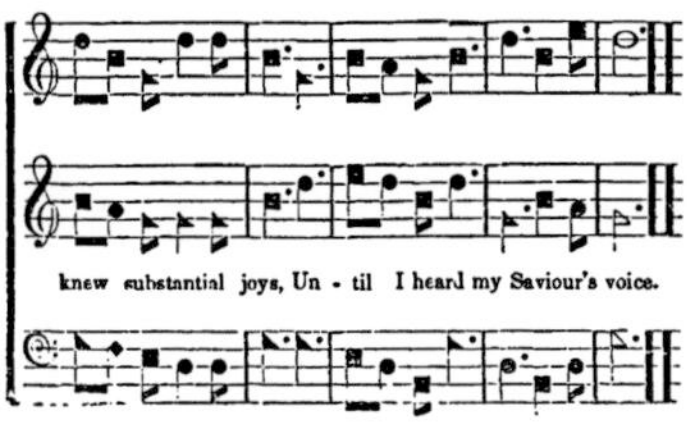
knew substantial joys, Un - til I heard my Saviour's voice.

2 He spake at once my sins forgiven,
And wash'd my load of guilt away;
He gave me glory, peace, and heaven,
And thus I found the heav'nly way
And now with trembling sense I view
The billows roll beneath your feet;
For death eternal waits for you,
Who slight the force of gospel truth

3 Youth, like the spring, will soon be gone
By fleeting time or conquering death,
Your morning sun may set at noon,
And leave you ever in the dark.
Your sparkling eyes and blooming cheeks
Must wither like the blasted rose;
The coffin, earth, and winding sheet
Will soon your active limbs enclose.

4 Ye heedless ones that wildly stroll,
The grave will soon become your bed,
Where silence reigns, and vapours roll
In solemn darkness round your head.
Your friends will pass the lonesome place,
And with a sigh move slow along;
Still gazing on the spires of grass
With which your graves are overgrown.

5 Your souls will land in darker realms,
Where vengeance reigns and billows roar,
And roll amid the burning flames,
When thousand thousand years are o'er.
Sunk in the shades of endless night,
To groan and howl in endless pain,
And never more behold the light,
And never, never rise again.

6 Ye blooming youth, this is the state
Of all who do free grace refuse;
And soon with you 'twill be too late
The way of life and Christ to choose.
Come, lay your carnal weapons by,
No longer fight against your God
But with the gospel now comply
And heav'n shall be your great reward.

He comes! he comes! to judge the world, Aloud th' archangel cries;
While thunders roll from pole to pole, And lightnings cleave the skies;
Th' affrighted nations hear the sound,
And upward lift their eyes;

The slumb'ring tenants of the ground In living armies rise.

2 Amid the shouts of numerous friends,
Of hosts divinely bright,
The Judge in solemn pomp descends,
Array'd in robes of light;
His head and hair are white as snow,
His eyes a fiery flame,
A radiant crown adorns his brow,
And Jesus is his name.

3 Writ on his thigh his name appears,
And scars his victories tell;
Lo! in his hand the conqueror bears
The keys of death and hell:
So he ascends the judgment-seat,
And at his dread command,
Myriads of creatures round his feet
In solemn silence stand.

4 Princes and peasants here expect
Their last, their righteous doom;
The men who dared his grace reject,
And they who dared presume.
"Depart, ye sons of vice and sin,"
The injured Jesus cries,
While the long kindling wrath within
Flashes from both his eyes.

5 And now in words divinely sweet,
With rapture in his face,
Aloud his sacred lips repeat
The sentence of his grace:
"Well done, my good and faithful sons,
The children of my love,
Receive the sceptres, crowns and thrones
Prepared for you above."

KINGWOOD. 8, 8, 6.

Humphreys.

My days, my weeks, my months, my years, Fly rapid as the whirling spheres, :‖: Around the steady pole; Time, like the tide, its motion

keeps, And I must launch thro' endless deeps, :‖: Where endless ages roll.

2 The grave is near, the cradle seen,
How swift the moments pass between,
And whisper as they fly;
Unthinking man, remember this,
Though fond of sublunary bliss,
That you must groan and die.

3 My soul, attend the solemn call,
Thine earthly tent must shortly fall
And thou must take thy flight
Beyond the vast expansive blue,
To sing above as angels do,
Or sink in endless night.

AN ADDRESS FOR ALL. C. M.

Wm. Walker.

I sing a song which doth be-long to all the hu-man race,
Con-cern-ing death, which steals the breath, and blasts the come-ly face;
Come lis-ten all un-to my call, which I do make to-

day . . . For you must die as well as I, And pass from hence a-way.

2. No human power can stop the hour, wherein a mortal dies;
A Cæsar may be great to-day, yet death will close his eyes:
Though some do strive and do arrive to riches and renown,
Enjoying health and swim in wealth, yet death will bring them down.

3. Though beauty grace your comely face, with roses white and red,
A dying fall will spoil it all, for Absalom is dead:
Though you acquire the best attire, appearing fine and fair,
Yet death will come into the room, and strip you naked there.

4. The princes high and beggars die, and mingle with the dust,
The rich, the brave, the negro slave, the wicked and the just:
Therefore prepare to meet thy God, before it be too late,
Or else you'll weep, lament and cry, lost in a ruin'd state

ELYSIAN. 7, 6, 7, 6, 7, 7, 7, 7.

Baptist Harmony, p. 471

Burst, ye emerald gates, and bring To my raptured vision
All th'ecstatic joys that spring Round the bright elysian.
Lo, we lift our longing eyes, Burst, ye intervening skies, Sun of

righteousness, arise, Ope the gates of para - dise.

2 Floods of everlasting light
Freely flash before him;
Myriads, with supreme delight,
Instantly adore him:
Angel trumps resound his fame,
Lutes of lucid gold proclaim
All the music of his name,
Heav'n echoing with the theme.

3 Four-and-twenty elders rise
From their princely station:
Shout his glorious victories,
Sing the great salvation:
Cast their crowns before his throne,
Cry in reverential tone,
Glory give to God alone;
'Holy, holy, holy One!'

4 Hark! the thrilling symphonies
Seem, methinks, to seize us
Join we too their holy lays,
Jesus, Jesus, Jesus!
Sweetest sound in seraphs' song—
Sweetest notes on mortal tongue
Sweetest carol ever sung—
Jesus, Jesus, roll along

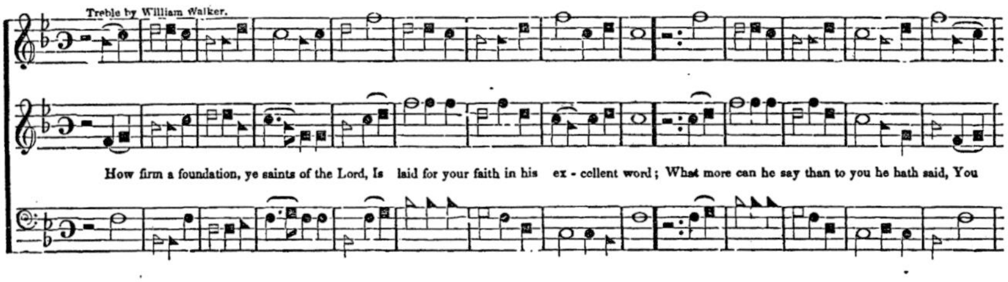
Treble by William Walker.
How firm a foundation, ye saints of the Lord, Is laid for your faith in his ex - cellent word; What more can he say than to you he hath said, You

who unto Jesus for refuge have fled?
1 2

2 In every condition—in sickness and health,
In poverty's vale, or abounding in wealth;
At home and abroad, on the land, on the sea,
As thy days may demand, shall thy strength ever be.

3 "Fear not, I am with thee, O be not dismay'd!
I, I am thy God, and will still give thee aid;
I'll strengthen thee, help thee, and cause thee to stand,
Upheld by my righteous, omnipotent hand.

4 "When through the deep waters I call thee to go,
The rivers of water shall not overflow;
For I will be with thee thy troubles to bless
And sanctify to thee thy deepest distress.

5 "When through fiery trials thy pathway shall lie,
My grace, all-sufficient, shall be thy supply;
The flame shall not hurt thee; I only design
Thy dross to consume, and thy gold to refine.

6 "E'en down to old age, all my people shall prove
My sovereign, eternal, unchangeable love:
And when hoary hairs shall their temples adorn,
Like lambs they shall still in my bosom be borne.

7 "The soul that on Jesus hath lean'd for repose,
I will not, I will not, desert to his foes;
That soul, though all hell should endeavour to shake
I'll never, no never, no never forsake."

DELIGHT. 7, 6.

Methodist Hymn Book, p. 325.

Vain, de - lusive world, adieu, With all of crea - ture good;
On - ly Jesus I pursue, Who bought us with his blood.
All thy pleasures I fore - go, I trample on thy wealth and pride; Only Jesus

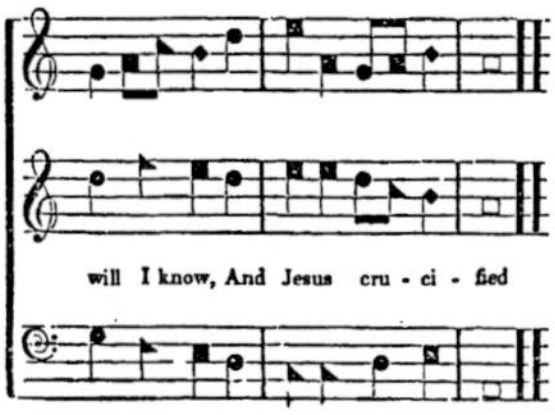
will I know, And Jesus cru - ci - fied

2 Other knowledge I disdain,
  'Tis all but vanity:
Christ, the Lamb of God, was slain,
  He tasted death for me!
Me to save from endless wo,
  The sin-atoning victim died!
Only Jesus will I know,
  And Jesus crucified!

3 Here will I set up my rest;
  My fluctuating heart
From the haven of his breast
  Shall never more depart:
Whither should a sinner go?
  His wounds for me stand open wide;
Only Jesus will I know
  And Jesus crucified

4 Him to know is life and peace,
  And pleasure without end;
This is all my happiness,
  On Jesus to depend;
Daily in his grace to grow,
  And ever in his faith abide,
Only Jesus will I know,
  And Jesus crucified!

5 O that I could all invite,
  This saving truth to prove:
Show the length, the breadth, the heigа
  And depth of Jesus' love!
Fain I would to sinners show
  The blood by faith alone applied!
Only Jesus will I know
  And Jesus crucified

Brethren, we have met to wor - ship, And a - dore the Lord our God;
Will you pray with all your power, While we try to preach the word.
All is vain, unless the Spirit Of the Holy One come down; Brethren, pray, and

ho - ly man - na Will be shower'd all around
1 2

2 Brethren, see poor sinners round you,
Trembling on the brink of wo;
Death is coming, hell is moving;
Can you bear to let them go?
See our fathers—see our mothers,
And our children sinking down;
Brethren, pray, and holy manna
Will be shower'd all around.

3 Sisters, will you join and help us?
Moses' sisters aided him;
Will you help the trembling mourners,
Who are struggling hard with sin?
Tell them all about the Saviour,
Tell them that he will be found;
Sisters, pray, and holy manna
Will be shower'd all around.

4 Is there here a trembling Jailer,
Seeking grace, and fill'd with fears?
Is there here a weeping Mary,
Pouring forth a flood of tears?
Brethren, join your cries to help them
Sisters, let your prayers abound;
Pray, O! pray, that holy manna
May be scatter'd all around.

5 Let us love our God supremely,
Let us love each other too;
Let us love and pray for sinners,
Till our God makes all things new
Then he'll call us home to heaven,
At his table we'll sit down.
Christ will gird himself, and serve us
With sweet manna all around.

THE SAINTS' DELIGHT.

F. Price. 65th hymn, 2d b. Watts.

When I can read my title clear To mansions in the skies, I'll bid farewell to every fear, And wipe my weeping eyes. I feel like, I feel like I'm

- on my journey home. I feel like, I feel like I'm on my journey home.

2 Should earth against my soul engage,
And fiery darts be hurl'd,
Then I can smile at Satan's rage,
And face a frowning world.

3 Let cares like a wild deluge come,
Let storms of sorrow fall,
So I but safely reach my home
My God, my heaven, my all.

4 There I shall bathe my weary soul
In seas of heavenly rest;
And not a wave of trouble roll
Across my peaceful breast.

COME AND TASTE WITH ME. 7,7,7,7,7,7,9,6.

Wm. Walker.

Come and taste, a - long with me, Con - so - la - tion run - ning free, Con - so - la - tion running free, And I will give him glo - ry.
'Tis re - li - gion we be-lieve, O, glo - ry, hal - le - lu - jah! Soon it will land our souls up yon-der; Glo - ry, hal - le - lu - jah!

2. From our Father's wealthy throne,
Sweeter than the honey-comb. ‡
And I will give, &c.

3. Wherefore should I feast alone?
Two are better far than one. ‡
And I will give, &c.

4. All that come with free good-will,
Make the banquet sweeter still. ‡
And I will give, &c.

5. Now I go to mercy's door,
Asking for a little more. ‡
And I will give, &c.

6. Jesus gives a double share,
Calling me his chosen heir. ‡
And I will give, &c.

7. Goodness, running like a stream
Through the New Jerusalem, ‡
And I will give, &c.

8. By a constant breaking forth,
Sweetens earth and heaven both. ‡
And I will give, &c.

9. Saints and angels sing aloud,
To behold the shining crowd, ‡
And I will give, &c.

10. Coming in at mercy's door,
Making still the number more. ‡
And I will give, &c.

11. Heaven's here, and heaven's there,
Comfort flowing everywhere. ‡
And I will give, &c.

12. And I boldly do profess
That my soul hath got a taste. ‡
And I will give, &c.

13. Now I'll go rejoicing home
From the banquet of perfume. ‡
And I will give, &c.

14. Finding manna on the road,
Dropping from the throne of God. ‡
And I will give, &c.

15. O, return, ye sons of grace,
Turn and see God's smiling face. ‡
And I will give, &c.

16. Hark! he calls backsliders home,
Then from him no longer roam. ‡
And I will give, &c.

THE PILGRIM'S SONG. L. M.

1. I am a atran-ger here be-low, And what I am 'tis hard to know; I am so vile, so prone to sin, I fear that I'm not born a-gain.
2. When I ex - pe-rience call to mind, My un-der-stand-ing is so blind— All feeling sense seems to be gone, Which makes me think that I am wrong.

PACOLET. 7, 6.

Wm. Golightly, jun. Dover Selection, p. 7.

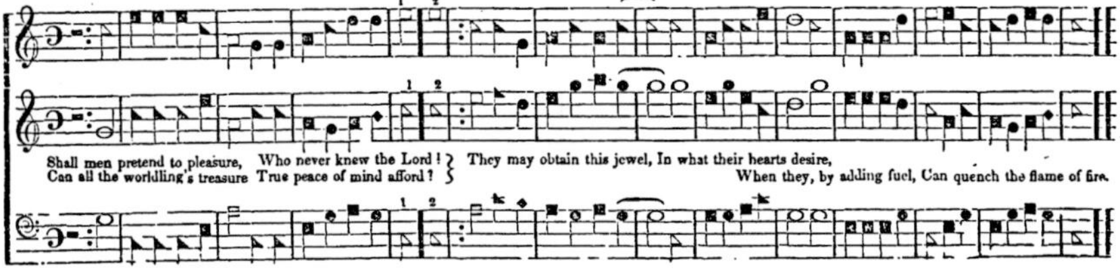
1
2
Shall men pretend to pleasure, Who never knew the Lord!
Can all the worldling's treasure True peace of mind afford?
They may obtain this jewel, In what their hearts desire,
When they, by adding fuel, Can quench the flame of fire.

HALLELUJAH. C. M

Wm. Walker. Dover Selection, p. 169.

Chorus.
And let this fee - ble bo - dy fail, And let die;
My soul shall quit this mournful vale, And soar to worlds on high.
And I'll sing hal - le - lu - jah, And
you'll sing hal - le - lu - jah, And we'll all sing hal - le - lu - jah, When we ar - rive at home.

REDEMPTION. L. M. 2 verses. *A. Benham, sen.*

Earth spreads, &c.
Hark! hark! glad tidings charm our ears, Angelic mu - sic fills the spheres; Earth spreads the sound with decent mirth, A God, a God is born
the hills reply;
A God, a God on earth is born!
on earth! A God is born! the valleys cry; A God is born!
Evening repeats to wondering morn,

WELCH. 8, 4.

There's a friend above all others, O, how he loves!
His is love beyond a brother's, O, how he loves!
Earthly friends may fail and leave us, This day kind, the next bereave us; But this friend will

ne'er deceive us, O, how he loves!

2 Blessed Jesus! wouldst thou know him,
O, how he loves!
Give thyself e'en this day to him,
O, how he loves!
Is it sin that pains and grieves thee?
Unbelief and trials tease thee?
Jesus can from all release thee,
O, how he loves!

3 Love this friend who longs to save thee,
O, how he loves!
Dost thou love? He will not leave thee
O, how he loves!
Think no more then of to-morrow,
Take his easy yoke and follow,
Jesus carries all thy sorrow,
O, how he loves!

4 All thy sins shall be forgiven,
O, how he loves!
Backward all thy foes be driven,
O, how he loves
Best of blessings he'll provide thee,
Naught but good shall e'er betide thee,
Safe to glory he will guide thee,
O, how he loves!

5 Pause, my soul! adore and wonder,
O, how he loves!
Naught can cleave this love asunder,
O, how he loves!
Neither trial, nor temptation,
Doubt, nor fear, nor tribulation,
Can bereave us of salvation;
O, how he loves!

6 Let us still this love be viewing;
O, how he loves!
And, though faint, keep on pursuing
O, how he loves!
He will strengthen each endeavour.
And when pass'd o'er Jordan's river
This shall be our song for ever
O, how he loves!

WOODLAND. C. M. or 8, 6, 8, 8, 6

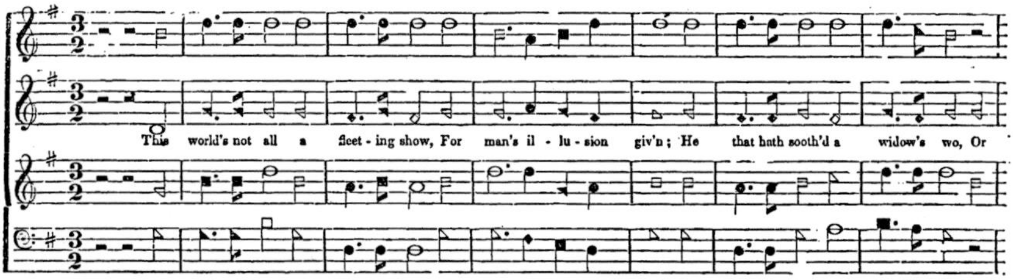
This world's not all a fleet - ing show, For man's il - lu - sion giv'n; He that hath sooth'd a widow's wo, Or

wiped an or - phan's tear, doth know There's something here of heav'n.

2 And he that walks life's thorny way,
With feelings calm and ev'n,
Whose path is lit from day to day
With virtue's bright and steady ray,
Hath something felt of heav'n.

3 He that the Christian's course has run,
And all his foes forgiv'n,
Who measures out life's little span
In love to God and love to man,
On earth hath tasted heav'n.

James Langston.
From Greenland's icy mountains,
From India's coral strand;
Where Afric's sunny fountains
Roll down their golden sand;
From many an ancient river,
From many a palmy plain,
They

call us to de - liver Their land from error's chain.

2 What though the spicy breeze
Blow soft o'er Ceylon's isle,
Though every prospect pleases,
And only man is vile;
In vain, with lavish kindness,
The gifts of God are strown;
The heathen, in his blindness,
Bows down to wood and stone.

3 Shall we, whose souls are lighted
With wisdom from on high,
Shall we, to men benighted,
The lamp of life deny?
Salvation! O salvation!
The joyful sound proclaim,
Till earth's remotest nation
Has learn'd Messiah's name.

4 Waft, waft, ye winds, his story,
And you, ye waters, roll
Till, like a sea of glory,
It spreads from pole to pole
Till o'er our ransom'd nature.
The Lamb for sinners slain,
Redeemer, King, Creator
In bliss returns to reign.

SOCIAL BAND. L. M

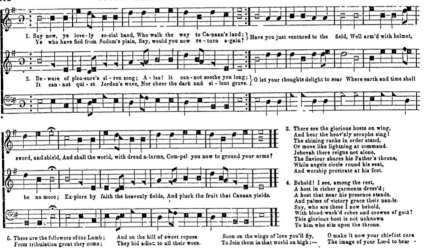

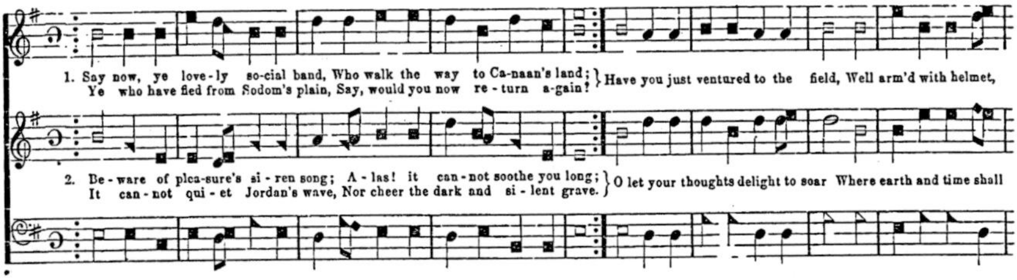
1. Say now, ye love-ly so-cial band, Who walk the way to Ca-naan's land; } Have you just ventured to the field, Well arm'd with helmet,
Ye who have fled from Sodom's plain, Say, would you now re-turn a-gain?
2. Be-ware of plea-sure's si-ren song; A-las! it can-not soothe you long; } O let your thoughts delight to soar Where earth and time shall
It can-not qui-et Jordan's wave, Nor cheer the dark and si-lent grave.

sword, and shield, And shall the world, with dread a-larms, Com-pel you now to ground your arms?
be no more; Ex-plore by faith the heavenly fields, And pluck the fruit that Canaan yields.

3. There see the glorious hosts on wing,
And hear the heav'nly seraphs sing!
The shining ranks in order stand,
Or move like lightning at command.
Jehovah there reigns not alone,
The Saviour shares his Father's throne,
While angels circle round his seat,
And worship prostrate at his feet.

4. Behold! I see, among the rest,
A host in richer garments dress'd;
A host that near his presence stands,
And palms of victory grace their hands.
Say, who are these I now behold,
With blood-wash'd robes and crowns of gold?
This glorious host is not unknown
To him who sits upon the throne.

5. These are the followers of the Lamb;
From tribulation great they came;
And on the hill of sweet repose
They bid adieu to all their woes.
Soon on the wings of love you'll fly,
To Join them in that world on high;—
O make it now your chiefest care
The image of your Lord to bear.

How splendid shines the morning star,
God's gracious light from darkness far The root of Jesse blessed.
Thou David's son of Jacob's stem, My bridegroom, king, and wondrous
Lamb, Thou hast my heart possessed. Sweetly, friendly, O thou handsome, precious ransom, Full of graces, set and kept in heav'nly places.

ALABAMA. C. M.

Those happy
Counter by William Walker.
Angels in shining order stand, Around the Saviour's throne; They bow with reverence at his feet, and make his glories known. Those happy spirits sing his

1 The cross of Christ inspires my heart,
To sing redeeming grace;
Awake, my soul, and bear a part
In my Redeemer's praise.
O! what can be compar'd to him
Who died upon the tree!
This is my dear, delightful theme
That Jesus died for me.

2 When at the table of the Lord
We humbly take our place,
The death of Jesus we record,
With love and thankfulness
These emblems bring my Lord to view,
Upon the bloody tree,
My soul believes and feels it's true,
That Jesus died for me.

3 His body broken, nail'd, and torn,
And stain'd with streams of blood,
His spotless soul was left forlorn,
Forsaken of his God.
'Twas then his Father gave the stroke
That justice did decree;
All nature felt the dreadful stroke.
When Jesus died for me.

4 Eli lama sabachthani,
My God, my God, he cried,
Why hast thou thus forsaken me!
And thus my Saviour died.
But why did God forsake his Son,
When bleeding on the tree?
He died for sins, but not his own,
For Jesus died for me

5 My guilt was on my Surety laid
And therefore he must die;
His soul a sacrifice was made,
For such a worm as I

spirits, &c.
Those,
Those,
praise, To all e - ter - ni - ty,
But I can sing redeeming grace, For Jesus died for me.

Was ever love so great as this?
Was ever grace so free!
This is my glory, joy and bliss,
That Jesus died for me.

6 He took his meritorious blood,
And rose above the skies,
And in the presence of his God,
Presents his sacrifice.
His intercession must prevail
With such a glorious plea

My cause can never, never fail,
For Jesus died for me

7 Angels in shining order sit
Around my Saviour's throne;
They bow with reverence at his feet
And make his glories known.
Those happy spirits sing his praise
To all eternity;
But I can sing redeeming grace
For Jesus died for me.

8 O! had I but an angel's voice
To bear my heart along,
My flowing numbers soon would raise
To an immortal song.
I'd charm their harps and golden lyres
In sweetest harmony,
And tell to all the heavenly choirs
That Jesus died for me.

JUBILEE. P. M.

Unknown.

Hark! the jubilee is sounding, O the joyful news is come;
Free salvation is proclaimed In and through God's only Son:
Now we have an in - vi - tation, To the meek and lowly Lamb, Glory, honour, and sal-

vation; Christ, the Lord, is come to reign.

2 Come, dear friends, and don't neglect it,
Come to Jesus in your prime;
Great salvation, don't reject it,
O receive it, now's your time;
Now the Saviour is beginning
To revive his work again.
Glory, honour, &c.

3 Now let each one cease from sinning,
Come and follow Christ the way;
We shall all receive a blessing,
If from him we do not stray;
Golden moments we've neglected,
Yet the Lord invites again!
Glory, honour, &c

4 Come, let us run our race with patience,
Looking unto Christ the Lord,
Who doth live and reign for ever,
With his Father and our God;
He is worthy to be praised,
He is our exalted king,
Glory, honour, &c.

5 Come, dear children, praise your Jesus,
Praise him, praise him evermore,
May his great love now constrain us,
His great name for to adore·
O then let us join together,
Crowns of glory to obtain!
Glory, honour, &c.

PART II.

CONTAINING

SOME OF THE MORE LENGTHY AND ELEGANT PIECES, COMMONLY USED AT CONCERTS, OR SINGING SOCIETIES.

TRIBULATION. C. M.

Chapin. Hymn 55, Book 2, Watts.

Death, 'tis a melan - choly day, To those who have no God, When the poor soul is forced a - way, To seek her last abode.

2 In vain to heaven she lifts her eyes,
For guilt, a heavy chain,
Still drags her downward from the skies,
To darkness fire, and pain.

3 Awake and mourn, ye heirs of hell,
Let stubborn sinners fear;
You must be driv'n from earth, and dwell
A long for ever there.

4 See how the pit gapes wide for you,
And flashes in your face;
And thou, my soul, look downward too,
And sing recovering grace.

5 He is a god of sovereign love,
That promised heaven to me.
And taught my thoughts to soar above.
Where happy spirits be.

6 Prepare me, Lord, for thy right hand,
Then come the joyful day;
Come, death, and some celestial band,
To bear my soul away.

FLORIDA S. M.

Wilmore.

Let sin - ners take their course, And choose the road to death; But in the wor - ship of my God, I'll spend my dai - ly
breath, I'll spend my daily breath, But in the worship of my God, I'll spend my dai - ly breath.

GREENFIELD. L. P. M.

God is our refuge in distress, A present help when dangers press; In him undaunted we'll confide, Though earth were from her centre toss'd, And
mountains in the o - cean lost, Torn piecemeal by the roar - ing tide, Torn piecemeal by the roar - ing tide.

FAITHFUL SOLDIER. 7, 6

Wm. Walker. Dover Selection, p. 129.

1
2
1
2
O when shall I see Jesus, And reign with him above ?
And from the flowing fountain, Drink everlasting love ?
When shall I be de - liver'd From this vain world of sin ?
And with my blessed
1
2

Je - sus, Drink endless pleasures in

2 But now I am a soldier,
  My Captain's gone before;
He's given me my orders,
  And bids me ne'er give o'er;
His promises are faithful—
  A righteous crown he'll give,
And all his valiant soldiers
  Eternally shall live.

3 Through grace I am determined
  To conquer, though I die,
And then away to Jesus,
  On wings of love I'll fly:
Farewell to sin and sorrow,
  I bid them both adieu!
And O, my friends, prove faithful,
  And on your way pursue

4 Whene'er you meet with troubles
  And trials on your way,
Then cast your care on Jesus,
  And don't forget to pray.
Gird on the gospel armour
  Of faith, and hope, and love,
And when the combat's ended,
  He'll carry you above.

5 O do not be discouraged,
  For Jesus is your friend;
And if you lack for knowledge,
  He'll not refuse to lend.
Neither will he upbraid you,
  Though often you request,
He'll give you grace to conquer,
  And take you home to rest.

6 And when the last loud trumpet
  Shall rend the vaulted skies,
And bid th' entombed millions
  From their cold beds arise;
Our ransom'd dust, revived,
  Bright beauties shall put on,
And soar to the blest mansions
  Where our Redeemer's gone.

7 Our eyes shall then with rapture,
  The Saviour's face behold;
Our feet, no more diverted,
  Shall walk the streets of gold
Our ears shall hear with transport
  The hosts celest'al sing;
Our tongues shall chant the glories
  Of our immortal King.

DISCIPLE. 8s & 7s. D.

Treble by Wm Houser. From Christian Lyre.

Rather Slow
*1. Je - sus, I my cross have ta - ken, All to leave and fol-low thee: Naked, poor, despised, for - saken, Thou from hence my all shalt be:
2. Let the world de-spise and leave me, They have left my Sa-viour, too; Human hearts and looks deceive me, Thou art not like them, un-true;
Per - ish ev' - ry fond am - bi - tion, All I've sought, or hoped, or known, Yet how rich is my con - di - tion, God and heav'n are still my own!
And whilst thou shalt smile up-on me, God of wisdom, love, and might, Foes may hate, and friends disown me; Show thy face and all is bright.

3. Go, then, earthly fame and treasure,
Come, disaster, scorn, and pain;
In thy service pain is pleasure,
With thy favour loss is gain.
I have called thee, Abba, Father,
I have set my heart on thee:
Storms may howl, and clouds may gather,
All must work for good to me.

4. Man may trouble and distress me,
'Twill but drive me to thy breast;
Life with trials hard may press me,
Heav'n will bring me sweeter rest.
Oh! 'tis not in grief to harm me,
While thy love is left to me;
Oh! 'twere not in joy to charm me,
Were that joy unmix'd with thee.

5. Soul, then know thy full salvation;
Rise o'er sin, and fear, and care;
Joy to find, in ev'ry station,
Something still to do or bear:
Think what Spirit dwells within thee;
Think what Father's smiles are thine;
Think that Jesus died to win thee;
Child of heaven, canst thou repine?

6. Haste thee on from grace to glory,
Arm'd by faith, and wing'd by prayer!
Heaven's eternal day's before thee,
God's own hand shall guide thee there:
Soon shall close thy earthly mission,
Soon shall pass thy pilgrim days;
Hope shall change to glad fruition,
Faith to sight, and prayer to praise.

* This glorious hymn is said to have been composed by a young English lady, a Methodist, who had suffered much affliction.

SHARON P. M.

How pleasant 'tis to see, Kindred and friends agree, Each in his proper station move, Each in his proper station move,
move, And each fulfil his part, With sympathizing heart, In all the cares of life, In all the cares of life and love.

My gracious Redeem - er   I   love,   His praises a - loud   I'll pro - claim, To   gaze   on the glories   di - vine, Shall be my   e - ter nal em-
And join with the armies   above,   To shout his a - do - ra - ble   name.

ploy,   And   feel them in - ces - sant   ly   shine,   My   boundless,   in - ef - fa - ble   joy.

SARDINA C. M

How did his flow - ing tears con - dole, As for a bro - thar dead, And fasting, mortified his soul, While for their lives he pray'd.

They groan'd and cursed him on their beds, Yet still he pleads and mourns ; And double blessings on his head, The righteous Lord re - turns

O, how happy are they, Who their Saviour obey, And whose treasure is laid up above; Tongue can never express The sweet comfort and

peace, Of a soul in its ear - li - est love.
1
2

2 That comfort was mine,
When the favour divine.
I first found in the blood of the Lamb;
When my heart first believed,
O! what joy I received!
What a heaven in Jesus's name.

3 'Twas a heaven below,
The Redeemer to know,
And the angels could do nothing more
Than to fall at his feet,
And the story repeat,
And the Saviour of sinners adore.

4 Jesus, all the day long,
Was my joy and my song;
O! that all his salvation might see!
He hath loved me, I cried,
He hath suffer'd and died,
To redeem such a rebel as me.

5 On the wings of his love,
I was carried above
All sin, and temptation, and pain;
I could not believe
That I ever should grieve,
That I ever should suffer again.

6 I rode on the sky,
Freely justified I,
Nor envied Elijah his seat;
My soul mounted higher,
In a chariot of fire,
And the world was put under my feet.

7 O, the rapturous height
Of that holy delight
Which I felt in the life-giving blood
Of my Saviour possess'd,
I was perfectly bless'd,
Overwhelm'd with the fulness of God.

8 What a mercy is this!
What a heaven of bliss!
How unspeakably favour'd am I!
Gather'd into the fold,
With believers enroll'd,
With believers to live and to die!

9 Now my remnant of days
Would I spend to his praise,
Who hath died my poor soul to redeem
Whether many or few,
All my years are his due;
May they all be devoted to him

LEANDER. C. M.

Austin.

My soul forsakes her vain delight, And bids the world farewell, Base as the dirt beneath thy feet, And mischievous as hell. No longer will I
ask your love, Nor seek your friendship more; The hap - pi - ness that I approve, Is not with - in your pow'r.
1
2

Mine eyes are now closing to rest, My body must soon be removed, And mould'ring, lie buried in dust, No more to be envied or
loved, No more to be envied or loved. Ah! what is this drawing my breath, And stealing my senses a - way.

O tell me, O tell me, O tell me, O tell me, my soul, is it death, Releasing me kindly from clay ! Now mounting, my soul shall de-
scry The regions of pleasure and love, My spirit triumphant shall fly, And dwell with my Saviour a - bove

THE CHRISTIAN'S CONFLICTS. 7, 6. *Wm. Walker* Dover Sel. p. 198

Very Brisk.
See how the wicked kingdom Is falling every day, And still our blessed Jesus Is winning souls a way; But
O how I am tempted, No mortal tongue can tell, So often I'm sur - rounded With enemies from hell.

BRUCE'S ADDRESS *Spiritualized.* 7, 7, 7, 5, 7, 7, 7, 5. *Wm. Walker.* Dover Sel. p. 152

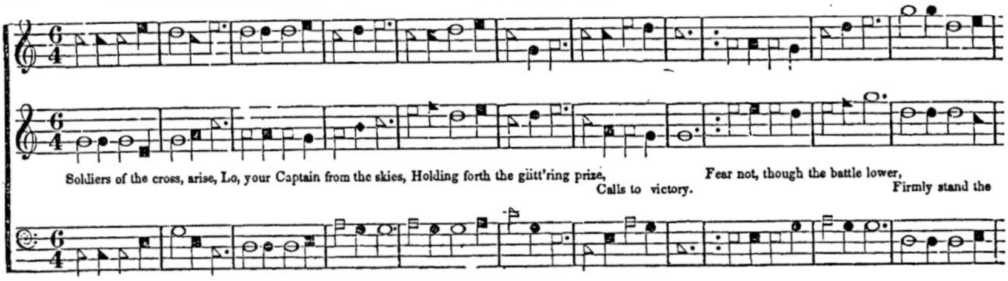
Soldiers of the cross, arise, Lo, your Captain from the skies, Holding forth the glitt'ring prize,
Calls to victory.
Fear not, though the battle lower,
Firmly stand the

trying hour, Stand the tempter's utmost power,
Spurn his slavery.

2 Who the cause of Christ would yield!
Who would leave the battle-field!
Who would cast away his shield!—
Let him basely go:
Who for Zion's King will stand!
Who will join the faithful band!
Let him come with heart and hand,
Let him face the foe.

3 By the mercies of our God,
By Emmanuel's streaming blood,
When alone for us he stood,
Ne'er give up the strife:
Even to the latest breath,
Hark to what your Captain saith;—
"Be thou faithful unto death;
Take the crown of life."

4 By the woes which rebels prove,
By the bliss of holy love,
Sinners, seek the joys above,
Sinners turn, and live!
Here is freedom worth the name;
Tyrant sin is put to shame;
Grace inspires the hallow'd flame
God the crown will give.

INDIAN CONVERT, (or NASHVILLE). 8,8,6.

Johnson

1. In de dark woods, no Indian nigh, Den me look Heb'n, and send up cry, Den me look Heb'n, and send up cry, Up - on my knee so low; But
2. God send he an - gel, take um care, He cum he self and hear um prayer, He cum he self and hear um prayer, (If In - dian heart do pray,) He
God on high, in shiny place, See me at night, wid teary face— See me at night, wid teary face— De preacher tell me so.
see me now, he know me here; He say, Poor In - dian, ne - ver fear, He say, Poor In - dian, ne - ver fear, Me wid you night and day.
1
2

3. So me lub God, wid inside heart,
He fight for me, he take um part,
He save um life before;
God hear poor Indian in de wood;
So me lub him, and dat be good
Me prize him evermore.

4. De joy I felt I cannot tell,
To tink dat I was saved from hell,
Through Jesus' streaming blood;
Dat I am saved by grace divine,
Who am de worst of all mankind,
O glory be to God;

5. Now I be here baptized to be,
Dat in de water you may see
De way my Jesus go;
Dis is de way I do believe
Dat Jesus here for us did leave,
To follow here below

The first three verses of this song were taken almost verbatim, by a Missionary, from an Indian's experience, while he was relating it: the last two verses were composed by David Walker the Author's brother.

IMANDRA. 11's.

A. Davison.

I love thee, my Saviour, I love thee, my Lord,
I love thy dear people, thy ways, and thy word;
With tender emotion I love sinners too, Since Jesus has died to redeem them from wo.

1 O Jesus, my Saviour, I know thou art mine,
For thee all the pleasures of sin I resign;
Of objects most pleasing, I love thee the best,
Without thee I'm wretched, but with thee I'm blest.

2 Thy Spirit first taught me to know I was blind,
Then taught me the way of salvation to find:
And when I was sinking in gloomy despair,
Thy mercy relieved me, and bid me not fear.

3 In vain I attempt to describe what I feel,
The language of mortals or angels would fail;
My Jesus is precious, my soul's in a flame,
I'm raised to a rapture while praising his name.

4 I find him in singing, I find him in prayer,
In sweet meditation he always is near;
My constant companion, O may we ne'er part!
All glory to Jesus, he dwells in my heart.

5 I love thee, my Saviour, &c.

6 My Jesus is precious—I cannot forbear,
Though sinners despise me, his love to declare;
His love overwhelms me; had I wings I'd fly
To praise him in mansions prepared in the sky.

7 Then millions of ages my soul would employ
In praising my Jesus, my love and my joy
Without interruption, when all the glad throng
With pleasures unceasing unite in the song.

WHITESTOWN. L. M *Ward*

Where nothing dwelt but beasts of prey, Or men as fierce and wild as they, He bids th' oppress'd and poor repair,
And build them towns and cities there.
They sow the fields, and
trees they plant,
Whose yearly fruit supplies their want;
Their race grows up from fruitful stocks, Their wealth increases with their flocks.

PORTUGUESE HYMN. P. M

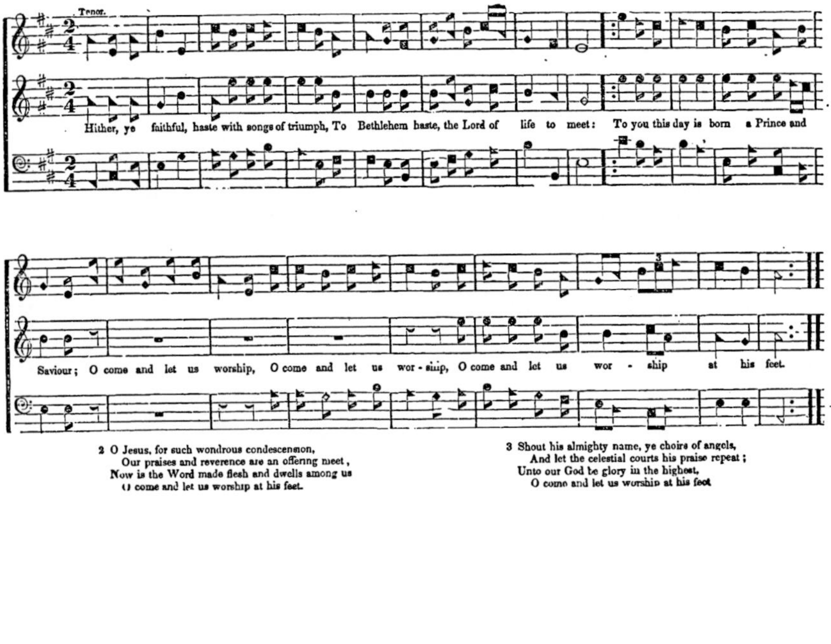
Tenor.
Hither, ye faithful, haste with songs of triumph, To Bethlehem haste, the Lord of life to meet: To you this day is born a Prince and
Saviour; O come and let us worship, O come and let us wor - siip, O come and let us wor - ship at his feet.

2 O Jesus, for such wondrous condescension,
Our praises and reverence are an offering meet,
Now is the Word made flesh and dwells among us
() come and let us worship at his feet.

3 Shout his almighty name, ye choirs of angels,
And let the celestial courts his praise repeat;
Unto our God be glory in the highest,
O come and let us worship at his feet

SWEET PROSPECT. C. M. *Wm. Walker* Dover Sel p. 171

On- Jor - dan's stormy banks I stand, And cast a wish - ful eye,
To Ca - naan's fair and hap - py land, Where my pos - sessions lie.
O the trans - port - ing, rapturous scene, That
ri - ses to my sight, Sweet fields ar - ray'd in liv - ing green, And ri - vers of de - light.

THE PILGRIM'S LOT. 8, 8, 6.

A. Gramblin. Mercer's Cluster, p. 224.

How happy is the pilgrim's lot, How free from anxious care and thought, How free from anxious care and thought, From worldly hope and fear; Con-
fined to neither court nor cell, His soul disdains on earth to dwell, His soul dis - dains on earth to dwell, He on - ly sojourns here.

HALLELUJAH. 8, 6, 8, 6, 8, 6, 8, 7. *Dr. Harrison.*

He comes! he comes! the Judge severe! halle, hal - le - lu - jah!
The seventh trum - pet speaks him near! halle, hal - le - lu - jah!
His lightning flash and thunder roll
halle, hal - le lu - jah!
How welcome to the faith - ful soul, O hal - le, hal - le - lu - jah!

KNOXVILLE. 8, 8, 8, 8, 7

R. Monday Dover Sel. p. 74.

Re - joice, my friends, the Lord is King,
Let all pre - pare to take him in,
Let Jacob rise, and Zi on sing, And all the earth with praises

ring, And give to Je - sus glory

2 O! may the desert land rejoice,
And mourners hear the Saviour's voice;
While praise their every tongue employs,
And all obtain immortal joys,
And give to Jesus glory.

3 O! may the saints of every name
Unite to praise the bleeding Lamb!
May jars and discords cease to flame,
And all the Saviour's love proclaim,
And give to Jesus glory.

4 I long to see the Christians join
In union sweet, and peace divine;
When every church with grace shall shine,
And grow in Christ the living vine,
And give to Jesus glory.

5 Come, parents, children, bond, and free,
Come, who will go along with me?
I'm bound fair Canaan's land to see,
And shout with saints eternally,
And give to Jesus glory

6 Those beauteous fields of living green,
By faith my joyful eyes have seen;
Though Jordan's billows roll between,
We soon shall cross the narrow stream,
And give to Jesus glory.

7 A few more days of pain and wo,
A few more suffering scenes below,
And then to Jesus we shall go,
Where everlasting pleasures flow,
And there we'll give him glory.

8 That awful trumpet soon will sound,
And shake the vast creation round,
And call the nations under ground,
And all the saints shall then be crown'd,
And give to Jesus glory.

9 Then shall our tears be wiped away,
No more our feet shall ever stray;
When we are freed from cumbrous clay
We'll praise the Lord in endless day
And give to Jesus glory

Hail, Columbia! happy land! Hail, ye heroes, heav'n-born band! Who fought and bled in freedom's cause, Who fought and bled in freedom's cause.
And when the storm of war is gone, Enjoy the peace your valour won; Let independence be your boast, Ever mindful what it cost; Ever grateful

for the prize, Let its altar reach the skies. Firm, united, let us be, Rallying round our lib - er - ty.
As a band of bre thers join'd, Peace and safe - ty we shall find.

Good morning, brother pilgrim,
What, bound for Canaan's coast!
March you towards Jerusalem,
To join the heav'nly host!
Pray, wherefore are you smiling,
While tears run down your face!
We
soon shall cease from toiling,
And reach that heav'nly place,
And reach that heav'nly place;
We soon shall cease from toiling, And reach that heav'nly place.

2 To Canaan's coast we'll hasten,
To join the heavenly throng,
Hark! from the banks of Jordan,
How sweet the pilgrims' song!
Their Jesus they are viewing,
By faith we see him too,
We smile, and weep, and praise him,
And on our way pursue

3 Though sinners do despise us,
And treat us with disdain,
Our former comrades slight us
Esteem us low and mean
No earthly joy shall charm us,
While marching on our way,
Our Jesus will defend us,
In the distressing day.

4 The frowns of old companions,
We're willing to sustain,
And in divine compassion,
To pray for them again;
For Christ, our loving Saviour,
Our Comforter and Friend,
Will bless us with his favour,
And guide us to the end.

4 With streams of consolation,
We're filled as with new wine
We die to transient pleasures,
And live to things divine
We sink in holy raptures
While viewing things above,
Why glory to my Saviour
My soul is full of love

O COME, COME AWAY

Treble by W. Houser.

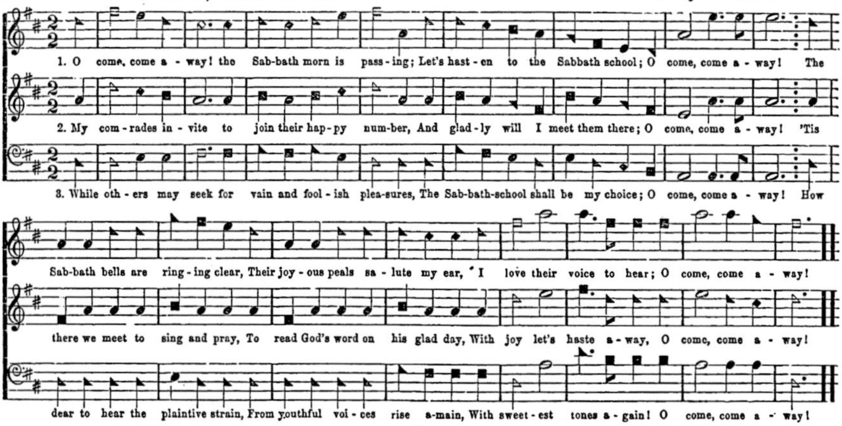
1. O come, come a - way! the Sab-bath morn is pass - ing; Let's hast - en to the Sabbath school; O come, come a - way! The
2. My com - rades in - vite to join their hap - py num-ber, And glad - ly will I meet them there; O come, come a - way! 'Tis
3. While oth - ers may seek for vain and fool - ish plea-sures, The Sab-bath-school shall be my choice; O come, come a - way! How
Sab-bath bells are ring - ing clear, Their joy - ous peals sa - lute my ear, I love their voice to hear; O come, come a - way!
there we meet to sing and pray, To read God's word on his glad day, With joy let's haste a - way, O come, come a - way!
dear to hear the plaintive strain, From youthful voi - ces rise a-main, With sweet - est tones a - gain! O come, come a - way!

4.
'Tis there I may learn the ways of heavenly wisdom,
To guide my feeble steps on high; O come, &c.
The flow'ry paths of peace to tread,
Where rays of heavenly bliss are shed,
My wand'ring steps to lead: O come, &c.

5.
I there hear the voice in heavenly accents speaking,
"Let little children come to me; O come, &c.
Forbid them not their hearts to give,
Let them on me in youth believe,
And I will them receive:" O come, &c.

6.
With joy I accept the gracious invitation;
My heart exults with rapturous hope; O come, &c
My deathless spirit, when I die,
Shall, on the wings of angels, fly
To mansions in the sky: O come, &c.

RHODE ISLAND. 8, 8, 6

Meth. Hymn Book, p. 107.

Thou great, mys - te - rious God unknown, Whose love hath gen - tly led me on, E'en from my in - fant days.
My in - most soul ex - pose to view, And tell me if I e - ver knew Thy jus - ti fy - ing grace.
1
2

12

ROYAL PROCLAMATION. 8, 8, 8, 8, 8, 3.

Dover Sel. p. 18

Hear the royal procla - mation, The glad tidings of sal - vation, Publish - ing to every creature, To the ruin'd sons of nature; Jesus
Chorus.

reigns, he reigns victorious, O - ver heav'n and earth most glorious, Jesus reigns.

2 See the royal banner flying,
Hear the heralds loudly crying,
"Rebel sinners, royal favour
Now is offer'd by the Saviour."
Jesus reigns, &c.

3 Hear, ye sons of wrath and ruin,
Who have wrought your own undoing,
Here is life and free salvation,
Offer'd to the whole creation.
Jesus reigns, &c.

4 Turn unto the Lord most holy,
Shun the paths of vice and folly;
Turn, or you are lost for ever,
O! now turn to God the Saviour.
Jesus reigns, &c.

PASTORAL ELEGY. 8's.

What sorrowful sounds do I hear Move slowly along. in the gale? How solemn they fall on my ear, As softly they pass through the vale. Sweet
Corydon's notes are all o'er, Now lonely he sleeps in the clay, His cheeks bloom with roses no more, Since death call'd his spirit away.
1
2

2 Sweet woodbines will rise round his feet,
And willows their sorrowing wave;
Young hyacinths freshen and bloom,
While hawthorns encircle his grave.
Each morn when the sun gilds the east,
(The green grass bespangled with dew,)
He'll cast his bright beams on the west,
To charm the sad Caroline's view.

3 O Corydon! hear the sad cries
Of Caroline, plaintive and slow;
O spirit! look down from the skies,
And pity thy mourner below;
'Tis Caroline's voice in the grove,
Which Philomel hears on the plain,
Then striving the mourner to soothe,
With sympathy joins in her strain.

4 Ye shepherds so blithesome and young,
Retire from your sports on the green,
Since Corydon's deaf to my song,
The wolves tear the lambs on the plain;
Each swain round the forest will stray
And sorrowing hang down his head,
His pipe then in symphony play,
Some dirge to sweet Corydon's shade.

5 And when the still night has unfurl'd
Her robes o'er the hamlet around,
Gray twilight retires from the world,
And darkness encumbers the ground,
I'll leave my own gloomy abode,
To Corydon's urn will I fiv.
There kneeling will bless the just Gol
Who dwelir [illegible] t mansions on bigh

MISSISSIPPI. 8, 8, 8, 7, 8, 8, 3, 3, 3, 3, 8.

Brasshaw.

When Gabriel's awful trump shall sound, And rend the rocks, convulse the ground,
And give to time her ut - most bound,
Ye dead, arise to judgment; See lightnings
flash and thunders roll, See earth wrapt up like parchment scroll;
Comets blaze, Sinners raise,
Dread amaze,
Horrors seize
The guilty sons of Adam's race, Unsaved from sin by Jesus.

The Christian fill'd with rapturous joy, Midst flaming worlds he mounts on high, To meet the Saviour in the sky, And see the face of Jesus;
The soul and body reunite, And fill'd with glory infinite, Blessed day, Christians say! Will you pray, That we may All join the happy company, To praise the name of Jesus.

LENA. 8, 7

See the Lord of glory dying! See him gasping! hear him crying! See his burden'd bosom heave!
Look, ye sinners, ye that hung him; Look, how deep your sins have stung him; Dy - ing sin ners, look and live.

PILGRIM. 8, 6, 8, 6, 8, 6, 8, 6. C. M.

Come, all ye mourning pilgrims dear, Who're bound for Canaan's land, } Our Captain's gone before us, Our Father's only Son,
Take courage and fight valiantly, Stand fast with sword in hand; } Then, pilgrims dear, pray, do not fear, But let us follow on.

2 We have a howling wilderness,
To Canaan's happy shore,
A land of dearth, and pits, and snares,
Where chilling winds do roar.
But Jesus will be with us,
And guard us by the way;
Though enemies examine us,
He'll teach us what to say

3 The pleasant fields of paradise,
So glorious to behold,
The valleys clad in living green,
The mountains paved with gold:
The trees of life with heavenly fruit,
Behold how rich they stand
Blow, gentle gales, and bear my soul
To Canaan's happy land.

4 Sweet rivers of salvation all
Through Canaan's land do roll,
The beams of day bring glittering scenes
Illuminate my soul;
There's ponderous clouds of glory,
All set in diamonds bright;
And there's my smiling Jesus,
Who is my heart's delight.

5 Already to my raptured sight,
The blissful fields arise,
And plenty spreads her smiling stores,
Inviting to my eyes.
O sweet abode of endless rest,
I soon shall travel there,
Nor earth nor all her empty joys
Shall long detain me here

6 Come, all you pilgrim travellers,
Fresh courage take by me;
Meantime I'll tell you how I came,
This happy land to see;
Through faith the glorious telescope
I view'd the worlds above,
And God the Father reconciled,
Which fills my heart with love

REPOSE. 8 7.

The Lamb appears to wipe our tears, And to complete our glory; Then shall we rest with all the blest, And tell the lovely story. To
sit and tell Christ loved us well, And that when we were sin - ners; Heaven will ring, while saints do sing, "Glory to the Redeem - er"

TRANSPORT. 12, 11

Ye children of Jesus, who're bound for the kingdom, Attune all your voices, and help me to sing
Sweet anthems of praises to my loving Jesus, For he is my prophet, my priest, and my king;
When Jesus first found me astray I was going, His
love did surround me, and saved me from ruin, He kindly embraced me, and freely he bless'd me, And taught me aloud his sweet praises to sing.
1
2

2 Why should you go mourning from such a physician,
Come to him believing, though bad your condition,
My soul he hath healed, my heart he rejoices,
I'll serve him, and praise him, and always adore him

Who's able and willing your sickness to cure.
His Father has promised your case to ensure:
He brought me to Zion, to hear the glad voices,
Till we meet in heaven where parting's no more

UPTON. L. M.

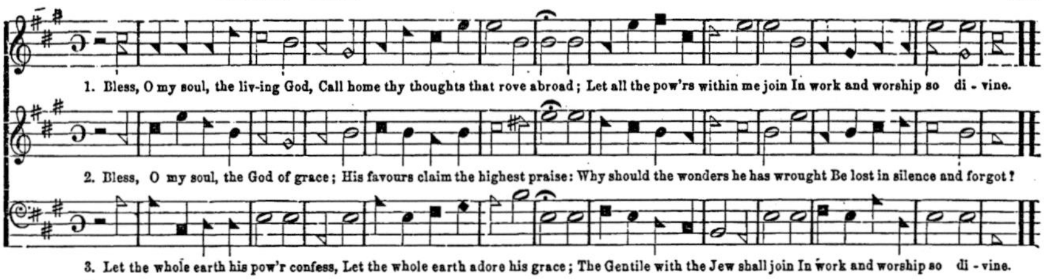
1. Bless, O my soul, the liv-ing God, Call home thy thoughts that rove abroad; Let all the pow'rs within me join In work and worship so di - vine.
2. Bless, O my soul, the God of grace; His favours claim the highest praise: Why should the wonders he has wrought Be lost in silence and forgot?
3. Let the whole earth his pow'r confess, Let the whole earth adore his grace; The Gentile with the Jew shall join In work and worship so di - vine.

WELTON. L. M.

Theme by Malan.

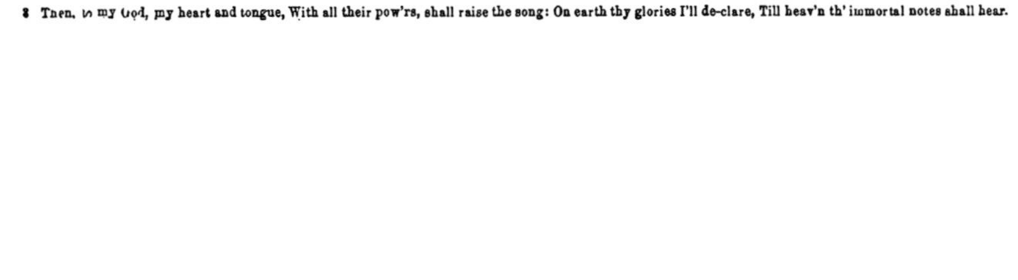
1 Thou great In-struc-tor, lest I stray, Oh! teach my err - ing feet thy way: Thy truth, with ever fresh delight, Shall guide my doubtful steps aright.
2. How oft my heart's af-fections yield, And wander o'er the world's wide field, My rov-ing passions, Lord, reclaim, Unite them all to fear thy name.
3 Then, O my God, my heart and tongue, With all their pow'rs, shall raise the song: On earth thy glories I'll de-clare, Till heav'n th' immortal notes shall hear.

KAMBIA. S. M.

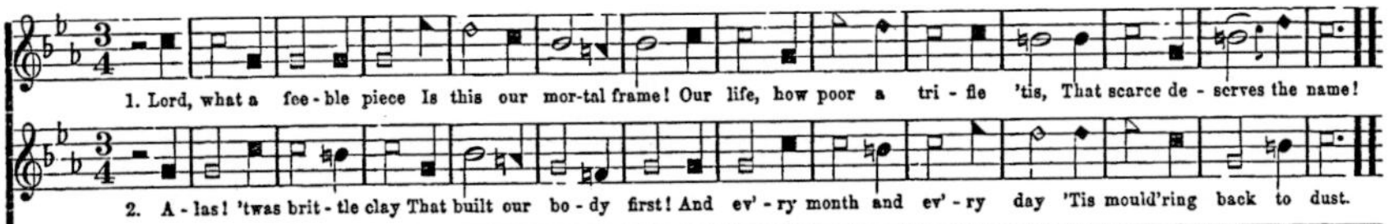
1. Lord, what a fee - ble piece Is this our mor-tal frame! Our life, how poor a tri - fle 'tis, That scarce de - serves the name!
2. A - las! 'twas brit - tle clay That built our bo - dy first! And ev' - ry month and ev' - ry day 'Tis mould'ring back to dust.

3. Our moments fly apace,
Our feeble powers decay;
Swift as a flood our hasty days
Are sweeping us away.

4. Yet if our days must fly,
We'll keep their end in sight,
We'll spend them all in wisdom's ways,
And let them speed their flight.

5. They'll waft us sooner o'er
This life's tempestuous sea:
Soon shall we reach the peaceful shore,
Of bloet eternity.

LISBON. S. M.

Theme by Read.

1. Wel-come, sweet day of rest, That saw the Lord a - rise; Wel - come to this re - vi - ving breast, And these re - joic - ing eyes.
2. The king him-self comes near, To feast his saints to - day; Here we may sit, and see him here, And love, and praise, and pray.
3. One day a - mid the place Where my dear God hath been, Is sweet - er than ten thou-sand days Of plea - sur - a - ble sin.
4 My will - ing soul would stay In such a frame as this, And sit and sing her - self a - way To ev - er - last - ing bliss

SWEET SOLITUDE. L. M

Hail, solitude! thou gentle queen, Of modest air and brow serene, 'Tis thou inspires the poet's theme, Wrapp'd in sweet vision's airy dream; Wrapp'd

in sweet vision's a - ry dream, Wrapp'd in sweet vision s airy dream.

2 Parent of virtue, muse of thought,
By thee are saints and patriots taught
Wisdom to thee her treasures owe,
And in thy lap fair science grow.

3 Whate'er's in thee, refines and charms,
Excites to thought, to virtue warms;
Whate'er is perfect, firm and good,
We owe to thee, sweet solitude.

4 With thee the charms of life shall last,
E'en when the rosy bloom is past;
When slowly pacing time shall spread
Thy silver blossoms o'er my head.

5 No more with this vain world perplex'd,
Thou shalt prepare me for the next
The spring of life shall gently cease,
And angels waft my soul to peace.

THE GOOD OLD WAY. L. M.

Wm. Walker. Dover Sel. p. 56

Lift up your heads, Immanuel's friends, O halle, halle - lujah,
And taste the pleasure Jesus sends, O halle, halle - lujah.
Let nothing cause you to delay, O halle, halle - lu - jah,

But hasten on the good old way, O halle, halle - lu - jah!

2 Our conflicts here, though great they be,
Shall not prevent our victory,
If we but watch, and strive, and pray,
Like soldiers in the good old way.

CHORUS.

And I'll sing hallelujah,
And glory be to God on high;
And I'll sing hallelujah,
There's glory beaming from the sky.

3 O good old way, how sweet thou art!
May none of us from thee depart,
But may our actions always say,
We're marching on the good old way.
And I'll sing, &c.

4 Though Satan may his power employ,
Our peace and comfort to destroy,
Yet never fear, we'll gain the day,
And triumph in the good old way
And I'll sing, &c.

5 And when on Pisgah's top we stand,
And view by faith the promised land,
Then we may sing, and shout, and pray
And march along the good old way.
And I'll sing, &c.

6 Ye valiant souls, for heaven contend;
Remember glory's at the end;
Our God will wipe all tears away,
When we have run the good old way.
And I'll sing, &c.

7 Then far beyond this mortal shore,
We'll meet with those who're gone before,
And him we'll praise in endless day,
Who brought us on the good old way
And I'll sing, &c.

WORCESTER. S. M.

Hy. 10. B. 1. Watts.

And words of peace reveal, Who, &c.
And, &c.
How, &c.
How beauteous are their feet Who stand on Zion's hill; Who bring salvation on their tongues, And words of peace reveal.
How charming is their voice.
Zion
He
Zion
How sweet the tidings are, Zion, behold thy Saviour king, He reigns and triumphs here.
Zion
He
Zion

PILGRIM'S FAREWELL. 12's 8's.

Dover Sel. p 195

1
2
1
2
Farewell, farewell, farewell, my friends, I must be gone, I have no home or stay with you; I'll take my staff and travel on, Till I a better world can view.
1
2
I'll march to Canaan's land, I'll land on Canaan's shore, Where pleasures never end, And troubles come no more. Farewell, :|: :|: my loving friends, farewell.

2 Farewell, &c. my friends, time rolls along,
Nor waits for mortal cares or bliss,
I'll leave you here, and travel on
Till I arrive where Jesus is.
I'll march. &c.
Farewel. &c

3 Farewell, &c. dear brethren in the Lord,
To you I'm bound with cords of love
But we believe his gracious word,
We all ere long shall meet above,
I'll march, &c.
Farewell. &c.

4 Farewell, &c. ye blooming sons of God,
Sore conflicts yet remain for you;
But dauntless keep the heavenly road
Till Canaan's happy land you view
I'll march. &c.
Farewell, farewell, farewell, my loving

LUTHER. S. M.

Hastings.

Vigoroso.
1. My soul, be on thy guard, Ten thousand foes a-rise; And hosts of sin are press-ing hard To draw thee from the skies, To draw thee from the skies.

2. O watch, and fight, and pray,
The battle ne'er give o'er;
Renew it loudly every day,
And help divine implore. ‡

3. Ne'er think the victory won,
Nor once at ease sit down;
Thy arduous work will not be done
Till thou hast got the crown. ‡

4. Fight on, my soul, till death
Shall bring thee to thy God;
He'll take thee at thy parting breath,
Up to his rest above. ‡

NEW HAVEN. 6,6,4,6,6,6,4.

Hastings.

1. Come, thou Al-might-y king, Help us thy name to sing, Help us to praise; Fa-ther, all glo - ri- ous, O'er all vic - to - ri-ous, Come and reign o - ver us, An-cient of days.

2. Come, thou incarnate Word,
Gird on thy mighty sword,
Our prayer attend;
Come, and thy people bless,
And give thy word success:
Spirit of holiness,
On us descend.

3. Come, holy Comforter,
Thy sacred witness bear
In this glad hour:
Thou who almighty art,
Now rule in every heart,
And ne'er from us depart,
Spirit of power!

4. To the great One and Three
The highest praises be,
Hence—evermore!
His sovereign majesty
May we in glory see,
And to eternity
Love and adore.

HYMN. 13,11. *Thou art gone to the grave.* (Scotland.) *Dr. John Clarke.*

Slowly and tenderly.
Thou art gone to the grave, but we will not de-plore thee; Tho' sor-rows and darkness en - com-pass the tomb; The Sa-viour has
pass'd thro' its portals be - fore thee, And the lamp of his love is thy guide thro' the gloom, And the lamp of his life is thy guide thro' the gloom.

REPENTANCE. C. M.

O, if my soul was form'd for wo, How would I vent my sighs! Repentance should like rivers flow, From both my streaming eyes. 'Twas for my sins my
dearest Lord Hung on that cursed tree, Hung, &c. And groan'd away his dying life, And groan'd, &c. For thee, my soul, for thee, For thee, &c.

BALLSTOWN. L. M

Great God, at - tend while Zion sings The joy that from thy presence springs; To spend one day with thee on earth, Exceeds a thousand
days of mirth.
To spend, &c.
To spend, &c.

NEW TOPIA. P. M.

Munday

Young people all, attention give, And hear what I do say; I want your souls in Christ to live, In eve-lasting day; Remember, you are hast'ning on, To death's dark, gloomy
shade Remember, you, &c.
Your joys on earth will soon be gone, Your flesh in dust be laid

BABYLONIAN CAPTIVITY. P. M

Dare

A - long the banks where Babel's cur - rent flows, Our captive bands in deep despondence stray'd, While Zi on's
fall in sad re - mem - brance rose, Her friends, her children, mingled with the dead.

IONIA. 7s.

W. Belcher.

1. Children of the heavenly King, As ye jour-ney, sweetly sing: Sing your Saviour's worthy praise, Glorious in his works and ways.
2. Ye are travelling home to God, In the way the fathers trod; They are hap-py now, and ye Soon their hap-pi-ness shall see.

WILMOT. 7s.

Slow. With tenderness and delicacy.
1. Sin-ner, art thou still se-cure? Wilt thou still re-fuse to pray? Can thy heart or hand en-dure, In the Lord's a-veng-ing day.

2. At his presence nature shakes,
Earth affrighted hastes to flee;
Solid mountains melt like wax,
What will then become of thee?

3. Who his coming may abide?
You that glory in your shame,
Will you find a place to hide
When the world is wrapp'd in flame?

4. Lord, prepare us by thy grace,
Soon we must resign our breath;
And our souls be call'd to pass
Through the iron gate of death.

SWEET RIVERS. C. M.

More. Bapt. Harmony, p. 468

Sweet ri - vers of re - deem - ing - love, Lie just be - fore mine eyes,
Had I the pi - nions of a dove, I'd to those ri - vers fly;
I'd rise su - pe - rior to my pain.
With joy out - strip the wind, I'd cross o'er Jordan's storm - y waves, And leave the world be - hind.

DELIGHT. P. M

Coan, Guilford, Ct.

No burning heats by day, Nor blasts of evening air, Shall take my health a - way, If God be with me there. Thou art my sun and thou my shade, To
guard my head by night or noon.
Thou art my sun, &c.

ROCKINGHAM. L. M.

Lowell Mason.

1. Thy praise, O Lord, shall tune the lyre, Thy love our joy - ful songs in-spire; To thee our cordial thanks be paid, Our sure defence, our constant aid.
2. Why then cast down, and why distress'd? And whence the grief that fills our breast? In God we'll hope, to God we'll raise Our songs of gra-ti-tude and praise.

LINDAN. L. M.

1. Lord, when my thoughts delighted rove A-mid the won-ders of thy love, Sweet hope revives my drooping heart, And bids in-trud-ing fears de - part.
2. Re-pent-ant sorrow fills my heart, But mingling joy al-lays the smart; O may my fu-ture life de - clare The sor-row and the joy sin-cere.
3. Be all my heart and all my days De - vo - ted to my Saviour's praise; And let my glad o-bedience prove How much I owe, how much I love.

HUNTINGTON. L. M

Lord, what a thoughtless wretch was I, To mourn, and murmur, and re - pine; To see the wicked placed on high, In
pride and robes of honour shine. But O their end! their dreadful end! Thy sanctuary taught me so;
1
2

HUNTINGTON. *Concluded.*

On slip - pery rocks I see them stand, And fiery billows roll below.

MONTGOMERY. C. M.

More.

Early, my God, without delay, I haste to seek thy face, My thirsty spirit faints a - - way, With

out thy cheering grace; So pilgrims on the scorching sand, Beneath a burning sky, Long for a
cooling stream at hand, And they must drink or die.
1 2
1 2
1 2
1 2

HUMBLE PENITENT. L. M.

Wm. Walker.

1. Show pi - ty, Lord, O Lord, for - give, O pi - ty me, dear Sa - viour!
Let a re - pent - ing re - bel live; O pi - ty me, dear Sa - viour!
Is there a - ny mer - cy here, O
Chorus.
2. Are not thy mer - cies large and free? O pi - ty me, dear Sa - viour!
May not a sin - ner trust in thee? O pi - ty me, dear Sa - viour!
Is there a - ny mer - cy here, &c.

pi - ty me, dear Lord, and I'll sing hal - le hal - le - lu - jah!

3. My crimes are great, but don't surpass
O pity me, dear Saviour,
The power and glory of thy grace;
O pity me, dear Saviour, &c.

4. Great God, thy nature hath no bound,
O pity me, dear Saviour,
So let thy pard'ning love be found,
O pity me, dear Saviour, &c.

5. O! wash my soul from every sin!
O pity me, dear Saviour,
And make my guilty conscience clean!
O pity me, dear Saviour, &c.

6. Here on my heart the burden lies,
O pity me, dear Saviour,
And past offences pain my eyes,
O pity me, dear Saviour, &c.

7. My lips with shame my sins confess,
O pity me, dear Saviour,
Against thy law, against thy grace;
O pity me, dear Saviour, &c.

8. Lord, should thy judgments grow severe,
O pity me, dear Saviour,
I am condemn'd, but thou art clear.
O pity me, dear Saviour, &c.

9. Should sudden vengeance seize my breath,
O pity me, dear Saviour,
I must pronounce thee Just in death
O pity me, dear Saviour, &c.

10. And if my soul were sent to hell,
O pity me, dear Saviour,
Thy righteous law approves it well,
O pity me, dear Saviour, &c.

11. Yet save a trembling sinner, Lord,—
O pity me, dear Saviour,
Whose hope, still hov'ring round thy word,
O pity me, dear Saviour, &c.

12. Would light on some sweet promise there,
O pity me, dear Saviour,
Some sure support against despair,
O pity me, dear Saviour, &c.

UXBRIDGE. L. M.

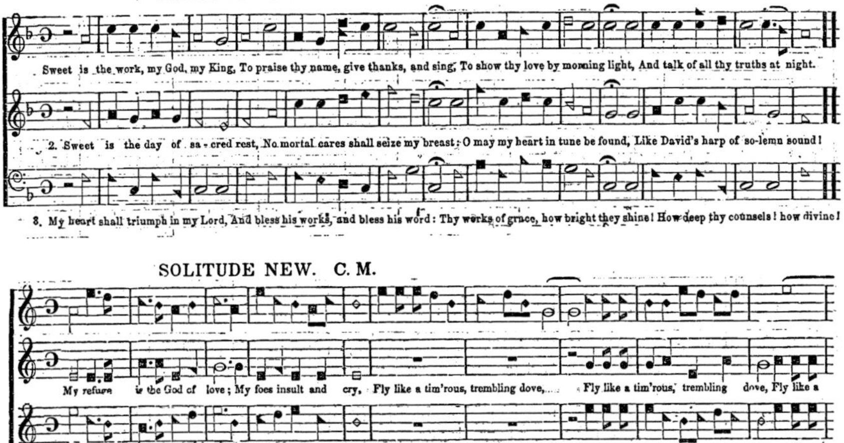
Sweet is the work, my God, my King, To praise thy name, give thanks, and sing; To show thy love by morning light, And talk of all thy truths at night.
2. Sweet is the day of sa - cred rest, No mortal cares shall seize my breast; O may my heart in tune be found, Like David's harp of so-lemn sound!
3. My heart shall triumph in my Lord, And bless his works, and bless his word: Thy works of grace, how bright they shine! How deep thy counsels! how divine!

SOLITUDE NEW. C. M.

My refuge is the God of love; My foes insult and cry, Fly like a tim'rous, trembling dove,... Fly like a tim'rous, trembling dove, Fly like a

trembling, tim'rous dove, To dis - tant moun - tains fly, Since I have placed my trust in God, A refuge always nigh.
Why should I like a tim'rous bird, To dis - tant mountains fly,

MOUNT ZION. S. M.

Brown.

The hill of Zi - on yields A thousand sa - cred sweets, Before we reach the heav'nly fields, Or walk the golden streets.
Then let your songs abound, And ev'ry tear be - dry; We're marching through Immanuel's ground, To fairer worlds on high.

MOUNT ZION. S M. *Concluded.*

We're marching through Immanuel's ground, To fairer worlds on high, To
fair - er worlds on high. We're marching through Im - ma - nuel's ground, To fair - er worlds on high.

EDOM. C. M. Sharp Key on F

With songs and honours sounding loud, Ad - dress the Lord on high, Over the heav'ns he spreads his clouds, And waters veil the
sky, And wa - ters veil the sky.
He sends his show rs of bless - ings down To cheer the plains be-

EDOM *Concluded.*

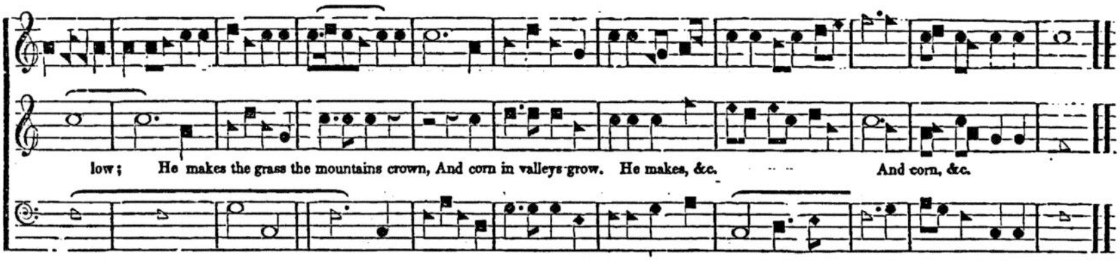
low; He makes the grass the mountains crown, And corn in valleys grow. He makes, &c. And corn, &c.

SCHENECTADY. L. M.

Shumway.

From all that dwell below the skies, Let the Cre - ator's praise arise; Let the Redeem - er's name be sung, Through ev'ry land by ev'ry

tongue. Eternal are thy mercies, Lord, Eternal truth attends thy word; Thy praise shall sound from shore to shore, Till sun
shall rise and set no more, Till sun shall rise and set no more.

OCEAN

Swan.

Thy works of glory, mighty Lord, That rul'st the boist'rous sea, The sons of courage shall record, Who tempt the dang'rous way. At thy command the winds arise, And
swell the tow'ring waves,
The men astonish'd mount the skies, And sink in gap - ing graves.
1
2

AZMON. C. M.

Arranged from Glaser.

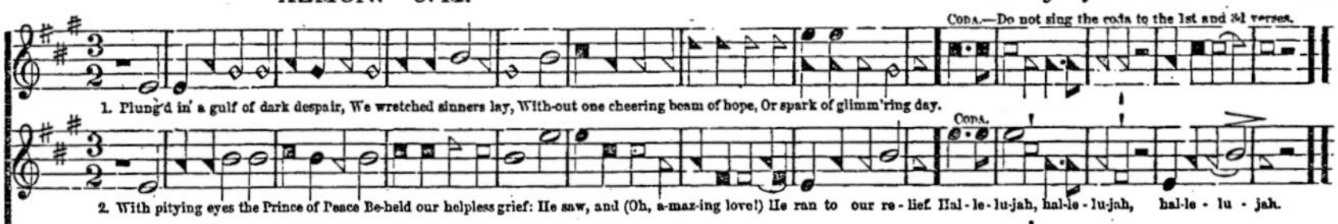
Coda.—Do not sing the coda to the 1st and 3d verses.
1. Plung'd in a gulf of dark despair, We wretched sinners lay, With-out one cheering beam of hope, Or spark of glimm'ring day.
Coda.
2. With pitying eyes the Prince of Peace Be-held our helpless grief: He saw, and (Oh, a-maz-ing love!) He ran to our re-lief. Hal-le-lu-jah, hal-le-lu-jah, hal-le-lu-jah.

3. Down from the shining seats above
With joyful haste he fled,
Enter'd the grave in mortal flesh,
And dwelt among the dead.

4. Oh! for this love let rocks and hills
Their lasting silence break,
And all harmonious human tongues
The Saviour's praises speak.

5. Angels, assist our mighty joys:
Strike all your harps of gold;
But when you raise your highest notes
His love can ne'er be told.

ETON. 7s. (Double.)

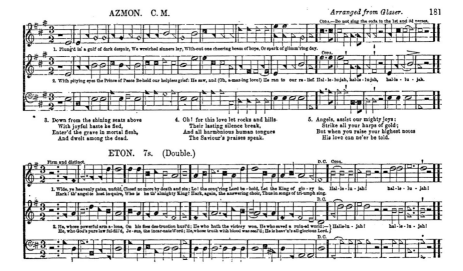

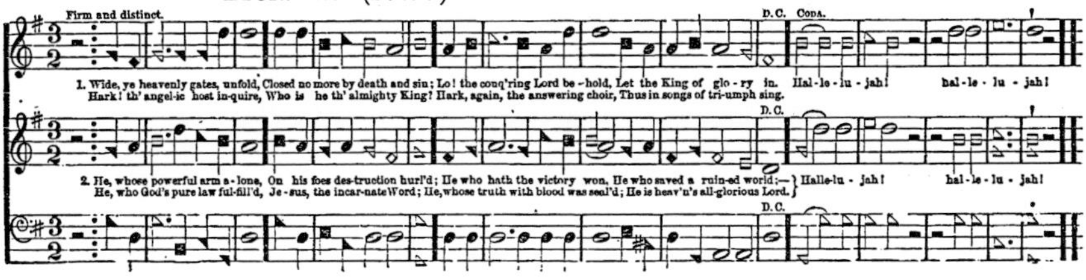
Firm and distinct.
D. C. Coda.
1. Wide, ye heavenly gates, unfold, Closed no more by death and sin; Lo! the conq'ring Lord be-hold, Let the King of glo-ry in. Hal-le-lu-jah! hal-le-lu-jah!
Hark! th' angel-ic host in-quire, Who is he th' almighty King? Hark, again, the answering choir, Thus in songs of tri-umph sing.
D. C.
2. He, whose powerful arm a-lone, On his foes des-truction hurl'd; He who hath the victory won, He who saved a ruin-ed world;— Halle-lu-jah! hal-le-lu-jah!
He, who God's pure law ful-fill'd, Je-sus, the incar-nate Word; He, whose truth with blood was seal'd; He is heav'n's all-glorious Lord.
D. C.

THE SAILOR'S HOME. L. M.   *By Wm. M. Caudill and Wm. Walker.*

1. When for e-ter-nal worlds we steer, And seas are calm, and skies are clear,
   And faith in live-ly ex-er-cise, And dis-tant hills of Ca-naan rise. } The soul, for joy then claps her wings, And loud her

2. With cheer-ful hope, his eyes ex-plore Each land-mark on the dis-tant shore;
   The trees of life— the pas-ture green, The crys-tal stream, de-light-ful scene: } A-gain for joy she plumes her wings, And loud her

3. The near-er still she draws to land, More eag-er all her pow'rs ex-pand;
   With stead-y helm, and free bent sail, Her an-chor drops with-in the vail: } And now for joy she folds her wings, And her ce-

love-ly son-net sings, I'm go-ing home, I'm go-ing home, And loud her love-ly son-net sings, I'm go-ing home.

love-ly son-net sings, I'm al-most home, I'm al-most home, And loud her love-ly son-net sings, I'm al-most home.

les-tial son-net sings, I'm home at last, I'm home at last, And her ce-les-tial son-net sings, I'm home at last

4. She meets with those who are gone before,   Around the dear Redeemer's feet,   And ceaseless hallelujahs ring,   And ceaseless hallelujahs ring
   On heaven's high and genial shore.   And loud they shout, Our God and King.   "We're safe at last, we're safe at last,   We're safe at last.

PETERBOROUGH. C. M.

Baptist Harmony, p. 2.

1. Approach, my soul, the mer - cy seat, Where Je - sus an - swers prayer; There hum-bly fall be - fore his feet, For none can per - ish there.
2. Thy pro-mise is my on - ly plea, With this I ven - ture nigh: Thou call'st the burden'd soul to thee, And such, O Lord, am I.

3. Bow'd down beneath a load of sin,
By Satan sorely prest,
By wars without, and fears within,
I come to thee for rest.

4. Be thou my shield and hiding-place,
That, shelter'd near thy side,
I may my fierce accuser face,
And tell him thou hast died.

5. O, wondrous love! to bleed and die,
To bear the cross and shame,
That guilty sinners, such as I,
Might plead his gracious name.

6. "Poor tempest-toss'd soul, be still,
My promised grace receive;"—
'Tis Jesus speaks—I must, I will,
I can, I do believe.

CLAREMONT.

Vital spark of heav'nly flame, Quit, O quit this mortal frame; Trembling, hoping, ling'ring, flying, flying, fly - ing, O! the pain, the bliss of dying.

Cease, fond nature, cease thy strife, And let me languish into life; And let me languish into life.
Hark!
Hark!
Hark! they whisper; angels say, Sister spirit, come away
Hark! they whisper; angels say, Sister spirit, come away; Sister spirit, come away.
What is this absorbs me quite—Steals my senses, shuts my sight?

Loud
Drowns my spirit, draws my breath, Tell me, my soul, can this be death? :|: :|:
Soft.
The world recedes, it dis - ap - pears, Heav'n opens on my eyes, My ears with sounds seraphic ring, My ears with sounds seraphic

Lively
Slow.
ring,
My ears, &c.
Lend, lend your wings! I mount, I fly! I mount! I fly! O grave! where is thy
victory! thy vic-to-ry! O grave! where is thy victory! thy vic-to-ry! O death! where is thy sting! Lend, lend your wings! I mount! I fly! I mount! I fly! I

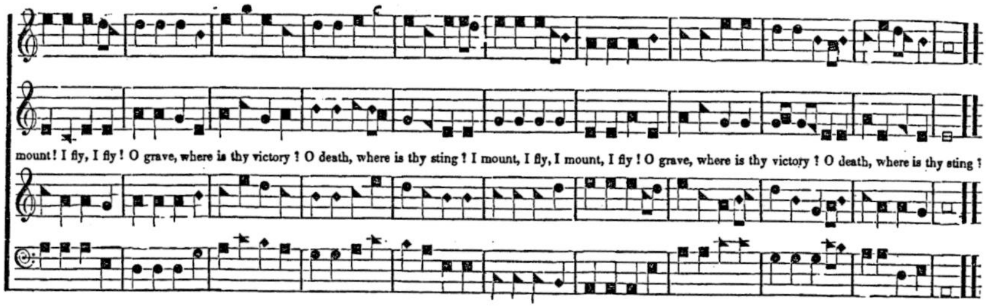
mount! I fly, I fly! O grave, where is thy victory? O death, where is thy sting? I mount, I fly, I mount, I fly! O grave, where is thy victory? O death, where is thy sting?

FUNERAL ANTHEM.

Rev. chap. xiv. ver. 13. *Billings.*

I heard a great voice from heav'n, saying unto me, Write, From henceforth, write, from, &c., write, From, &c. Blessed are the dead that die in the Lord.

Yea, saith the Spirit, for they rest, for they rest for they rest. for they rest from their labours, from their labours,
from their la - bours and their works, which do fol - low, fol - low, fol - low, which do fol - low, fol - low them. Which do follow them.

The Lord is ris'n in - deed! Hal - - - le - lujah! The Lord is ris'n in - deed! Hal - le - lu - jah!
Now is Christ ris'n from the dead, And become the first-fruit of them that slept. Now is Christ, &c.

Halle - lujah, halle - lujah, halle lu - jah. And did he rise? And did he rise? And did he rise? did he rise? hear it, ye

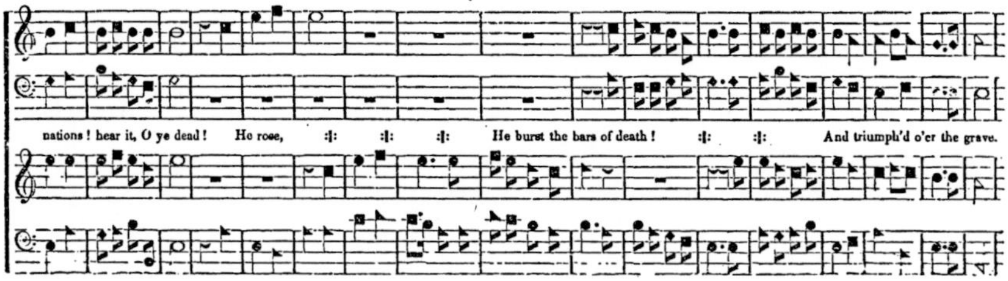
nations! hear it, O ye dead! He rose, :|: :|: :|: He burst the bars of death! :|: :|: And triumph'd o'er the grave.

Then, then, then I rose, then I rose, then I rose, then first hu-
manity triumphant past the crystal ports of light, and seiz'd e - ter - nal youth. Man all im - mortal hail,

hail, Heaven, all lavish of strange gifts to man, Thine's all the glory, man's the boundless bliss; Thine's all the glory, man's the boundless bliss.

HARWELL. 8,7,7.

Animated.
See he sits, &c.
1. Hark! ten thousand harps and voices Sound the note of praise above;
Jesus reigns, and heav'n rejoices; Jesus reigns, the God of love:
See, he sits on yonder throne; Jesus rules the world alone. Hal-le-lu-jah! hal-le-lu-jah! hal-le-lu-jah! A-men.

BOUND FOR CANAAN. 7,6.

Mercer's Cluster, p. 356. *E. J. King.*

1
2
Chorus.
Oh when shall I see Je-sus, And reign with him a-bove?
And from the flowing fountain, Drink ev-er - last-ing love?
I'm on my way to Canaan, I'm on my way to Ca-naan, I'm on my way to Ca-naan, To the New Je-ru-sa-lem.

INVOCATION. 8,7.

Chorus.
1. Je - sus, grant us all a bless-ing, Send it down, Lord, from a-bove;
May we all re-turn home pray-ing, And re - joic-ing in thy love:
Farewell, brethren; farewell sis-ters, Till we all shall meet a - gain.

2 Jesus, pardon all our follies,
Since together we have been;
Make us humble, make us holy,
Cleanse us all from every sin:
Farewell, brethren; farewell, sisters,
Till we all shall meet above.

3. May thy blessing, Loru, go with us
To each one's respective home;
And the presence of our Jesus
Rest upon us every one:
Farewell, brethren; farewell, sisters,
Till we all shall meet at home.

IN THAT MORNING. L. M

Wm. Walker.

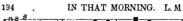

1. Je-sus, my all, to heav'n is gone, And we'll all shout to-geth-er in that morn-ing;
He whom I fix my hopes up-on, And we'll all shout to-geth-er in that morn-ing.
In that morn-ing, in that
2. His track I see, and I'll pur-sue, And we'll all shout to-geth-er in that morn-ing;
The nar-row way, till him I view, And we'll all shout to-geth-er in that morn-ing.
In that morn-ing, &c.

morn-ing, And we'll all shout to-geth-er in that morning.

3. The way the holy prophets went,
And we'll all shout together, &c.
The road that leads from banishment,
And we'll all shout together, &c.

4. The King's highway of holiness,
And we'll all shout together, &c.
I'll go, for all his paths are peace,
And we'll all shout together, &c.

5. This is the way I long have sought,
And we'll all shout together, &c.
And mourn'd because I found it not;
And we'll all shout together, &c

6. My grief a burden long has been,
And we'll all shout together, &c.
Because I was not saved from sin;
And we'll all shout together, &c.

7. The more I strove against its power,
And we'll all shout together, &c.
I felt its weight and guilt the more;
And we'll all shout together, &c.

8. Till late I heard my Saviour say,
And we'll all shout together, &c.
"Come hither, soul, I am the way,"
And we'll all shout together, &c.

9. Lo! glad I come, and thou, blest Lamb,
And we'll all shout together, &c.
Shalt take me to thee, whose I am;
And we'll all shout together, &c.

10. Nothing but sin have I to give,
And we'll all shout together, &c.
Nothing but love shall I receive:
And we'll all shout together, &c.

11. Then will I tell to sinners round,
And we'll all shout together, &c.
What a dear Saviour I have found;
And we'll all shout together, &c

12. I'll point to thy redeeming love,
And we'll all shout together, &c.
And say, "Behold the way to God!
And we'll all shout together, &c.

Chorus.
1. Oh when shall I see Jesus, And reign with him above? And shall hear the trumpet sound in that morning.
And from the flowing fountain, Drink everlasting love? And shall hear the trumpet sound in that morning.
Shout, O glo - ry! for I shall
When shall I be de-li-ver'd From this vain world of sin? And shall hear the trumpet sound in that morning.
And with my blessed Jesus Drink endless pleasures in? And shall hear the trumpet sound in that morning.
Shout, O glo - ry! for I shall

mount above the skies, When I hear the trumpet sound in that morning.
mount above the skies, When I hear the trumpet sound in that morning.

2. But now I am a soldier,
My Captain's gone before;
He's given me my orders,
And bids me ne'er give o'er;
His promises are faithful—
A righteous crown he'll give,
And all his valiant soldiers
Eternally shall live,
Shout, &c.

3. Through grace I feel determined
To conquer, though I die,
And then away to Jesus,
On wings of love I'll fly:
Farewell to sin and sorrow,
I bid them both adieu!
And O my friends, prove faithful,
And on your way pursue.
Shout, &c.

4. Whene'er you meet with troubles
And trials on your way,
Then cast your care on Jesus,
And don't forget to pray.
Gird on the gospel armour
Of faith, and hope, and love,
And when the combat's ended,
He'll carry you above.
Shout, &c.

5. Oh do not be discouraged,
For Jesus is your friend;
And if you lack for knowledge,
He'll not refuse to lend.
Neither will he upbraid you,
Though often you request,
He'll give you grace to conquer,
And take you home to rest.
Shout, &c

Rev. Samuel Wakefield.
Words by Rev. Wm Hunter.

DRUMMOND. 11s.

Treble by Wm. Houser.

"Tell my brethren that I died at my post."—*Last words of Rev Thomas Drummond.*

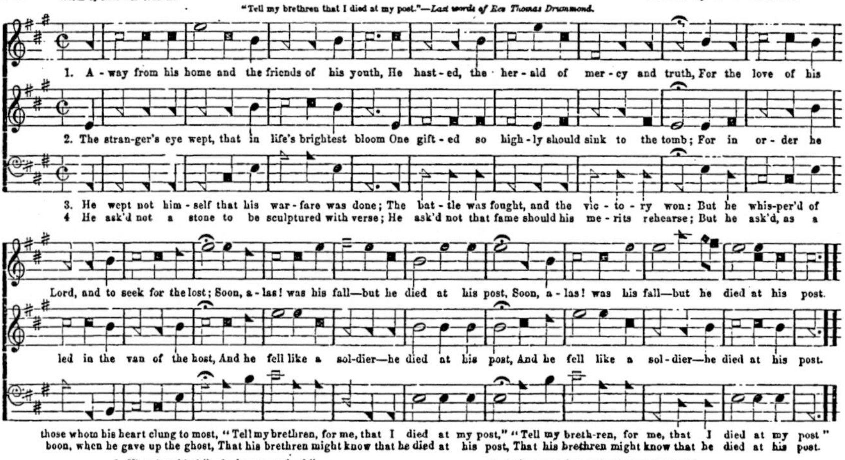
1. A - way from his home and the friends of his youth, He hast - ed, the her - ald of mer - cy and truth, For the love of his
2. The stran-ger's eye wept, that in life's brightest bloom One gift - ed so high - ly should sink to the tomb; For in or - der he
3. He wept not him - self that his war - fare was done; The bat - tle was fought, and the vic - to - ry won: But he whis-per'd of
4 He ask'd not a stone to be sculptured with verse; He ask'd not that fame should his me - rits rehearse; But he ask'd, as a
Lord, and to seek for the lost; Soon, a - las! was his fall—but he died at his post, Soon, a - las! was his fall—but he died at his post.
led in the van of the host, And he fell like a sol-dier—he died at his post, And he fell like a sol - dier—he died at his post.
those whom his heart clung to most, "Tell my brethren, for me, that I died at my post," "Tell my breth-ren, for me, that I died at my post"
boon, when he gave up the ghost, That his brethren might know that he died at his post, That his brethren might know that he died at his post.

5. Victorious his fall—for he rose as he fell,
With Jesus, his Master, in glory to dwell;
He has pass'd o'er the stream, and has reach'd the bright coast,
For he fell like a martyr—he died at his post.

6. And can we the words of his exit forget?
Oh, no! they are fresh in our memory yet:
An example so brilliant shall never be lost.
We will fall in the work—we will die at our post.

MISSIONARY SONG. 8,7,4.

S. B. Pond, principally.

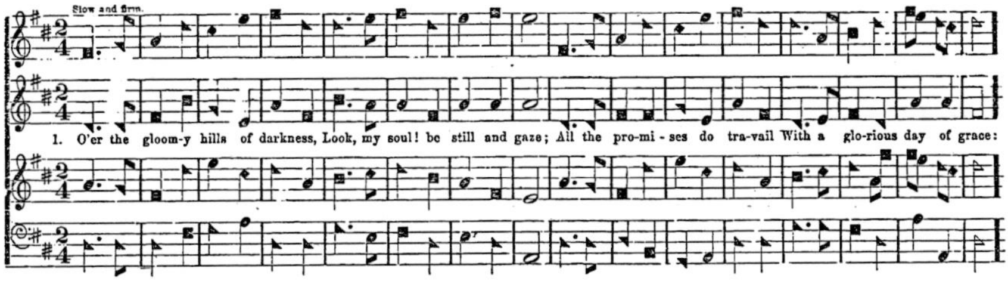
Slow and firm.
1. O'er the gloom-y hills of darkness, Look, my soul! be still and gaze; All the pro-mi - ses do tra-vail With a glo-rious day of grace:

Bless-ed jub'-lee! Blessed jub'lee! Let thy glo-rious morning dawn.

2.

Let the Indian, let the Negro,
Let the rude barbarian see
That divine and glorious conquest
Once obtain'd on Calvary;
Let the gospel,
Loud resound from pole to pole.

3.

Kingdoms wide, that sit in darkness,
Grant them, Lord, the glorious light,
And from eastern coast to western
May the morning chase the night:
And redemption
Freely purchased, win the day.

4.

May the glorious day approaching,
On the grossest darkness dawn;
And the everlasting gospel
Spread abroad thy holy name—
All the borders
Of the great Emmanuel's land.

5.

Fly abroad, thou mighty Gospel,
Win and conquer, never cease;
May thy lasting, wide dominions
Multiply and still increase;
Sway the sceptre,
Saviour, all the world around.

NEVER PART AGAIN. C. M.

Chorus.
1. Je - ru-sa-lem, my happy home, Oh how I long for thee! When will my sorrows have an end? Thy joys, when shall I see? } We're marching thro' Emmanuel's ground;
We soon shall hear the welcome trumpet sound.—
Oh, there we shall with Jesus dwell, And
2. Jesus, my Lord, to glory's gone; Him will I go and see; And all my brethren, here below, Will soon come after me. } We're marching, &c.
3. Reach down, O Lord, thine arm of grace, And cause me to as-cend Where congregations ne'er break up, And Sab-baths never end. } We're marching, &c.
Pia.
For.
nev - er part a - gain: What, nev-er part a-gain? No, never part a-gain, No, never part a-gain, No, nev-er part again: Oh, there we shall with Jesus dwell, And nev - er part a - gain.

Christmas Hymn.

DERRICK. C. M. D.

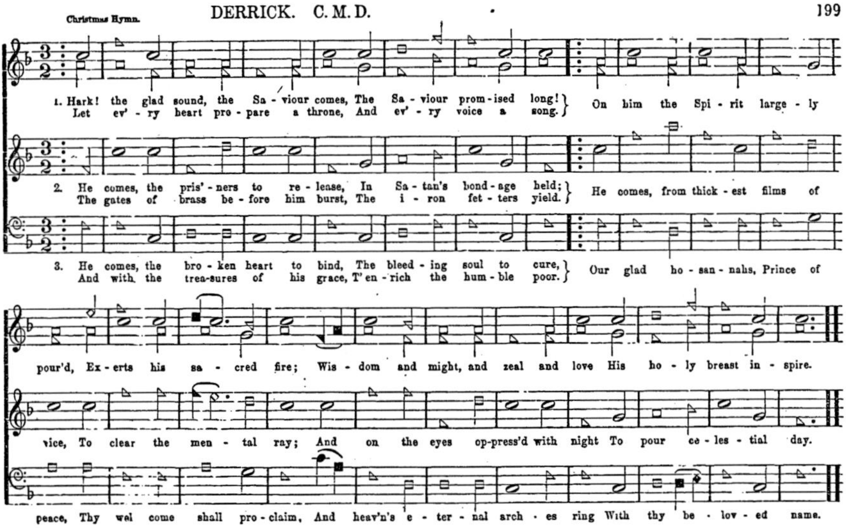
1. Hark! the glad sound, the Sa - viour comes, The Sa - viour prom - ised long! On him the Spi - rit large - ly
Let ev' - ry heart pre - pare a throne, And ev' - ry voice a song.
2. He comes, the pris' - ners to re - lease, In Sa - tan's bond - age held; He comes, from thick - est films of
The gates of brass be - fore him burst, The i - ron fet - ters yield.
3. He comes, the bro - ken heart to bind, The bleed - ing soul to cure, Our glad ho - san - nahs, Prince of
And with the trea-sures of his grace, T' en - rich the hum - ble poor.
pour'd, Ex - erts his sa - cred fire; Wis - dom and might, and zeal and love His ho - ly breast in - spire.
vice, To clear the men - tal ray; And on the eyes op-press'd with night To pour ce - les - tial day.
peace, Thy wel come shall pro - claim, And heav'n's e - ter - nal arch - es ring With thy be - lov - ed name.

SWEET GLIDING KEDRON. 11s.

Wm. Houser.

1. Thou sweet gliding Kedron, by thy silver stream Our Saviour at midnight, when moonlight's pale beam
Shone bright on thy wa-ters, would frequently stray,
And lose in thy murmurs the toils of the day.

2. How damp were the vapors that fell on his head!
How hard was his pillow! how humble his bed!
The angels, astonish'd, grew sad at the sight,
And follow'd their Master with solemn delight.

3. O garden of Olivet, dear honour'd spot!
The fame of thy wonder shall ne'er be forgot;
The theme most transporting to seraphs above,
The triumph of sorrow, the triumph of love.

4. Come, saints and adore him; come, bow at his feet!
Oh, give him the glory, the praise that is meet;
Let joyful hosannas unceasingly rise,
And join the full chorus that gladdens the skies.

ROSE OF SHARON.

Sol. Song ii. *Billings.*

I am the rose of Sharon, and the lily of the valley; I am the rose of Sharon, and the li - ly of the valley,

As the lily among the thorns, so is my love among the daughters;
As the apple tree, the apple tree a - mong the trees of the wood,
so is my be - loved among the sons, so is my be - loved among the sons.
I sat down un - der his shadow with great delight.

And his fruit was sweet to my taste; And his fruit, and his fruit was sweet to my taste.
And his fruit was sweet to my taste.
And his fruit, and his fruit was sweet to my taste, And his fruit, and his fruit, &c.
He brought me to the banqueting house,
his banner over me was love, He brought me to the banqueting house, his banner over me was love.
Stay me with flagons, comfort me with

ap ples, For I am sick, for I am sick, for I am sick of love: I charge you, O ye daughters of Je - rusalem,

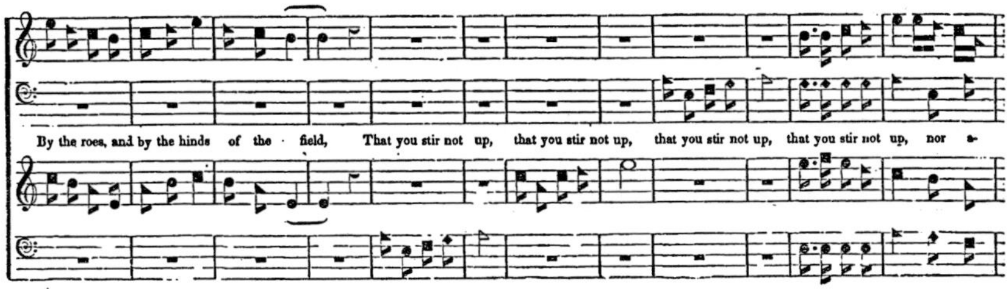
By the roes, and by the hinds of the field, That you stir not up, that you stir not up, that you stir not up, that you stir not up, nor a-

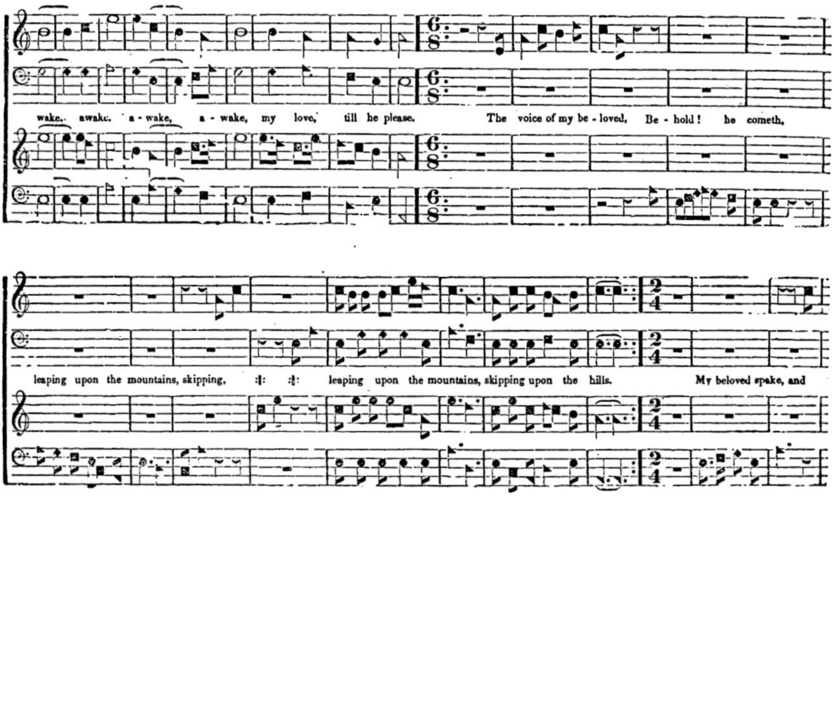
wake, awake, a - wake, a - wake, my love, till he please. The voice of my be - loved, Be - hold! he cometh,
leaping upon the mountains, skipping, :‖: :‖: leaping upon the mountains, skipping upon the hills. My beloved spake, and

said unto me, Rise up, rise up, rise up, rise up, my love, my fair one, and come away. For lo, the winter is
past, the rain is over and gone. For lo, &c. the rain is o ver, the
tr

ROSE OF SHARON. *Concluded.*

rain is over, the rain is over and gone. For lo, &c.

HEAVENLY VISION.

Taken from Rev. v. 11. *Billings.*

I beheld, and lo a great multitude, which no man could number, Thousands of thousands, and ten times thousands, thousands, &c.

thousands of thousands, and ten times thousands, Thousands, &c.
Stood before the Lamb, and they had palms in the

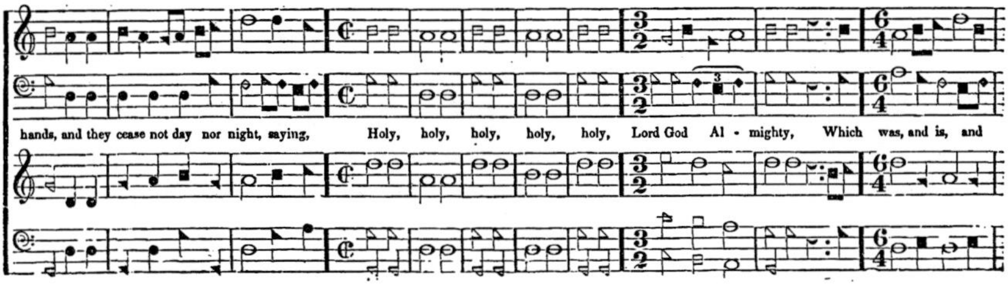
hands, and they cease not day nor night, saying,
Holy, holy, holy, holy, holy, Lord God Al - mighty, Which was, and is, and

is to come, Which was, &c.
And I heard a mighty angel fly - - ing through the midst of heav'n,
crying with a loud voice, We wo, wo, - wo,
Be unto the earth by reason of the trumpet which is

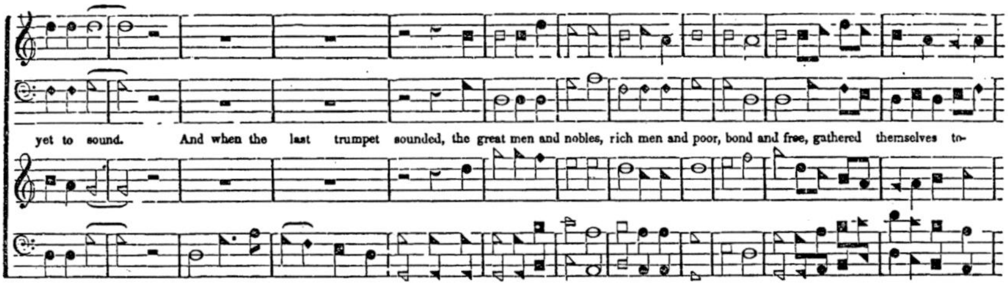
yet to sound. And when the last trumpet sounded, the great men and nobles, rich men and poor, bond and free, gathered themselves to-

gether, and cried to the rocks and mountains to fall up - on them, and hide them from the face of Him that sitteth on the throne,

HEAVENLY VISION. *Concluded.*

For the great day of the Lord is come, and who shall be able to stand! And who shall be a - ble to stand!

ODE ON SCIENCE. Sharp Key on G.

The morn - ing sun shines from the east, And spreads his glo - ries to the west, All nations with his beams are

blest, Where'er the ra - diant light appears. So sci - ence spreads her lu - cid ray O'er lands which long in

darkness lay She vi - sits fair Co - lum - bi - a, And sets her sons a - mong the stars. Fair

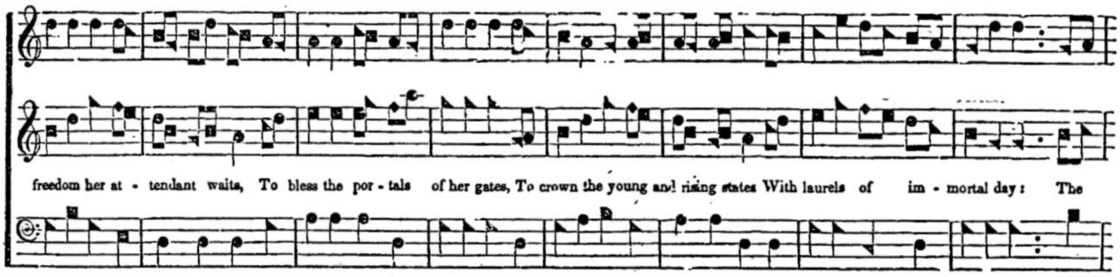
freedom her at - tendant waits, To bless the por - tals of her gates, To crown the young and rising states With laurels of im - mortal day: The

British yoke, the Gallic chain, Was urged upon our necks in vain, All haughty tyrants we disdain, And shout, Long live A - me - ri - ca.
1
2

DAVID'S LAMENTATION.

2 Sam. xviii. 33. *Billings*

David the king was grieved and moved, He went to his chamber, his chamber, and wept; And as he went he wept, and said,
O my son! :‖: Would to God I had died, :‖: :‖: For thee, O Absalom, my son, my son!

My friends,
I am going, I am going a long and
My friends, I am going a long and te - dious jour - ney,
Never to return ; I am going a long journey, never to return. I am
tedious journey, Never to return: I am going a long journey, Never to re - turn.
Never to re - turn.
Never to re turn.
Never to re-
going a long journey, Never to return.
I am going a long journey, Never to re - turn.
Never to return.

Fare you well,
turn; never, never, never, never, to re - turn; Fare you well, my friends. :|:
never to re - turn. never, never to - re - turn; Fare you well, my friends.
Fare you well, my friends, And God grant we may meet together in that world a - bove, Where trouble shall cease and harmony shall abound,

FAREWELL ANTHEM. *Concluded*

hark! hark! my dear friends, for death hath call'd me, And I must go, and lie down in the cold and silent grave, Where the mourners cease from mourning,
and the pris'ner is set free; Where the rich and the poor are both alike; Fare you well, fare you well, fare you well, fare you well, fare you well, my friends.

APPENDIX:

CONTAINING

SEVERAL TUNES ENTIRELY NEW.

INTERROGATION. 7's. *Christopher.* Baptist Harmony, 141.

Hark! my soul, it is the Lord; 'Tis the Saviour, hear his word; Jesus speaks, he speaks to thee— Say, poor sinner, :‖: Say, poor sinner, Say, poor sinuer, lov'st thou me?

DUDLEY. C. M.

Wm. Walker

When I can read my ti - tle clear to man - sions in the skies, I'll bid fare - well to ev - ry
fear, And wipe my weep - ing eyes. I'll bid fare - well to ev - ry fear, I'll bid fare-well to ev - ry fear, And wipe my weep-ing eyes.

2 Should earth against my soul engage,
And hellish darts be hurl'd,
Then I can smile at Satan's rage,
And face a frowning world.

3 Let cares like a wild deluge come,
And storms of sorrow fall;
May I but safely reach my home
My God, my heaven, my all.

4 There shall I bathe my weary soul
In seas of heavenly rest.
And not a wave of trouble roll
Across my peaceful breast.

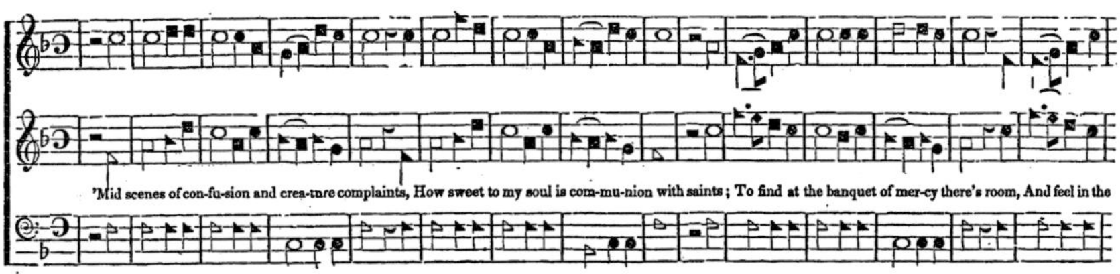

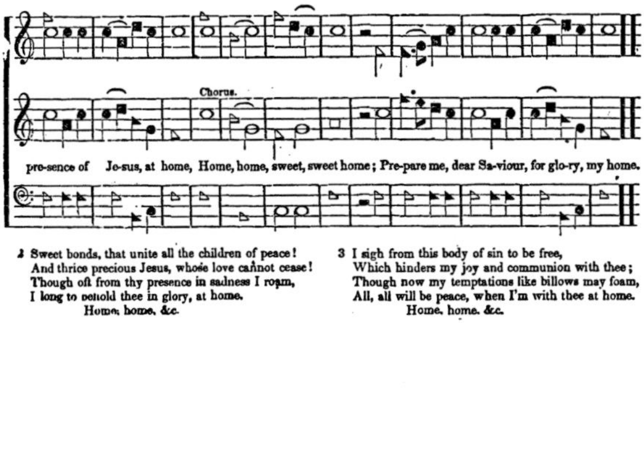

'Mid scenes of con-fu-sion and crea-ture complaints, How sweet to my soul is com-mu-nion with saints; To find at the banquet of mer-cy there's room, And feel in the

pre-sence of   Je-sus, at home, Home, home, sweet, sweet home; Pre-pare me, dear Sa-viour, for glo-ry, my home.

4 While here in the valley of conflict I stay,
  O give me submission, and strength as my day;
  In all my afflictions to thee I would come,
  Rejoicing in hope of my glorious home.
        Home, home, &c.

5 Whate'er thou deniest, O give me thy grace,
  The Spirit's sure witness, and smiles of thy face;
  Indulge me with patience to wait at thy throne,
  And find, even now, a sweet foretaste of home.
        Home, home, &c.

6 I long, dearest Lord, in thy beauties to shine,
  No more, as an exile in sorrow to pine,
  And in thy dear image, arise from the tomb,
  With glorified millions to praise thee, at home.
        Home, home, sweet, sweet, home,
        Receive me, dear Saviour, in glory, my home.

1 Sweet bonds, that unite all the children of peace!
  And thrice precious Jesus, whose love cannot cease!
  Though oft from thy presence in sadness I roam,
  I long to behold thee in glory, at home.
        Home, home, &c.

3 I sigh from this body of sin to be free,
  Which hinders my joy and communion with thee;
  Though now my temptations like billows may foam,
  All, all will be peace, when I'm with thee at home.
        Home, home, &c.

WONDROUS LOVE. 12, 9, 6, 6, 12, 9

Christopher.

What won-drous love is this, oh! my soul! oh! my soul! What won-drous love is this, oh! my soul! What won-drous love is this! That
caused the Lord of bliss, To bear the dread-ful curse for my soul, for my soul, To bear the dread-ful curse for my soul.

Chorus.
On Jor-dan's storm-y banks I stand, And cast a wish-ful eye To Ca-naan's fair and hap-py land, Where my possessions lie.
To see the right-eous a march-ing home, and the
an-gels bid them come,
To wel-come trav'-lers home, to wel-come trav'-lers home.
And Je-sus stands a wait-ing, to wel-come trav'-lers home,
And Je-sus stands a wait-ing, to wel-come trav'-lers hom

SOMETHING NEW. C. M.

1 Since man by sin has lost his God, He seeks cre - a - tion through; And vain-ly strives for - so - lid bliss, In try - ing some - thing new, In

try - ing some - thing new, And vain - ly strives for so - lid bliss, In try - ing some - thing new.

4 But when we feel the power of Christ,
  All good in him we view;
' The soul forsakes her vain pursuits,
  In Christ finds something new.

5 The joy the dear Redeemer gives,
  Will bear a strict review '
Nor need we ever change again,
  For Christ is always new

6 Come, sinners, then and seek the joys
  Which Christ bids you pursue;
And keep the glorious theme in view,
  In Christ seek something new.

2 The new possessed like fading flowers,
  Soon loses its gay hue;
The bubble now no longer stays,
  The soul wants something new

3 Now could we call all Europe ours,
  With India and Peru;
The mind would feel an aching void,
  And still want something new.

7 But soon a change awaits us all.
  Before the great review;
And at his feet with rapture fell,
  And Heaven brings something new

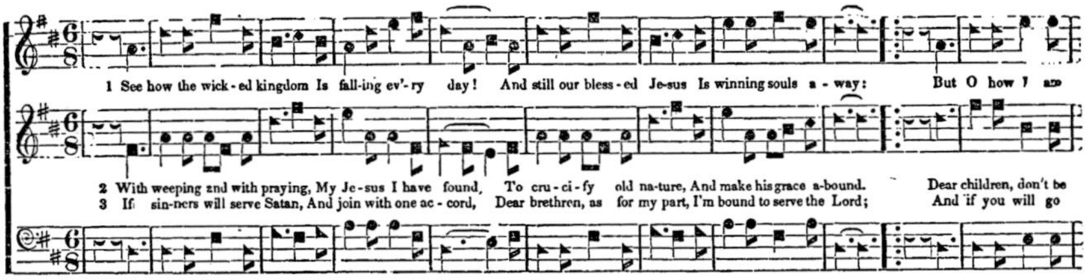
1 See how the wick-ed kingdom Is fall-ing ev'-ry day! And still our bless-ed Je-sus Is winning souls a-way: But O how I am
2 With weeping and with praying, My Je-sus I have found, To cru-ci-fy old na-ture, And make his grace a-bound. Dear children, don't be
3 If sin-ners will serve Satan, And join with one ac-cord, Dear brethren, as for my part, I'm bound to serve the Lord; And if you will go

tempted, No mortal tongue can tell! So oft-en I'm surrounded With enemies from hell.
wea-ry, But march on in the way; For Je-sus will stand by you, And be your guard and stay.
with me, Pray give to me your hand, And we'll march on together, Unto the promised land.

4 Through troubles and distresses,
We'll make our way to God;
Though earth and hell oppose us,
We'll keep the heavenly road.
Our Jesus went before us,
And many sorrows bore,
And we who follow after,
Can never meet with more.

5 Thou dear to me, my brethren,
Each one of you I find.
My duty now compels me
To leave you all behind:
But while the parting grieves us,
I humbly ask your prayers,
To bear me up in trouble,
And conquer all my fears.

6 And now, my loving brothers,
I bid you all farewell!
With you my loving sisters,
I can no longer dwell.
Farewell to every mourner!
I hope the Lord you'll find,
To ease you of your burden,
And give you peace of mind

7 Farewell, poor careless sinners!
I love you dearly well;
I've labour'd much to bring you
With Jesus Christ to dwell,
I now am bound to leave you—
O tell me, will you go?
But if you won't decide it,
I'll bid you all adieu!

8 We'll bid farewell to sorrow,
To sickness, care, and pain,
And mount aloft with Jesus
For evermore to reign;
We'll join to sing his praises
Above the ethereal blue.
And then, poor careless sinners
What will become of you?

THE LONE PILGRIM. 11,8,11,8.

Wm. Walker.

1. I came to the place where the lone pil-grim lay, And pen-sive-ly stood by the tomb, When in a low whis-per I

heard some-thing say, How sweet-ly I sleep here a-lone!

2. The tempest may howl, and the loud thunder roar,
   And gathering storms may arise,
   Yet calm is my feeling, at rest is my soul,
   The tears are all wiped from my eyes.

3. The cause of my Master compell'd me from home,
   I bade my companions farewell;
   I blest my dear children, who now for me mourn—
   In far distant regions they dwell.

4. I wander'd an exile and stranger from home,
   No kindred or relative nigh;
   I met the contagion, and sank to the tomb,
   My soul flew to mansions on high.

5. Oh tell my companion and children most dear,
   To weep not for me now I'm gone;
   The same hand that led me through scenes most severe,
   Has kindly assisted me home.

*6. And there is a crown that doth glitter and shine,
   That I shall for evermore wear:
   Then turn to the Saviour, his love's all divine,
   All you that would dwell with me there.

* The sixth verse was composed by J. J. Hicks, of North Carolina.

Thou art gone to the grave—but we will not deplore thee, Though sorrows and darkness encompass the tomb; The Saviour has pass'd through its por-tals before thee, And the

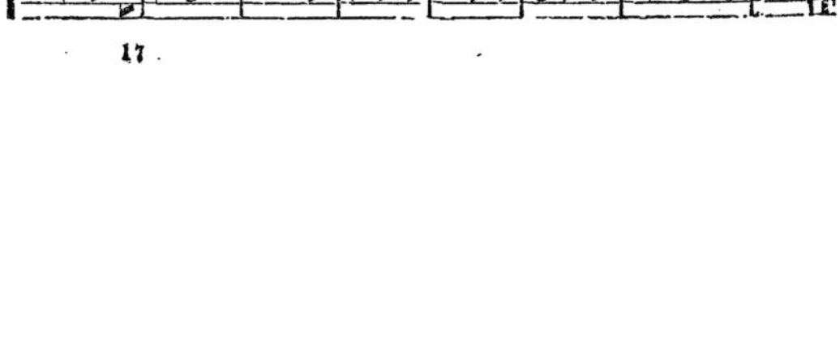
lamp of his love is thy guide through the gloom, And the lamp of his love is thy guide through the gloom.

2 Thou art gone to the grave—we no longer behold thee,
Nor tread the rough paths of the world by thy side;
But the wide arms of mercy are spread to enfold thee
And sinners may hope, since the Saviour hath died.

3 Thou art gone to the grave—and thy cradle's forsaken,
With us thy fond spirit did not tarry long,
But the sunshine of heaven beam'd bright on thy waking,
And the sound thou didst hear was the seraphim's song.

4 Thou art gone to the grave, but 'twere wrong to deplore thee,
When God was thy ransom, and guardian, and guide,
He gave thee, and took thee, and soon will restore thee,
Where death hath no sting, since the Saviour hath died.

THE SAINTS BOUND FOR HEAVEN. 12, 9.

by J. King and W. Walker

1 Our bondage it shall end, by and by, by and by, Our bondage it shall end, by and by; From Egypt's yoke set free; Hail the glorious jubi-

lee, And to Canaan we'll re-turn, by and by, by and by, And to Canaan we'll return, by and by.

4 Though Marah has bitter streams, we'll go on;
Though Baca's vale be dry,
And the land yield no supply;
To a land of corn and wine, we'll go on.

5 And when to Jordan's floods, we are come,
Jehovah rules the tide,
And the waters he'll divide,
And the ransom'd host shall shout, we are come,

6 Then friends shall meet again, who have loved,
Our embraces shall be sweet
At the dear Redeemer's feet,
When we meet to part no more, who have loved.

7 Then with all the happy throng, we'll rejoice
Shouting glory to our King,
Till the vaults of heaven rung,
And through all eternity we'll rejoice

2 Our deliverer he shall come, by and by,
And our sorrows have an end,
With our threescore years and ten,
And vast glory crown the day, by and by

3 Though our enemies are strong, we'll go on
Though our hearts dissolve with fear,
Lo, Sinai's God is near,
While the fiery pillar moves, we'll go on.

I ; the floods of tri-bu - la-tion, While the bil-lows o'er me roll, Hal-le - 'u-jah, Hal-le - lu-jah, Hal-le - lu - jah, praise the Lord, Hal-le - lu-jah,
Je-sus whis-pers con-so-la-tion, And sup-ports my faint - ing soul,

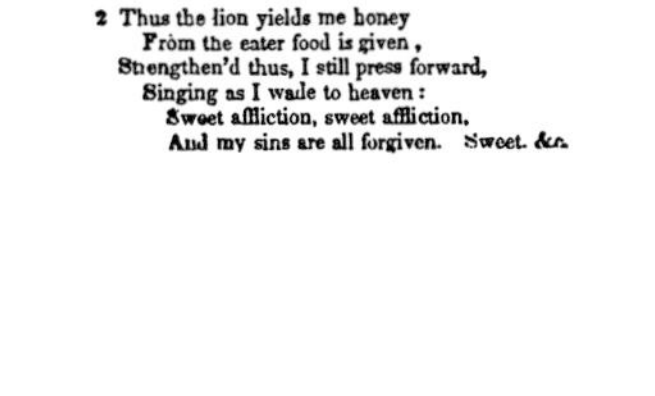
Hal - le - lu - jah, Hal-le - lu-jah, praise the Lord.

2 Thus the lion yields me honey
From the eater food is given,
Strengthen'd thus, I still press forward,
Singing as I wade to heaven:
Sweet affliction, sweet affliction,
And my sins are all forgiven. Sweet, &c.

3 Mid the gloom the vivid lightning,
With increasing brightness play
Mid the thorn bright beauteous flowrets
Look more beautiful and gay.
Hallelujah, Hallelujah,
Hallelujah, praise the Lord. Hallelujah, &c.

4 So in darkest dispensations
Doth my faithful Lord appear,
With his richest consolations
To reanimate and cheer.
Sweet affliction, sweet affliction,
Thus to bring my Saviour near. Sweet, &c.

5 Floods of tribulations brighten,
Billows still around me roar;
Those that know not Christ ye frighten,
But my soul defies your power.
Hallelujah, Hallelujah,
Hallelujah, praise the Lord. Hallelujah, &c.

6 In the sacred page recorded;
Thus the word securely stands,
Fear not, I'm in trouble near thee,
Nought shall pluck thee from my hands.
Sweet affliction, sweet affliction,
Every word my love demands. Sweet, &c.

7 All I meet I find assist me,
In my path to heavenly joy;
Where the trials now attend me,
Trials never more annoy.
Hallelujah, Hallelujah,
Hallelujah, praise the Lord. Hallelujah, &c.

8 Wearing there a weight of glory,
Still the path I'll near forget
But exulting cry it led me
To my blessed Saviour's feet.
Sweet affliction, sweet affliction,
Which has brought to Jesus' feet. Sweet, &c.

STAR OF COLUMBIA. 11's. *Miss M. T Durham.* Words bv Dr. Dwignt

1 Co - lum-bia! Co - lum-bia! to glo - ry a-rise, The queen of the world, and the child of the skies, Thy ge-nius com-mands thee, with
2 To con-quest and slaugh-ter let Eu-rope as-pire, Whelm na - tions in blood, or wrap ci-ties in fire; Thy he-roes the rights of man-
rap-tures be-hold, While a - ges on a - ges thy splen-dours un-fold: Thy reign is the last and the no - blest of time, Most
kind shall de-fend, And tri - umph pur - sue them and glo-ry at - tend. A world is thy realm, for a world be thy laws, En-

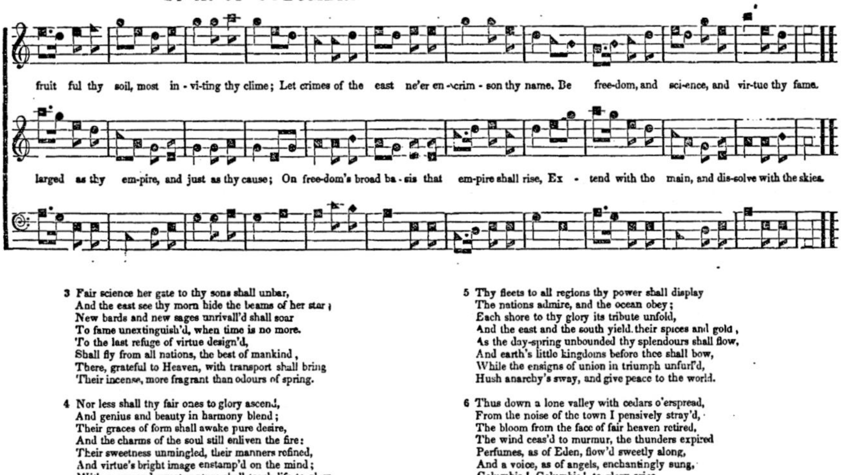
fruit ful thy soil, most in - vi-ting thy clime; Let crimes of the east ne'er en -crim - son thy name. Be free-dom, and sci-ence, and vir-tue thy fame.
larged as thy em-pire, and just as thy cause; On free-dom's broad ba - sis that em-pire shall rise, Ex - tend with the main, and dis-solve with the skies.

3 Fair science her gate to thy sons shall unbar,
And the east see thy morn hide the beams of her star;
New bards and new sages unrivall'd shall soar
To fame unextinguish'd, when time is no more.
To the last refuge of virtue design'd,
Shall fly from all nations, the best of mankind,
There, grateful to Heaven, with transport shall bring
Their incense, more fragrant than odours of spring.

4 Nor less shall thy fair ones to glory ascend,
And genius and beauty in harmony blend;
Their graces of form shall awake pure desire,
And the charms of the soul still enliven the fire:
Their sweetness unmingled, their manners refined,
And virtue's bright image enstamp'd on the mind;
With peace and sweet rapture shall teach life to glow
And light up a smile in the aspect of wo

5 Thy fleets to all regions thy power shall display
The nations admire, and the ocean obey;
Each shore to thy glory its tribute unfold,
And the east and the south yield.their spices and gold,
As the day-spring unbounded thy splendours shall flow,
And earth's little kingdoms before thee shall bow,
While the ensigns of union in triumph unfurl'd,
Hush anarchy's sway, and give peace to the world.

6 Thus down a lone valley with cedars o'erspread,
From the noise of the town I pensively stray'd,
The bloom from the face of fair heaven retired,
The wind ceas'd to murmur, the thunders expired
Perfumes, as of Eden, flow'd sweetly along,
And a voice, as of angels, enchantingly sung,
Columbia! Columbia! to glory arise,
The queen of the world. and the child of the skies.

PLENARY. C. M.

By A. Clark

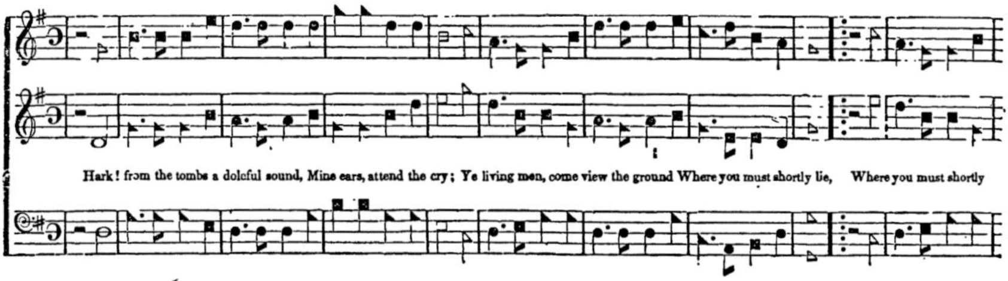

Hark! from the tombs a doleful sound, Mine ears, attend the cry; Ye living men, come view the ground Where you must shortly lie, Where you must shortly

lie. :‖: Ye living men, come view the ground Where you must shortly lie.
Where you must shortly lie,

2\. "Princes, this clay must be your bed,
In spite of all your towers;
The tall, the wise, the reverend head
Must lie as low as ours."

3\. Great God, is this our certain doom?
And are we still secure?
Still walking downward to the tomb,
And yet prepare no more!

4\. Grant us the power of quickening grace,
To fit our souls to fly;
Then, when we drop this dying flesh,
We'll rise above the sky.

OH! TURN, SINNER. L. M.

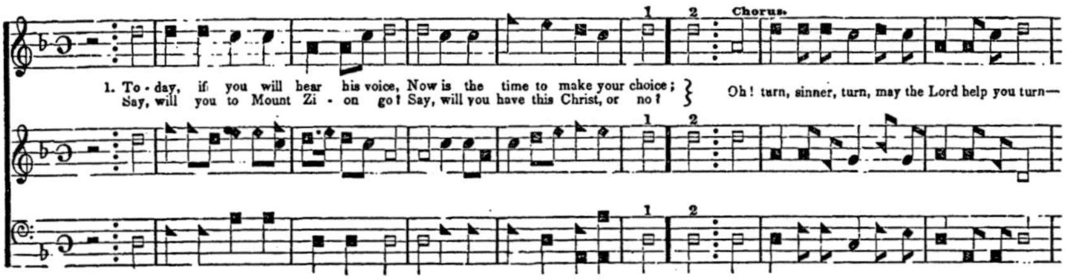
1 2
Chorus.
1. To - day, if you will hear his voice, Now is the time to make your choice;
Say, will you to Mount Zi - on go? Say, will you have this Christ, or no?
Oh! turn, sinner, turn, may the Lord help you turn—
1 2
1 2

2. Say, will you be for ever blest,
And with this glorious Jesus rest?
Will you be saved from guilt and pain?
Will you with Christ for ever reign?
Oh! turn, sinner, &c.

3. Make now your choice, and halt no more;
He now is waiting for the poor:
Say now, poor souls, what will you do?
Say, will you have this Christ, or no?
Oh! turn, sinner, &c.

4. Ye dear young men, for ruin bound,
Amidst the Gospel's joyful sound,
Come, go with us, and seek to prove
The joys of Christ's redeeming love.
Oh! turn, sinner, &c.

5. Your sports, and all your glittering toys,
Compared with our celestial joys,
Like momentary dreams appear:—
Come, go with us—your souls are dear.
Oh! turn, sinner, &c.

6. Young women, now we look to you,
Are you resolved to perish too?
To rush in carnal pleasures on;
And sink in flaming ruin down?
Oh! turn, sinner, &c.

7. Then, dear young friends, a long farewell,
We're bound to heav'n, but you to hell.
Still God may hear us, while we pray,
And change you ere that burning day.
Oh! turn, sinner, &c.

8. Once more I ask you, in his name;
(I know his love remains the same)
Say, will you to Mount Zion go?
Say, will you have this Christ, or no?
Oh! turn, sinner, &c.

9. Come, you that love th' incarnate God,
And feel redemption in his blood,
Let's watch and pray, and onward move,
Till we shall meet in realms above.
Oh! turn sinner, &c

THE SINGING CHRISTIAN. 7.6

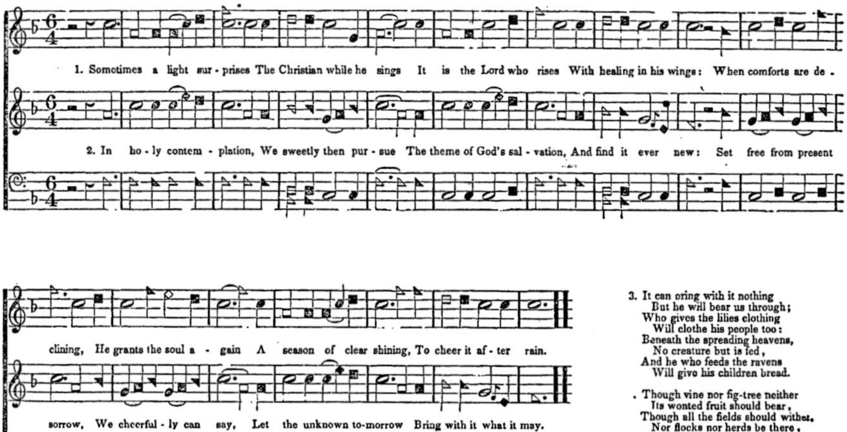
1. Sometimes a light sur - prises The Christian while he sings It is the Lord who rises With healing in his wings: When comforts are de -
2. In ho - ly contem - plation, We sweetly then pur - sue The theme of God's sal - vation, And find it ever new: Set free from present

clining, He grants the soul a - gain A season of clear shining, To cheer it af - ter rain.
sorrow, We cheerful - ly can say, Let the unknown to-morrow Bring with it what it may.

3. It can bring with it nothing
But he will bear us through;
Who gives the lilies clothing
Will clothe his people too:
Beneath the spreading heavens,
No creature but is fed,
And he who feeds the ravens
Will give his children bread.

. Though vine nor fig-tree neither
Its wonted fruit should bear,
Though all the fields should wither,
Nor flocks nor herds be there,
Yet God, the same abiding,
His praise shall tune my voice;
For while in him confiding
I cannot but rejoice.

FRENCH BROAD. L. M.

Wm. Walker.

Slow.
1. *High o'er the hills the mountains rise, Their summits tow - er toward the skies; But far a - bove them I must dwell,
2. Oh, God! for - bid that I should fall And lose my ev - er - last - ing all; But may I rise on wings of love,

Or sink be - neath the flames of hell.
And soar to the blest world a - bove.

3. Although I walk the mountains high,
Ere long my body low must lie,
And in some lonesome place must rot,
And by the living be forgot.

4. There it must lie till that great day,
When Gabriel's awful trump shall say,
Arise, the judgment day is come,
When all must hear their final doom.

5. If not prepared, then I must go
Down to eternal pain and wo,
With devils there I must remain,
And never more return again.

6. But if prepared, oh, blessed thought!
I'll rise above the mountain's top,
And there remain for evermore
On Canaan's peaceful, happy shore.

7. Oh! when I think of that blest world,
Where all God's people dwell in love,
I oft-times long with them to be
And dwell in heaven eternally.

8. Then will I sing God's praises there,
Who brought me through my troubles here
I'll sing, and be forever blest,
Find sweet and everlasting rest.

* This song was composed by the Author, in the fall of 1831, while travelling over the mountains, on French Broad River, in North Carolina and Tennessee.

HEBREW CHILDREN * 7,6,8,8,8,6

David Walker

1. Where are the Hebrew children? Where are the Hebrew children? Where are the Hebrew children? Safe in the promised land: Tho' the furnace flamed around them,
2. Where are the twelve apostles? Where are the twelve apostles? Where are the twelve apostles? Safe in the promised land: They went thro' the flaming fire,
3. Where are the holy martyrs? Where are the holy martyrs? Where are the holy martyrs? Safe in the promised land: Those who wash'd their robes, and made them

God while in their trouble found them; He with love and mercy bound them, Safe in the promised land.
Trusting in the great Messiah, Holy grace did raise them higher, Safe in the promised land.
White and spotless pure, and laid them Where no earthly stain could fade them, Safe in the promised land.

4. Where are the holy Christians? ‡
Safe in the promised land:
There our souls will join the chorus,
Saints and angels sing before us,
While all heaven is beaming o'er us,
Safe in the promised land.

5. By and by we'll go and meet them, ‡
Safe in the promised land:
There we'll sing and shout together,
There we'll sing and shout hosanna,
There we'll sing and shout forever,
Safe in the promised land.

6. Glory to God Almighty, ‡
Who called us unto him,
Who are blind by sinful nature,
Who have sinned against our Maker,
Who did send his son to save us,
Safe in the promised land.

7. Where is our blessed Saviour? ‡
Safe in the promised land:
He was scourged and crucified
He by Romans was derided,
Thus the Lord of glory died,
To raise our souls above.

* This tune was set to music by DAVID WALKER, in 1841: also the last two verses of the song are his composition

BALLERMA. C. M.

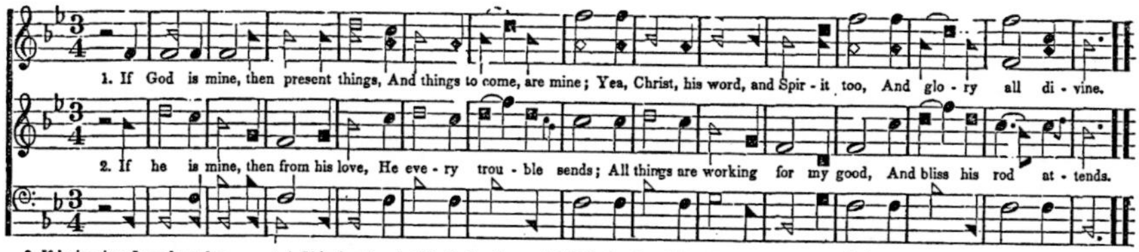
1. If God is mine, then present things, And things to come, are mine; Yea, Christ, his word, and Spir - it too, And glo - ry all di - vine.
2. If he is mine, then from his love, He eve - ry trou - ble sends; All things are working for my good, And bliss his rod at - tends.

3. If he is mine, I need not fear
The rage of earth and hell;
He will support my feeble frame,
Their utmost force repel.

4. If he is mine, let friends forsake,—
Let wealth and honours flee—
Sure he, who giveth me *himself*,
Is more than these to me.

5. If he is mine, I'll boldly pass
Through death's tremendous vale:
He is a solid comfort, when
All other comforts fail.

6. Oh, tell me, Lord! that thou art mine;
What can I wish beside?
My soul shall at the *fountain* live,
When all the *streams* are dried.

SHEPHERD. S. M.

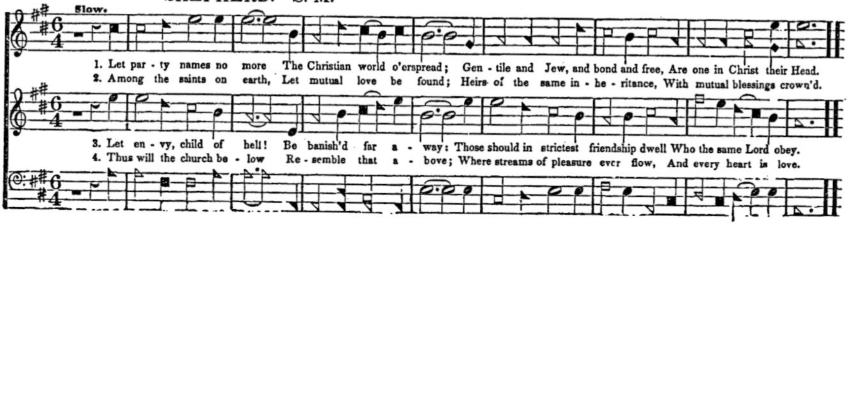
Slow.
1. Let par - ty names no more The Christian world o'erspread; Gen - tile and Jew, and bond and free, Are one in Christ their Head.
2. Among the saints on earth, Let mutual love be found; Heirs of the same in - he - ritance, With mutual blessings crown'd.
3. Let en - vy, child of hell! Be banish'd far a - way: Those should in strictest friendship dwell Who the same Lord obey.
4. Thus will the church be - low Re - semble that a - bove; Where streams of pleasure ever flow, And every heart is love.

PARDONING LOVE. C. M.

Wm. Walker.

3. Alas! I knew not what I did;
But now my tears are vain:
Where shall my trembling soul be hid?
For I the Lord have slain.
A second look he gave, which said,
"I freely all forgive;
This blood is for thy ransom paid,
I'll die that thou may'st live."

4. Thus, while his death my sin displays
In all its blackest hue;
(Such is the mystery of grace,)
It seals my pardon too.
With pleasing grief and mournful joy
My spirit now is fill'd,
That I should such a life destroy,
Yet live by him I kill'd.

THE INDIAN'S PETITION. 12,12,12,12.11

Slow.

1. "Let me go to my home in the far distant west, To the scenes of my childhood, in innocence blest, Where the tall cedars wave, and the bright waters

2. Let me go to the spot where the cataracts play, Where I often have sported in boyhood's bright day, And there greet my fond mother whose heart will o'er-

flow, Where my fathers repose, let me go, let me go, - - - Where my fathers repose, oh! there let me go.

flow At the sight of her child, let me go, let me go, - - - At the sight of her child, oh! there let me go.

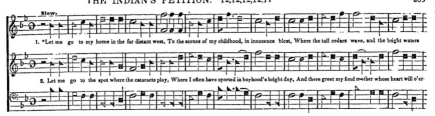

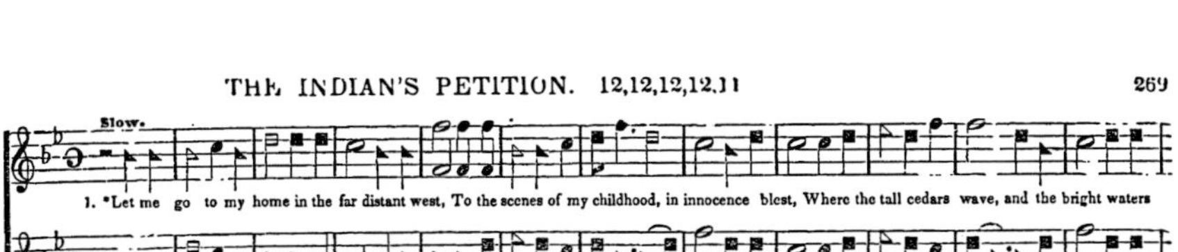

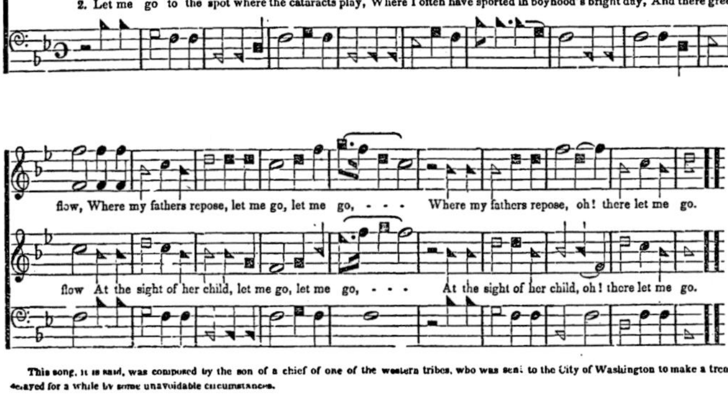

3. Let me go to my sire, by whose battle-scarr'd si 'e
I have sported as oft in the noon of my pride,
And exulted to conquer the insolent foe;
To my father, the chief, let me go, let me go,
To my father, the chief, oh! there let me go.

4. And, oh! do let me go to my flushing eyed maid,
Who hath taught me to love 'neath the green willow's
shade;
Whose heart like the fawn leaps, and is pure as the
snow;
To the bosom I love, let me go, let me go,
To the bosom I love, oh! there let me go.

5. And, oh! do let me go to my wild forest home,
No more from its life-cheering haed pleasures to roam
'Neath the green of the glen let my tomb lie low;
To my home in the word let me go, let me go,
To my home in the wood, oh! there let me go.

This song, it is said, was composed by the son of a chief of one of the western tribes, who was sent to the City of Washington to make a treaty with the United States, which trea'y wa. delayed for a while by some unavoidable circumstances.

ZION'S LIGHT. 7,6.

Chorus.
1. The glorious light of Zion Is spreading all around, And sinners now are heark'ning Unto the gospel sound: To see the saints in glo - ry, And the angels
2. The standard of King Jesus Triumphant doth arise, And mourners crowd around it, With bitter groans and cries. To see the saints in glory, &c.

stand inviting, The angels stand in - viting, to welcome pilgrims home.

3. The suffering, bleeding Saviour,
Who died on Calvary,
Is now proclaim'd to sinners
To set the guilty free;
To see the saints in glory, &c.

4. And while the glorious message
Was circulating round,
Some souls, exposed to ruin,
Redeeming love have found.
To see the saints in glory, &c.

5. And of that favour'd number,
I hope that I am one;
And Christ, I trust, will finish
The work he has begun;
To see the saints in glory, &c.

6. He'll perfect it in righteousness,
And I shall ever be
A monument of mercy,
To all eternity.
To see the saints in glory, &c.

7. I am but a young convert,
Who lately did enlist
A soldier under Jesus,
My Prophet, King, and Priest;
To see the saints in glory, &c.

8. I have received my bounty,
Likewise my martial dress,
A ring of love and favour,
A robe of righteousness.
To see the saints in glory, &c.

9. Now down into the water
Will we young converts go;
There went our Lord and Master
When he was here below;
To see the saints in glory, &c.

10. We lay our sinful bodies
Beneath the yielding wave,
An emblem of the Saviour,
When he lay in the grave.
To see the saints in glory, &c.

11. Poor sinners, think what Jesus
Has done for you and me:
Behold his mangled body
Hung tortured on the tree!
To see the saints in glory, &c.

12. His hands, his feet, his bleeding side
To you he doth display;—
Oh! tell me, brother sinner,
How can you stay away?
To see the saints in glory, &c.

13. Come, all you elder brethren
Ye soldiers of the cross:
Who, for the sake of Jesus,
Have counted all things loss.—
To see the saints in glory, &c.

14. Come [illegible] pray for us, young converts,
That we may travel on,
And meet you all in glory,
Where our Redeemer's gone.
To see the saints in glory, &c.

GOSPEL TRUMPET, (OR WOODSTOCK). C. M.

1. Let ev'-ry mor-tal ear attend, And ev'-ry heart re-joice, The trum-pet of the gos-pel sounds With an in-vi-ting voice.
2. Ho, all ye hun-gry starv-ing souls, That feed up-on the wind, And vain-ly strive with earth-ly toys To fill an emp-ty mind;
3. E-ter-nal wis-dom has prepared A soul-re-vi-ving feast, And bids your longing ap-pe-tites The rich pro-vi-sion taste.
4. Ho, ye that pant for liv-ing streams, And pine a-way and die, Here you may quench your ra-ging thirst With springs that ne-ver dry.
5. Riv-ers of love and mer-cy here In a rich o-cean join; Sal-va-tion in a-bundance flows, Like floods of milk and wine.
6. Ye per-ish-ing and na-ked poor, Who work with migh-ty pain To weave a gar-ment of your own That will not hide your sin;
7. Come, naked, and a-dorn your souls In robes pre-pared by God, Wrought by the la-bours of his Son, And dyed in his own blood.
8. Dear God, the treasures of thy love Are e-ver-last-ing mines, Deep as our help-less mis'ries are, And boundless as our sins.
9. The hap-py gates of gos-pel grace Stand o-pen night and day, Lord, we are come to seek sup-plies, And drive our wants a-way.

NASHVILLE. L. M. 6 lines.

1. I love the volume of thy word;
What light and joy these leaves afford,
To souls benighted and distrest,
Thy precepts guide my doubtful way,
Thy fear forbids my feet to stray,
Thy promise leads my heart to rest.
2. Thy threat'nings wake my slumb'ring eyes,
And warn me where my danger lies;
But 'tis thy blessed gospel, Lord,
That makes my guilty conscience clean,
Converts my soul, subdues my sin,
And give a free and large reward.

HOPE. S. M.

Pia.
1. My God, my life, my love, To thee, to thee I call, I cannot live if thou remove, For thou art all in all: I cannot live if
2. Thy shining grace can cheer This dungeon where I dwell; 'Tis paradise when thou art here, If thou depart, 'tis hell: 'Tis pa - ra - dise when

For.
thou re - move, For thou art all in all.
thou art here, If thou de - part, 'tis hell.

3. The smilings of thy face,
How amiable they are!
'Tis heaven to rest in thine embrace,
And no where else but there.

4. To thee, and thee alone,
The angels owe their bliss;
They sit around thy gracious throne,
And dwell where Jesus is.

5. Not all the harps above
Can make a heavenly place,
If God his residence remove,
Or but conceal his face.

6. Nor earth, nor all the sky
Can one delight afford,
No, not a drop of real joy,
Without thy presence, Lord.

7. Thou art the sea of love,
Where all my pleasures roll,
The circle where my passions move,
And centre of my soul.

8. To thee my spirits fly
With infinite desire,
And yet how far from thee I lie!
Dear Jesus raise me nigher.

GOSPEL TIDINGS. S. M.

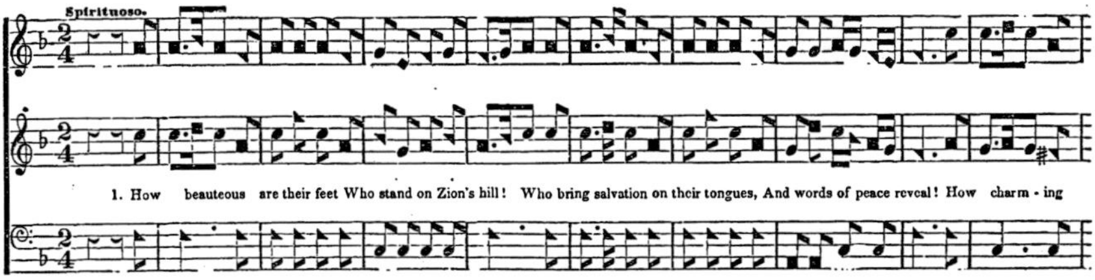

Spirituoso.
1. How beauteous are their feet Who stand on Zion's hill! Who bring salvation on their tongues, And words of peace reveal! How charm - ing

is their voice! How sweet tne tidings are! 'Zi - on, behold tny Saviour King, He reigns ana triumphs here.'

2. How happy are our ears
   That hear this joyful sound
Which kings and prophets waited for,
   And sought, but never found!
How blessed are our eyes
   That see this heavenly light
Prophets and kings desired it long,
   But died without the sight.

3. The watchmen join their voice,
   And tuneful notes employ;
Jerusalem breaks forth in songs
   And deserts learn the joy.
The Lord makes bare his arm
   Through all the earth abroad
Let every nation now behold
   Their Saviour and their God.

STANTON. 6 lines. 7's.

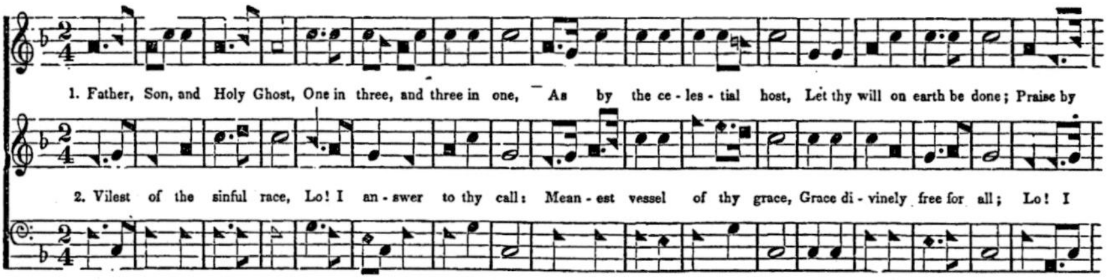
1. Father, Son, and Holy Ghost, One in three, and three in one, As by the ce - les - tial host, Let thy will on earth be done; Praise by
2. Vilest of the sinful race, Lo! I an - swer to thy call: Mean - est vessel of thy grace, Grace di - vinely free for all; Lo! I

all to thee be given, Gracious Lord of earth and heaven!
come to do thy will, All thy counsel to ful - fil.

3. If so poor a worm as I
   May to thy great glory live,
All my actions sanctify,
   All my words and thoughts receive;
Claim me for thy service, claim
All I have, and all I am.

4. Take my soul and body's powers,
   Take my memory, mind, and will:
All my goods, and all my hours,
   All I know, and all I feel;
All I think, or speak, or do;
Take my heart, but make it new!

5. Now, my God, thine own I am,
   Now I give thee back thine own:
Freedom, friends, and health, and fame
   Consecrate to thee alone:
Thine I live, thrice happy I!
Happier still if thine I die.

6. Father, Son, and Holy Ghost,
   One in three, and three in one
As by the celestial host,
   Let thy will on earth be done.
Praise by all to thee be given,
Glorious Lord of earth and heaven

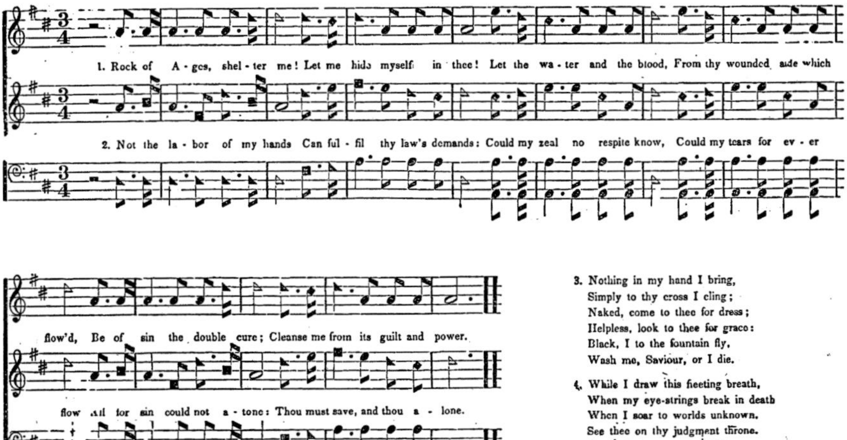
1. Rock of A - ges, shel - ter me! Let me hide myself in thee! Let the wa - ter and the blood, From thy wounded side which
2. Not the la - bor of my hands Can ful - fil thy law's demands: Could my zeal no respite know, Could my tears for ev - er

flow'd, Be of sin the double cure; Cleanse me from its guilt and power.
flow All for sin could not a - tone: Thou must save, and thou a - lone.

3. Nothing in my hand I bring,
Simply to thy cross I cling;
Naked, come to thee for dress;
Helpless, look to thee for grace:
Black, I to the fountain fly,
Wash me, Saviour, or I die.

4. While I draw this fleeting breath,
When my eye-strings break in death
When I soar to worlds unknown,
See thee on thy judgment throne.
Rock of Ages, shelter me:
Let me hide myself in thee!

DUNLAP'S CREEK. C. M.

F. Lewis.

1 My God, my por - tion, and my love,--My ev - er - last - ing all, I've none but thee in heaven a - bove, Or on this earth - ly ball.
2 What emp - ty things are all the skies, And this in - fe - rior clod! There's nothing here de - serves my joys, There's nothing like my God.
3. In vain the bright, the burning sun Scatters his - fee - ble light; 'Tis thy sweet beams cre - ate my noon; If thou withdraw 'tis night.
4. And whilst up - on my restless bed, Amongst the shades I roll, If my Re - deem - er shows his head, 'Tis morning with my soul.

5. To thee I owe my wealth, and friends,
And health, and safe abode;
Thanks to thy name for meaner things,
But they are not my God.

6. How vain a toy is glitt'ring wealth,
If once compared to thee;
Or what's my safety, or my health,
Or all my friends to me?

7. Were I possessor of the earth,
And call'd the stars my own,
Without thy graces and thyself
I were a wretch undone.

8. Let others stretch their arms like seas,
And grasp in all the shore,
Grant me the visits of thy face,
And I desire no more.

CHINA. C. M.

Swan.

1. Why do we mourn de - part - ing friends? Or shake at death's a - larms? 'Tis but the voice that Je - sus sends To call them to his - arms.
2. Are we not tending up - ward too As fast as time can move? Nor would we wish the hours more slow, To keep us from our love.
3. Why should we tremb e to con - vey Their bo - dies to the tomb? There the dear flesh of Je - sus lay, And left a long per - fume.
4. The graves of all his saints he bless'd, And sof - ten'd ev' - ry bed; Where should the dy - ing members rest, But with their dy - ing Head?
5. Thence he a - rose, as - cend - ed high, And show'd our feet the way; Up to the Lord our souls shall fly At the great ris - ing - day
6. Then let the last loud trumpet sound, And bid our kin dred rise A - wake, ye na - tions un - der ground, Ye saints, as - cend the skies

WILLOUGHBY. 8,8,6.

SLOW AND DISTINCT.
1. How pre - cious, Lord, thy sa - cred word, What light and joy those leaves af - ford, To souls in deep dis - tress;
2. Thy threat'nings wake our slumb'ring eyes, And warn us where our dan - ger lies, But 'tis thy gos - pel, Lord,
Thy pre - cepts guide our doubt - ful way, Thy fear for - bids our feet to stray, Thy pro - mise leads to rest.
That makes the guil - ty con - science clean, Con - verts the soul and con - quers sin, And gives a free re - ward

WELLS L. M.

Holdroyd

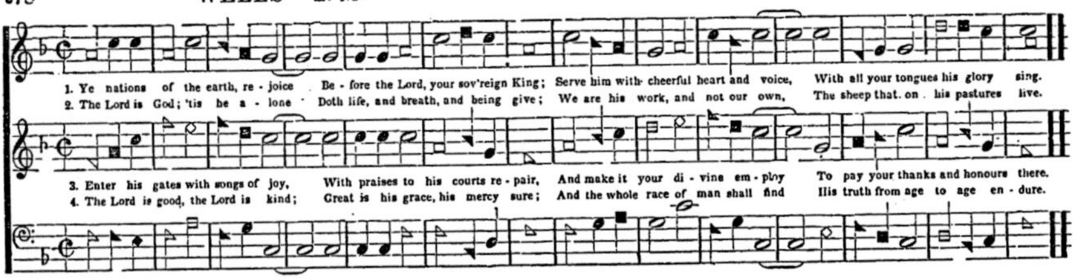
1. Ye nations of the earth, re - joice Be - fore the Lord, your sov'reign King; Serve him with cheerful heart and voice, With all your tongues his glory sing.
2. The Lord is God; 'tis he a - lone Doth life, and breath, and being give; We are his work, and not our own, The sheep that on his pastures live.
3. Enter his gates with songs of joy, With praises to his courts re - pair, And make it your di - vine em - ploy To pay your thanks and honours there.
4. The Lord is good, the Lord is kind; Great is his grace, his mercy sure; And the whole race of man shall find His truth from age to age en - dure.

ZION. 8,7,4.

Thos. Hastings.

1 2
1. On the mountain's top appearing, Lo! the sacred herald stands,
Welcome news to Zion bearing, Zi - on long in hostile lands,
Mourning captive, God himself shall loose thy bands,
Mourning captive, God himself shall loose thy bands.
2. Lo! thy sun is ris'n in glory, God himself appears thy friend,
All thy foes shall flee before thee, Here thy boasted triumphs end;
Great deliv'rance Zion's king vouchsafes to send: Great deliv'rance, &c.
3. En - e - mies no more shall trouble, All thy wrongs shall be redress'd,
For thy shame thou shalt have double, In thy Maker's favor blest;
All thy conflicts end in an eternal rest All thy conflicts &c.

ROCHESTER. C. M.

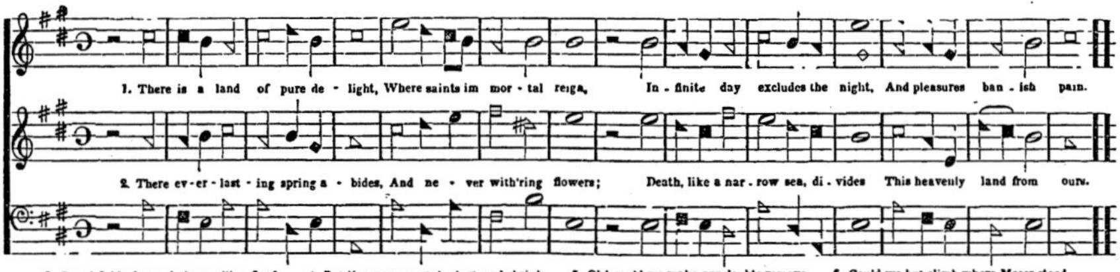
1. There is a land of pure de - light, Where saints im mor - tal reign, In - finite day excludes the night, And pleasures ban - ish pain.
2. There ev - er - last - ing spring a - bides, And ne - ver with'ring flowers; Death, like a nar - row sea, di - vides This heavenly land from ours.

3. Sweet fields, beyond the swelling flood,
Stand dress'd in living green:
So to the Jews old Canaan stood,
While Jordan roll'd between.

4. But timorous mortals start and shrink
To cross this narrow sea,
And linger, shivering, on the brink,
And fear to launch away.

5. Oh! could we make our doubts remove,
Those gloomy doubts that rise,
And see the Canaan that we love,
With unbeclouded eyes.

6. Could we but climb where Moses stood,
And view the landscape o'er;
Not Jordan's stream, nor death's cold flood
Should fright us from the shore.

STONINGTON. S. M.

1. Ye trembling captives hear! The gos - pel trum - pet sounds, No mu - sic more can charm the ear, Or heal thy heart - felt wounds.
2. 'Tis not the trump of war, Nor Si - nai's aw - ful roar, Sal - va - tion's news it spreads a - far, And vengeance is no more.

SILVER STREET. S. M.

J. Street.

1. Come, sound his name a - broad, And hymns of glo - ry sing; Je - ho - vah is the sov' - - reign God, The u - - ni - ver - sal King.
2. He form'd the deeps unknown: He gave the seas their bound; The wat' - ry worlds are all his own, And all the so - lid ground.

3. Come, worship at his throne,
Come, bow before the Lord:
We are his works and not our own;
He form'd us by his word.

4. To-day attend his voice,
Nor dare provoke his rod;
Come, like the people of his choice,
And own your gracious God.

5. But if your ears refuse
The language of his gmce,
And hearts grow hard like stubborn Jews,
That unbelieving race;

5. The Lord, in vengeance drest,
Will lift his hand and swear,
"You that despise my promised rest
Shall have no nortion there."

SHERBURNE. L. M.

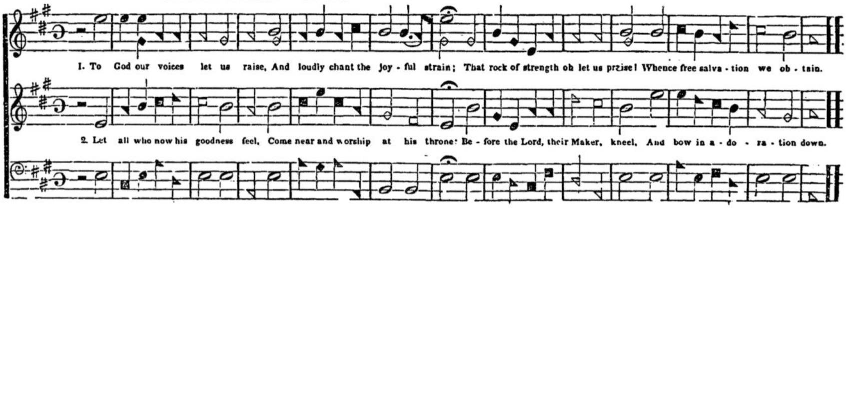
1. To God our voices let us raise, And loudly chant the joy - ful strain; That rock of strength oh let us praise! Whence free salva - tion we ob - tain.
2. Let all who now his goodness feel, Come near and worship at his throne: Be - fore the Lord, their Maker, kneel, And bow in a - do - ra - tion down.

AYLESBURY. S. M. *Chetham.*

1. And am I born to die? To lay this bo - dy down? And must my trembling spi - rit fly In - to a world un known?
2. A land of deep - est shade, Unpierced by human thought; The drea - ry re - gions of the dead, Where all things are for - got!
3. Soon as from earth I go, What will be - come of me? E - ter - nal hap - pi - ness or wo Must then my por - tion be:
4. Waked by the trumpet's sound, I from my grave shall rise! And see the Judge with glo - ry crown'd, And see the flaming skies!

5. How shall I leave my tomb?
With triumph or regret?
A fearful, or a joyful doom,
A curse, or blessing meet?

6. Will angel bands convey
Their brother to the bar?
Or devils drag my soul away,
To meet its sentence there?

7. Who can resolve the doubt
That tears my anxious breast?
Shall I be with the damn'd cast out,
Or number'd with the bless'd?

8. I must from God be driven,
Or with my Saviour dwell;
Must come at his command to heaven,
Or else—depart to hell.

JOY TO THE WORLD, (OR PAXTON). C. M.

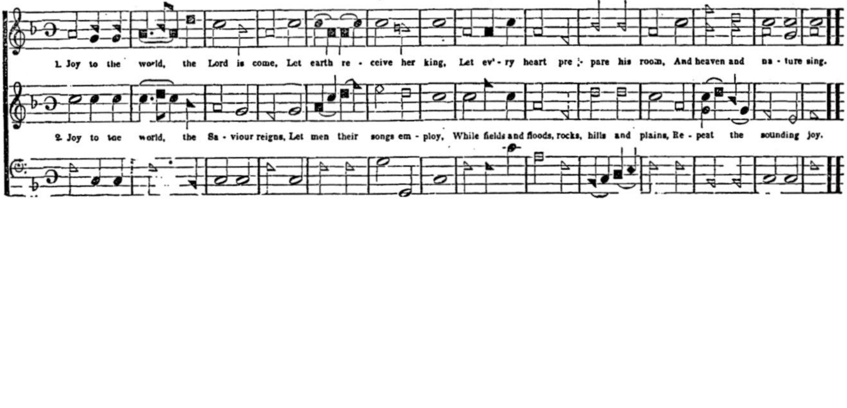
1. Joy to the world, the Lord is come, Let earth re - ceive her king, Let ev' - ry heart pre - pare his room, And heaven and na - ture sing.
2. Joy to the world, the Sa - viour reigns, Let men their songs em - ploy, While fields and floods, rocks, hills and plains, Re - peat the sounding joy.

AMITY. 6,6,8,6,6,8

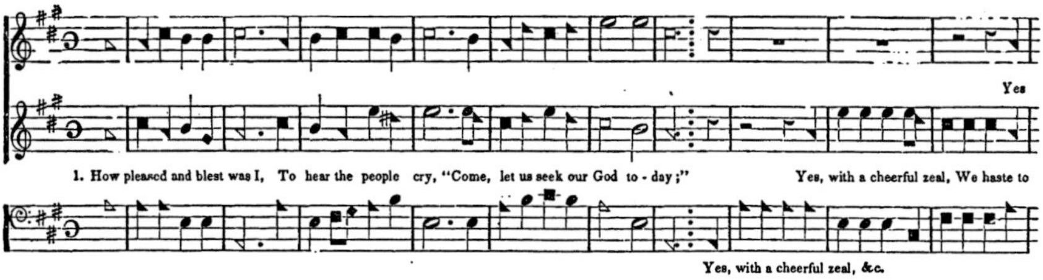
Yes
1. How pleased and blest was I, To hear the people cry, "Come, let us seek our God to - day;" Yes, with a cheerful zeal, We haste to
Yes, with a cheerful zeal, &c.

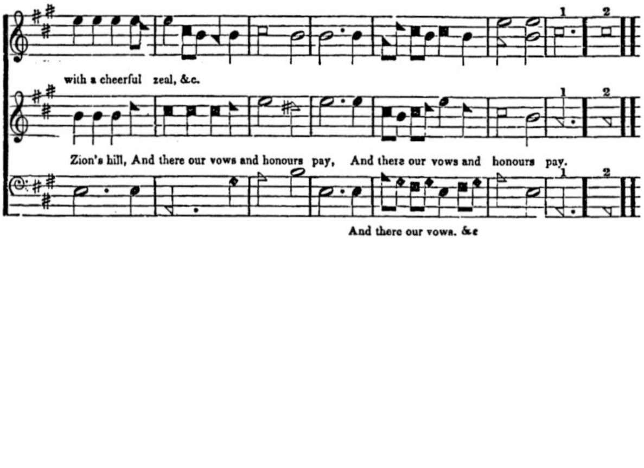
1 2
with a cheerful zeal, &c.
1 2
Zion's hill, And there our vows and honours pay, And there our vows and honours pay.
1 2
And there our vows. &c

2. Zion, thrice happy place,
Adorn'd with wondrous grace,
And walls of strength embrace thee r. and
In thee our tribes appear,
To pray, and praise, and hear
The sacred gospel's joyful sound.

3. There David's greater Son
Has fix'd his royal throne:
He sits for grace and judgment there
He bids the saint be glad,
He makes the sinner sad,
And humble souls rejoice with fea.

4. May peace attend thy gate,
And joy within thee wait,
To bless the soul of ev'ry guest;
The man that seeks thy peace,
And wishes thine increase,
A thousand blessings on him rest!

5. My tongue repeats her vows,
"Peace to this sacred house!"
For here my friends and kindred dwelt;
And since my glorious God
Makes thee his blest abode,
My soul shall ever [illegible] thee [illegible]

NORTHFIELD. C. M.

Ingalls.

How long, dear Je - sus, oh! how long Shall that bright hour de - lay;
Fly swiftly round, ye
Fly swift - ly round, ye wheels of time, Fly
Fly swift - ly round, &c.
And bring, &c.
wheels of time, And bring the pro - mised day, And bring the pro - - mised day.
swift - ly round, ye wheels of time, And bring, &c.
1
2

WATCHMAN. S. M

1. Shall wisdom cry a - loud, And not her speech be heard? The voice of God's e - ter - nal Word, De - serves it no re - gard?
2. "I was his chief de - light, His ev - er - last - ing Son, Be - fore the first of all his works, Cre - a - tion was be - gun.
3. "Be - fore the fly - ing clouds, Be - fore the so - lid land, Be - fore the fields, be - fore the floods, I dwelt at his righ. hand.
4. "When he a - dorn'd the skies, And built them, I was there To or - der when the sun should rise, And mar - shal ev' - ry star.

5. "When he pour'd out the sea,
And spread the flowing deep,
I gave the flood a firm decree
In its own bounds to keep.

6. "Upon the empty air
The earth was balanced well;
With joy I saw the mansion where
The sons of men should dwell.

7. "My busy thoughts at first
On their salvation ran,
Ere sin was born, or Adam's dust
Was fashion'd to a man.

8. "Then come, receive my grace,
Ye children, and be wise;
Happy the man that keeps my ways;
The man that shuns them dies."

SPRAGUE. C. M.

Arranged from J. Smith.

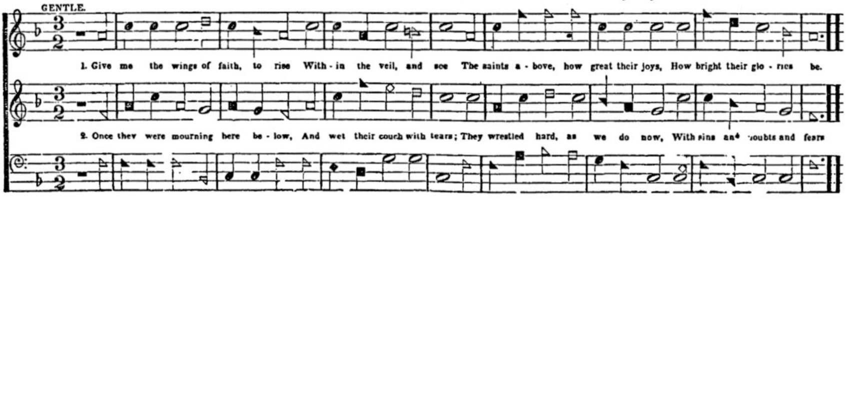
GENTLE.
1. Give me the wings of faith, to rise With - in the veil, and see The saints a - bove, how great their joys, How bright their glo - ries be.
2. Once thev were mourning here be - low, And wet their couch with tears; They wrestled hard, as we do now, With sins an* 'oubts and fears

ARLINGTON. C. M.

Dr. Arne.

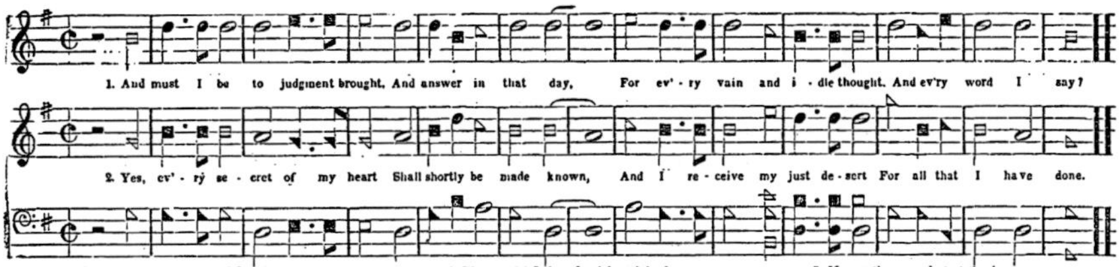
1. And must I be to judgment brought, And answer in that day, For ev' - ry vain and i - dle thought, And ev'ry word I say?
2. Yes, ev' - ry se - cret of my heart Shall shortly be made known, And I re - ceive my just de - sert For all that I have done.

3. How careful then ought I to live!
With what religious fear,
Who such a strict account must give
For my behaviour here!

4. Thou awful Judge of quick and dead,
The watchful power bestow;
So shall I to my ways take heed,
To all I speak or do.

5. If now thou standest at the door,
O let me feel thee near!
And make my peace with God, before
I at thy bar appear

MORNING WORSHIP, (OR NATCHEZ). S. M.

SLOW.
1. How sweet the melting lay Which breaks up - on the ear, When, at the hour of ris - ing day, Chris - tians u - nite in prayer.
2. The breezes waft their cries Up to Je - ho - vah's throne; He lis - tens to their heaving sighs, And sends his bless - ing down.
3. So Je - sus rose to pray Be - fore the morning light, Or on the chill - ing mount did stay, And wrestle all the night.
4. Glo - ry to God, on high, Who sends his blessings down, To res - cue souls condemn'd to die, And make his peo - ple one.

SHIRLAND. S. M

Slow.
1. My God, my life, my love, To thee, to thee I call, I can - not live if thou re-
2. Thy shi - ning grace can cheer This dungeon where I dwell; 'Tis pa - ra - dise when thou art

move, For thou art all in all.
here If thou de - part, 'tis hell.

3. The smilings of thy face,
   How amiable they are!
   'Tis heaven to rest in thine embrace,
   And no where else but there.

4. To thee, and thee alone,
   The angels owe their bliss;
   They sit around thy gracious throne,
   And dwell where Jesus is.

5. Not all the harps above
   Can make a heavenly place,
   If God his residence remove,
   Or but conceal his face.

6. Nor earth, nor all the sky
   Can one delight afford,
   No, not a drop of real joy,
   Without thy presence, Lord.

7. Thou art the sea of love,
   Where all my pleasures roll,
   The circle where my passions move
   And centre of my soul.

8. To thee my spirits fly
   With infinite desire,
   And yet how far from thee I lie.
   Dear Jesus, raise me nigher.

PORTUGAL. L. M

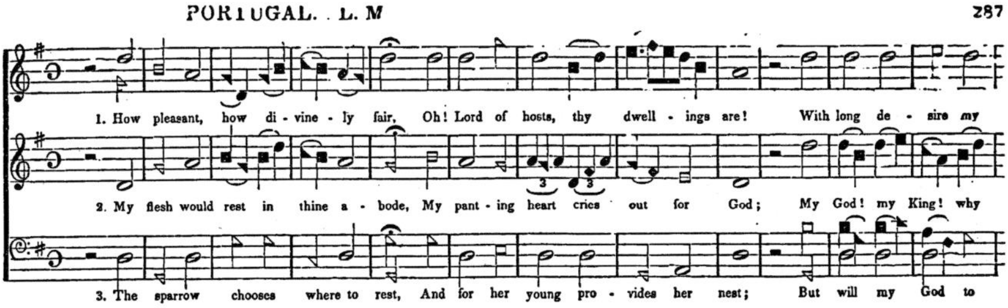
1. How pleasant, how di - vine - ly fair, Oh! Lord of hosts, thy dwell - ings are! With long de - sire my
2. My flesh would rest in thine a - bode, My pant - ing heart cries out for God; My God! my King! why
3. The sparrow chooses where to rest, And for her young pro - vides her nest; But will my God to

spi - rit faints To meet th' as - sem - blies of thy saints.
should I be So far from all my joys and thee!
spar rows grant That pleasure which his children want!

4. Blest are the saints who sit on high,
Around thy throne of majesty;
Thy brightest glories shine above,
And all their work is praise and love.

5. Blest are the souls that find a place
Within the temple of thy grace;
There they behold thy gentler rays,
And seek thy face, and learn thy praise.

6. Blest are the men whose hearts are set
To find the way to Zion's gate;
God is their strength, and through the road
They lean upon their helper, God.

7. Cheerful they walk with growing strength,
Till all shall meet in heaven at length,
Till all before thy face appear,
And join in nobler worship there

HEBRON. L. M.

1. Thus far the Lord has led me on, Thus far his pow'r prolongs my days, And ev' - ry evening shall make known Some fresh me - morial of his grace.
2. Much of my time has run to waste, And I, perhaps, am near my home; But he forgives my fol - lies past, He gives me strength for days to come.
3. I lay my bo - dy down to sleep, Peace is the pil - low for my head, While well - appoint - ed an - gels keep Their watchful stations round my bed.
4. In vain the sons of earth or hell Tell me a thousand frightful things; My God in safe - ty makes me dwell Be - neath the sha - dow of his wings.
5. Thus when the night of death shall come, My flesh shall rest be - neath the ground, And wait thy voice to rouse the tomb, With sweet sal - va - tion in the sound.

ROCKBRIDGE. L. M.

Chapin.

1. Life is the time to serve the Lord, The time t' ensure the great re - ward; And while the lamp holds out to burn, The vi - lest sin - ner may re - turn.
2. Life is the hour that God has giv'n To 'scape from hell, and fly to heaven; The day of grace, and mortals may Se - cure the blessings of the day.

3. The living know that they must die.
But all the dead forgotten lie,
Their memory and their sense is gone,
Alike unknowing and unknown

4. Their hatred and their love is lost,
Their envy buried in the dust;
They have no share in all that's done
Beneath the circuit of the sun.

5. Then what my thoughts design to do,
My hands with all your might pursue,
Since no device, nor work is found,
Nor faith, nor hope, beneath the ground.

6. There are no acts of pardon past
In the cold grave to which we haste.
But darkness, death, and long despair
Reign in eternal silence there

THE NARROW WAY. L. M.

Rev. Andrew Grambling.

3
4
1. Come ye who know the Lord in - deed, Who are from sin and bondage freed, Sub - mit to all the ways of
3
4
2. Great tri - bu - la - tion you shall meet, But soon shall walk the gold - en street; Though hell may rage and vent her
3
4

1
God And walk the nar - - row hap - py road.
1 2
spite, Yet Christ will save his heart's de - light
1 2

3.
That awful day will soon appear,
When Gabriel's trumpet you shall hear
Sound through the earth, yea down to hell,
To call the nations great and small.

4.
To see the earth in burning flames,
The trumpet louder here proclaims,
"The world shall hear and know her doom,
The separation now is come."

5.
Behold the righteous marching home,
And all the angels bid them come;
While Christ, the judge, with joy proclaims,
"Here come my saints, I'll own their names

6.
"Ye everlasting doors fly wide,
Make ready to receive my bride;
Ye trumps of heaven proclaim abroad,
Here comes the purchase of my blood."

7.
In grandeur see the royal line
In glitt'ring robes the sun outshine;
See saints and angels join in one
And march in splendour to the throne

8.
They stand and wonder, and look on—
They join in one eternal song,
Their great Redeemer to admire,
While raptures set thy souls on fire

THE PENITENT'S PRAYER, (OR AVON). C. M.

Scottish.

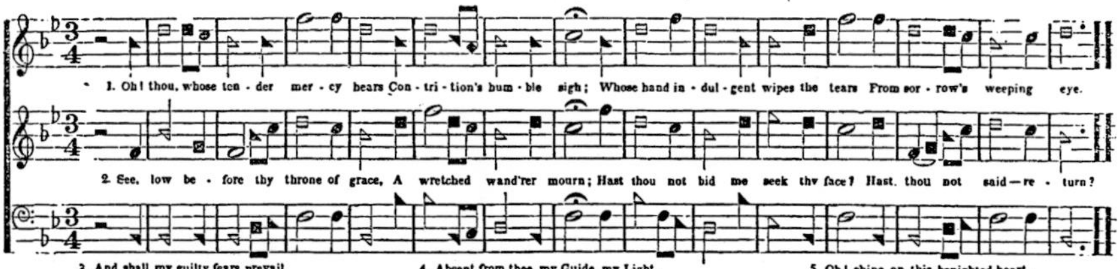
1. Oh! thou, whose ten - der mer - cy hears Con - tri - tion's hum - ble sigh; Whose hand in - dul - gent wipes the tears From sor - row's weeping eye.
2. See, low be - fore thy throne of grace, A wretched wand'rer mourn; Hast thou not bid me seek thy face? Hast thou not said—re - turn?

3. And shall my guilty fears prevail
To drive me from thy feet?
Oh! let not this dear refuge fail,
This only safe retreat.

4. Absent from thee, my Guide, my Light,
Without one cheering ray;
Through dangers, fears, and gloomy night,
How desolate my way!

5. Oh! shine on this benighted heart,
With beams of mercy shine!
And let thy healing voice impart
A taste of joys divine.

MISSIONARY'S ADIEU. C. M.

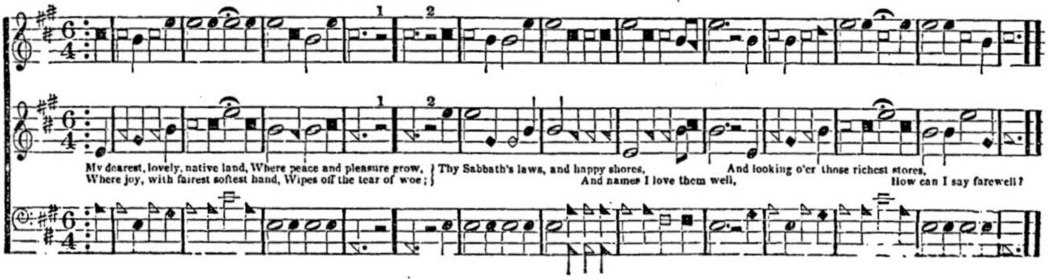
1
2
My dearest, lovely, native land, Where peace and pleasure grow,
Where joy, with fairest softest hand, Wipes off the tear of woe;
Thy Sabbath's laws, and happy shores,
And names I love them well,
And looking o'er those richest stores,
How can I say farewell?

DUKE STREET. L. M.

Hutton.

Slow.
1. 'Tis by the faith of joys to come We walk through deserts dark as night, Till we ar - rive at heaven our home, Faith is our guide, and faith our light.
2. The want of sight she well sup - plies; She makes the pearly gates ap - pear; Far in - to dis - tant worlds she pries, And brings e - ter - nal glo - ries near.
3. Cheerful we tread the de - sert through, While faith inspires a heavenly ray, Though lions roar and tem - pests blow, And rocks and dan - gers fill the way.
4. So Abraham, by di - vine com - mand, Left his own house to walk with God; His faith be - held the pro - mised land, And fired his zeal a - long the road.

WARWICK: C. M.

J. Stanley.

1. Lord, in the morning thou shalt hear My voice a - scend - ing high; To thee will I di - rect my prayer, To thee lift up mine eye.
2. Thou art a God, be - fore whose sight The wicked shall not stand; Sin - ners shall ne'er be thy de - light, Nor dwell at thy right hand.
3. But to thy house will I re - sort, To taste thy mer - cies there; I will fre - quent thine ho - ly court, And wor - ship in thy fear.
4. O may thy spi - rit guide my feet In ways of righteous - ness; Make every path of du - ty straight, And plain be - fore my face.

RIPLEY. 8,7.

Arranged from a Gregorian Chant, by L. Mason

1. Je - sus, I my cross have taken, All to leave and fol - low thee;
Naked, poor, despised, for - saken, Thou, from hence, my all shalt be:
Let the world ne - glect and leave me, They have left my

Saviour too; Hu - man hopes have oft deceived me, Thou art faithful, thou art true.

2.

Perish earthly fame and treasure,
Come disaster, scorn and pain,
In thy service pain is pleasure,
With thy favour loss is gain:
Oh! 'tis not in grief to harm me,
While thy bleeding love I see:
Oh! 'tis not in joy to charm me,
When that love is hid from me

WINTER. C. M.

Reed.

His hoary frost, his flee - cy snow, Descend and clothe the ground, The li - quid streams for - bear to flow, In i - cy fet - ters bound

THIS WORLD IS NOT MY HOME. C. M.

As sung by Rev. Mr. Gamewell.

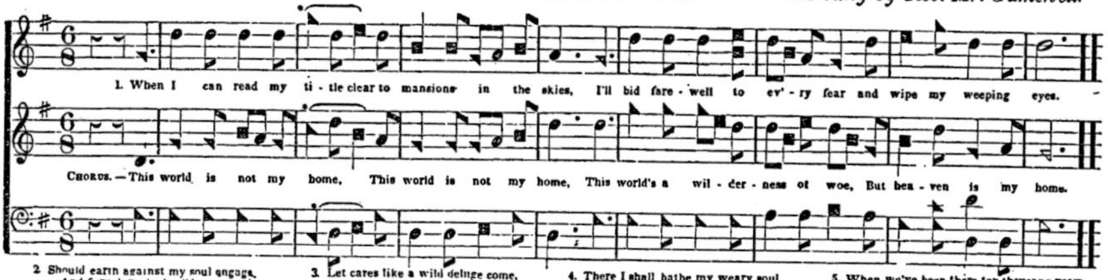
1. When I can read my ti - tle clear to mansions in the skies, I'll bid fare - well to ev' - ry fear and wipe my weeping eyes.
CHORUS. — This world is not my home, This world is not my home, This world's a wil - der - ness of woe, But hea - ven is my home.

2 Should earth against my soul engage,
And fiery darts be hurl'd,
Then I can smile at Satan's rage,
And face a frowning world.

3. Let cares like a wild deluge come,
And storms of sorrow fall,
May I but safely reach my home,
My God, my heaven, my all.

4. There I shall bathe my weary soul
In seas of heavenly rest,
And not a wave of trouble roll
Across my peaceful breast.

5. When we've been there ten thousand years,
Bright shining as the sun,
We've no less days to sing God's praise,
Than when we first begun.

* The slur is only used in singing the chorus; in singing the verses, sing as if there was no slur.

COME, YE DISCONSOLATE. 11.10.

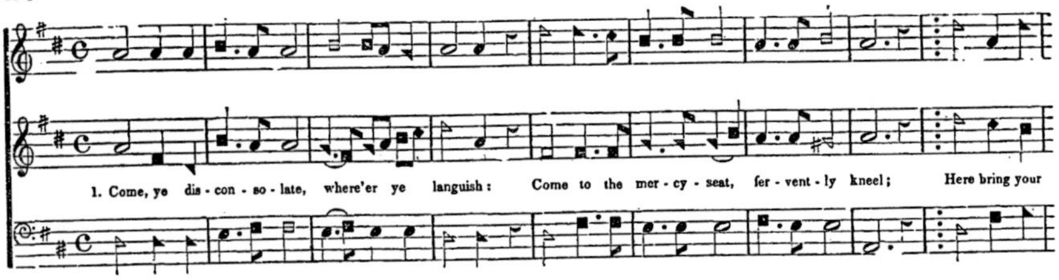
1. Come, ye dis - con - so - late, where'er ye languish: Come to the mer - cy - seat, fer - vent - ly kneel; Here bring your

wounded hearts, here tell your anguish; Earth has no sor - row that heaven car - not heal.

2.

Joy of the desolate, light of the straying,
Hope of the penitent, fadeless and pure,
Here speaks the Comforter, tenderly saying,
Earth has no sorrow that heaven cannot cure.

3.

Here see the bread of life; see waters flowing
Forth from the throne of God, pure from above:
Come to the feast of love; come, ever knowing
Earth has no sorrow but heaven can remove

GLASGOW. L. M.

Dare.

Slow.
This life's a dream, an emp - ty show, But the bright world to which I go Hath
joys sub - stan - tial and sin - cere; When shall I wake, when shall I wake and find me there.
Pia.
Fort.

NEWBURGH. S. M.

Manson.

Ye
1. Let eve - ry creature join To praise th' e - ter - - nal God; Ye heaven - ly hosts, the song be - gin, Ye
Ye heavenly hosts, the song - - - - be - gin, Ye
heavenly hosts, the song be - gin, And sound his name a - broad. And moon with pa - ler
heavenly hosts, the song be - gin, And sound his name a - broad. And moon with pa - ler
heavenly hosts, &c. Thou sun with gold - en beams. And moon with pa - ler

rays, Ye starry lights, ye twinkling flames, Shine to your Maker's praise. Ye starry lights, &c.
rays, Ye starry lights, ye twinkling flames, Shine to your Maker's praise.
rays, Ye starry lights, &c.

2. He built those worlds above,
And fix'd their wond'rous frame;
By his command they stand or move,
And ever speak his name.
Ye vapours, when ye rise,
Or fall in showers or snow,
Ye thunders murm'ring round the skies,
His power and glory show.

3. Wind, hail, and flashing fire,
Agree to praise the Lord,
When ye in dreadful storms conspire
To execute his word.
By all his works above
His honours be exprest;
But saints that taste his saving love
Should sing his praises best.

PAUSE I.

4. Let earth and ocean know
They owe their Maker praise;
Praise him, ye watery worlds below,
And monsters of the seas.
From mountains near the sky
Let his high praise resound,
From humble shrubs and cedars high,
And vales and fields around.

5. Ye lions of the wood,
And tamer beasts that graze,
Ye live upon his daily food,
And he expects your praise.
Ye birds of lofty wing,
On high his praises bear;
Or sit on flowery boughs, and sing
Your Maker's glory there.

6. Ye creeping ants and worms,
His various wisdom show,
And flies, in all your shining swarms,
Praise him that dress'd you so.
By all the earth-born race
His honours be exprest:
But saints that know his heavenly grace
Should learn to praise him best.

PAUSE II.

7. Monarchs of wide command,
Praise ye th' eternal King;
Judges, adore that sovereign hand
Whence all your honours spring.
Let vigorous youth engage
To sound his praises high;
While growing babes, and withering age,
Their feebler voices try.

8. United zeal be shown
His wond'rous fame to raise;
God is the Lord: his name alone
Deserves our endless praise.
Let nature join with art,
And all pronounce him blest;
But saints that dwell so near his heart
Should sing his praises best.

THE WEARY PILGRIM'S CONSOLATION. 12,11,12,11,12,12.12.11.

C. H. Parr

1. How sweet to reflect on the joys that await me In yon blissful region, the haven of rest,
Where glorified spirits with welcome shall greet me, And lead me to mansions prepared for the blest; } En - circled in light, and with glory en - shrouded,
My hap - piness per - fect, my mind's sky unclouded, I'll bathe in the ocean of pleasure unbounded, And range with delight through the Eden of love.

2. While angelic legions, with harps tuned celestial,
   Harmoniously join in the concert of praise,
The saints, as they flock from the regions terrestrial,
   In loud hallelujah their voices will raise;
Then songs to the Lamb shall re-echo through heaven,
My soul will respond, to Immanuel be given
All glory, all honour, all might and dominion,
Who brought us, through grace to the Eden of love.

3. Then hail, blessed state! hail, ye songsters of glory!
   Ye harpers of bliss, soon I'll meet you above,
And join your full choir in rehearsing the story,
   Salvation from sorrow through Jesus's love;
Though prison'd in earth, yet by anticipation
Already my soul feels a sweet prelibation
Of joys that await me when freed from probation
My heart 's now in heaven .he Eden of love.

CORONATION.* C. M.

Holden.

1. All hail the power of Jesus' name! Let angels prostrate fall; Bring forth the royal di - a - dem, And crown him Lord of all. Bring
All hail the power of Jesus' name! Let angels prostrate fall;
And crown him Lord of all. Bring

forth the royal di - adem, And crown him Lord of all.
forth the royal di - adem, &c.

2.

Crown him, ye martyrs of our God,
Who from his altar call;
Extol the stem of Jesse's rod,
And crown him Lord of all.

3

Ye chosen seed of Israel's race,
A remnant weak and small.
Hail him who saves you by his grace,
And crown him Lord of all.

4.

Ye Gentile sinners, ne'er forget
The wormwood and the gall;
Go— spread your trophies at his feet,
And crown him Lord of all.

5.

Babes, men, and sires, who know his love,
Who feel your sin and thrall,
Now join with all the hosts above,
And crown him Lord of all.

6.

Let every kindred, every tribe,
On this terrestrial ball,
To him all majesty ascribe,
And crown him Lord of all.

7.

Oh that, with yonder sacred throng,
We at his feet may fall!
We'll join the everlasting song,
And crown him Lord of all.

* This tune was a great favourite with the late Dr. Dwight. It was often sung by the College Choir, while he, "catching, as it were, the inspiration of the heavenly world, would join them and lead them with the most ardent devotion."—*Incidents in the Life of President Dwight*, p. 36

MILLEDGEVILLE. C. M.

Original parts from Rev. A. Grambling

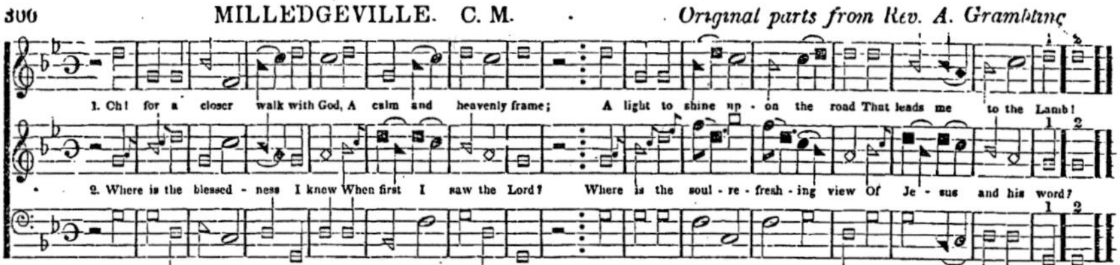
1. Oh! for a closer walk with God, A calm and heavenly frame; A light to shine up - on the road That leads me to the Lamb!
2. Where is the blessed - ness I knew When first I saw the Lord? Where is the soul - re - fresh - ing view Of Je - sus and his word?
1 2

3. What peaceful hours I then enjoy'd?
How sweet their memory still!
But now I find an aching void
The world can never fill.

4. Return, oh holy Dove! return,
Sweet messenger of rest!
I hate the sins that made thee mourn,
And drove thee from my breast.

5. The dearest idol I have known,
Whate'er that idol be,
Help me to tear it from thy throne,
And worship only thee.

6. So shall my walk be close with God,
Calm and serene my frame;
So purer light shall mark the road
That leads me to the Lamb.

ROCKINGHAM. C. M.

Chapin.

1. Come, hap - py souls, ap - proach your God With new me - lo - dious songs; Come, tender to Al - migh - ty grace The tri - butes of your tongues.
2. So strange, so boundless was the love That pitied dy - ing men, The Fa - ther sent his e - qual Son To give them life a - gain.

3. Thy hands, dear Jesus, were not arm'd
With a revenging rod:
No hard commission to perform
The vengeance of a God

4. But all was mercy, all was mild,
And wrath forsook the throne,
When Christ on the kind errand came,
And brought salvation down.

5. Here, sinners, you may heal your wounds,
And wipe your sorrows dry;
Trust in the mighty Saviour's name,
And you shall never die.

6. See, dearest Lord, our willing souls
Accept thine offer'd grace,
We bless the great Redeemer's love,
And give the Father praise

1. Hark! lis - ten to the trum - pet - ers! They sound for vol - un - teers! | Their horses white, their garments bright With crows and
On Zi - on's bright and flow' - ry mount De - hold the of - fi - cers—

2. It sets my heart all in a flame; A sol - dier I will be; | They want no cowards in their band, (They will their
I will en - list, gird on my arms, And fight for lib - er - ty.

Now they stand, En - list - ing sol - diers for their King, To march for Canaan's land.

co - lours fly,) But call for valiant - hearted men, Who're not a - fraid to die.

4. The trumpet sounds, the armies shout,
   And drive the hosts of hell;
How dreadful is our God in arms!
   The great Immanuel !—
Sinners, enlist with Jesus Christ
   Th' eternal Son of God,
And march with us to Canaan's land,
   Beyond the swelling flood.

5. There is a green and flow'ry field,
   Where fruits immortal grow ;
There, clothed in white, the angels bright
   Our great Redeemer know.
We 'll shout and sing for evermore
   In that eternal world ;
But Satan and his armies too,
   Shall down to hell be hurl'd.

6. Hold up your heads, ye soldiers bold,
   Redemption 's drawing nigh
We soon shall hear the trumpet sound
   'T will shake both earth and sky ;
In fiery chariots then we 'll fly.
   And leave the world on fire
And meet around the starry throne
   To tune th' immortal lyre.

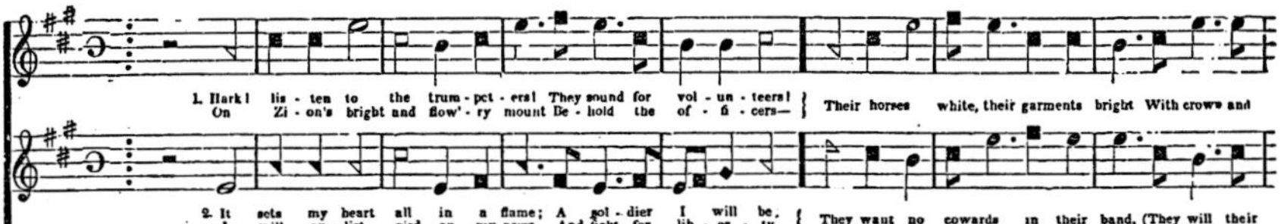

3. The armies now are in parade,
   How martial they appear!
All arm'd and dress'd in uniform.
   They look like men of war !

They follow their great General,
   The great Eternal Lamb.
His garments stain'd with his own blood,
   King Jesus is his name.

LONG SOUGHT HOME. C. M.

William Bobo.

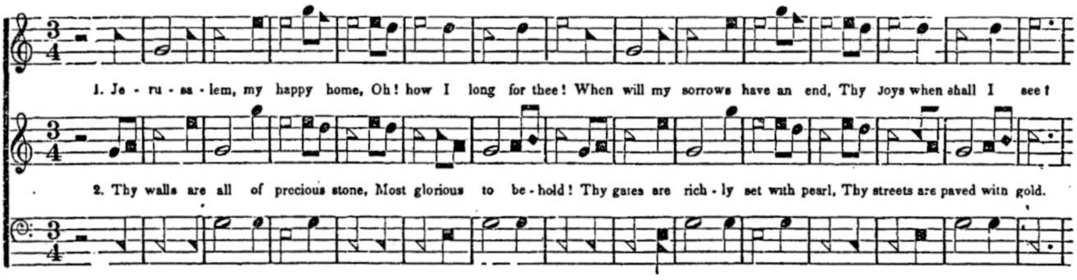
1. Je - ru - sa - lem, my happy home, Oh! how I long for thee! When will my sorrows have an end, Thy joys when shall I see!
2. Thy walls are all of precious stone, Most glorious to be - hold! Thy gates are rich - ly set with pearl, Thy streets are paved with gold.

Chorus.
Home, sweet home, my long sought home, My home in heaven a - bove.
Home, sweet home, my long sought home, My home in heaven a - bove.

3. Thy gardens and thy pleasant greens,
My study long have been;
Such sparkling light, by human sight,
Has never yet been seen.
Home, sweet home, &c.

4. If heaven be thus glorious, Lord,
Why should I stay from thence:
What folly 't is that I should dread
To die and go from hence!

5. Reach down, reach down thine arm of grace,
And cause me to ascend,
Where congregations ne'er break up,
And sabbaths never end.

6. Jesus, my love, to glory 's gone;
Him will I go and see;
And all my brethren here below
Will soon come after me.

7. My friends, I bid you all adieu!
I leave you in God's care;
And if I never more see you,
Go on,—I'll meet you there.
Home, sweet home, &c.

8. There we shall meet and no more part,
And heaven shall ring with praise;
While Jesus' love, in every heart,
Shall tune the song *free grace.*

9. And if our fellowship below
In Jesus be so sweet,
What heights of rapture shall we know
When round the throne we meet!

10. Millions of years around may run—
Our songs shall still go on,
To praise the *Father* and the *Son*.
And *Spirit,—Three* in **One.**
Home, sweet home, &c.

INVITATION. 8,7,4. (New.)

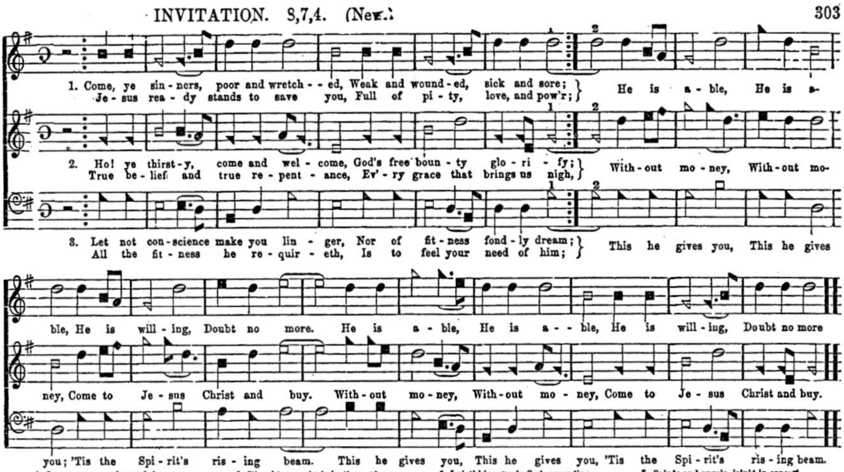

1. Come, ye sin - ners, poor and wretch - - ed, Weak and wound - ed, sick and sore;
Je - sus rea - dy stands to save you, Full of pi - ty, love, and pow'r;
He is a - ble, He is a - ble, He is will - ing, Doubt no more. He is a - ble, He is a - - ble, He is will - ing, Doubt no more
2. Ho! ye thirst - y, come and wel - come, God's free boun - ty glo - ri - fy;
True be - lief and true re - pent - ance, Ev' - ry grace that brings us nigh,
With - out mo - ney, With - out mo - ney, Come to Je - sus Christ and buy. With - out mo - ney, With - out mo - ney, Come to Je - sus Christ and buy.
3. Let not con - science make you lin - ger, Nor of fit - ness fond - ly dream;
All the fit - ness he re - quir - eth, Is to feel your need of him;
This he gives you, This he gives you; 'Tis the Spi - rit's ris - ing beam. This he gives you, This he gives you, 'Tis the Spi - rit's ris - ing beam.

4. Come, ye weary, heavy laden,
Lost and ruin'd by the fall;
If you tarry till you're better,
You will never come at all:
Not the righteous—
Sinners Jesus came to call.

5. View him prostrate in the garden;
On the ground your Saviour lies!
On the bloody tree behold him;
Hear him cry, before he dies,
"It is finished!"
Sinners, will not this suffice?

6. Lo! th' incarnate God, ascending,
Pleads the merit of his blood:
Venture on him, venture wholly,
Let no other trust intrude:
None but Jesus
Can do helpless sinners good.

7. Saints and angels, join'd in concert,
Sing the praises of the Lamb:
While the blissful seats of heaven
Sweetly echo with his name.
Hallelujah!
Sinners here may sing the same.

MERCY'S FREE. 9,6,9,8,8,8,6.

Leonard P. Breedlove.

1. What's this that in my soul is ris-ing? Is it grace? Is it grace?
Which makes me keep for mer-cy cry-ing, Is it grace? Is it grace?
This work that's in my soul be-gun, It makes me strive all
2. Great God of love, I can but won-der, Mer-cy's free! Mer-cy's free!
Though I've no price at all to ten-der, Mer-cy's free! Mer-cy's free!
Though mercy's free, our God is just, And if a soul should

sin to shun, It plants my soul be-neath the sun, Mer-cy's free! Mer-cy's free!
ere be lost, This will tor-ment the sin-ner most, Mer-cy's free! Mer-cy's free!

3. Swell, O swell the heavenly chorus,
Mercy's free! Mercy's free!
The devil's kingdom falls before us,
Mercy's free! Mercy's free!
Sinners, repent, inquire the road
That leads to glory and to God,
Come, wash in Christ's atoning blood,
Mercy's free! Mercy's free!

4. This truth through all our life shall cheer us,
Mercy's free! Mercy's free!
And through the vale of death shall bear us,
Mercy's free! Mercy's free!
And when to Jordan's banks we come,
And cross the raging billow's foam,
We'll sing, when safely landed home,
Mercy's free! Mercy's free!

WHEN I AM GONE. 10s & 8s.

M. H. Turner.

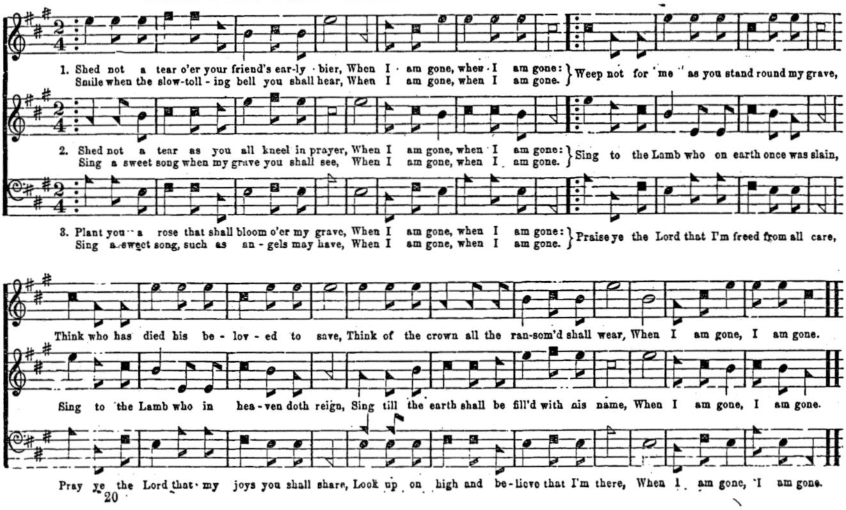
1. Shed not a tear o'er your friend's ear-ly - bier, When I - am gone, when I am gone:
Smile when the slow-toll - ing bell you shall hear, When I am gone, when I am gone.
Weep not for me as you stand round my grave,
2. Shed not a tear as you all kneel in prayer, When I am gone, when I am gone:
Sing a sweet song when my grave you shall see, When I am gone, when I am gone.
Sing to the Lamb who on earth once was slain,
3. Plant you a rose that shall bloom o'er my grave, When I am gone, when I am gone:
Sing a sweet song, such as an - gels may have, When I am gone, when I am gone.
Praise ye the Lord that I'm freed from all care,
Think who has died his be - lov - ed to save, Think of the crown all the ran-som'd shall wear, When I am gone, I am gone.
Sing to the Lamb who in hea - ven doth reign, Sing till the earth shall be fill'd with his name, When I am gone, I am gone.
Pray ye the Lord that my joys you shall share, Look up on high and be - lieve that I'm there, When I am gone, I am gone.

ALL IS WELL. P. M.

J. T. White.

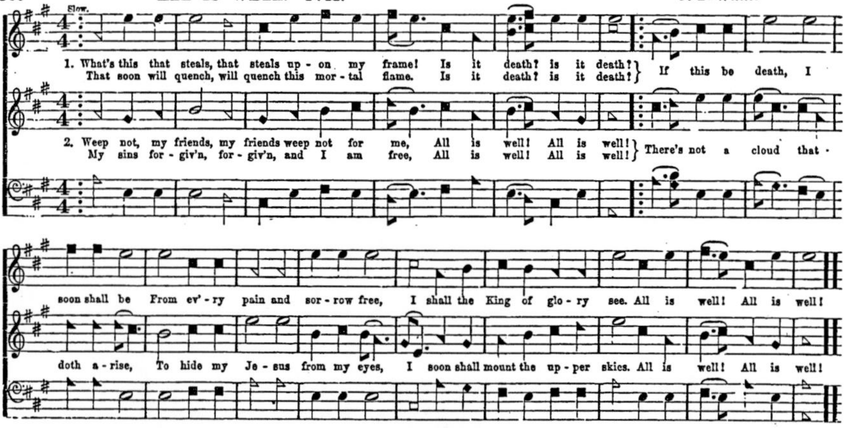
Slow.
1. What's this that steals, that steals up - on my frame! Is it death? is it death?
That soon will quench, will quench this mor - tal flame. Is it death? is it death?
If this be death, I soon shall be From ev'-ry pain and sor-row free, I shall the King of glo-ry see. All is well! All is well!
2. Weep not, my friends, my friends weep not for me, All is well! All is well!
My sins for-giv'n, for-giv'n, and I am free, All is well! All is well!
There's not a cloud that doth a-rise, To hide my Je-sus from my eyes, I soon shall mount the up-per skies. All is well! All is well!

3. Tune, tune your harps, your harps, ye saints on high,
All is well, All is well!
I too will strike my harp with equal joy,
All is well, All is well!
Bright angels are from glory come,
They're round my bed, they're in my room,
They wait to waft my spirit home.
All is well, All is well!

4. Hark! hark! my Lord, my Lord and Master's voice,
Calls away, Calls away!
I soon shall see—enjoy my happy choice,
Why delay, Why delay!
Farewell, my friends, adieu, adieu,
I can no longer stay with you,
My glittering crown appears in view.
All is well, All is well

5. Hail! hail! all hail! all hail! ye blood-wash'd throng,
Saved by grace, Saved by grace—
I come to join, to join your rapturous song,
Saved by grace, Saved by grace
All, all is peace and joy divine,
And heaven and glory now are mine,
Loud hallelujahs to the Lamb!
All is well, All is well.

ELTHAM. 7s. (Double.) *L. Mason.* From the Carmina Sacra.

Slow.
1. Hast - en, Lord, the glo - rious time, When, be - neath Mes - si - ah's sway, Ev' - ry na - tion, ev' - ry clime
D. C. Sa - tan and his host, o'er - thrown, Bound in chains, shall hurt no more.
2. Then shall wars and tu - mults cease, Then be ban - ish'd grief and pain; Right - eous - ness and joy and peace
D. C. All his might - y acts re - cord, All his wond - rous love pro - claim.
Shall the gos - pel call o - bey.
Might-iest kings his pow'r shall own,
Hea-then tribes his name a - dore;
D. C.
Un - dis - turbed shall ev - er reign.
Bless we, then, our gra - cious Lord,
Ev - er praise his glo-rious name,
D. C.
D. C.

THE YOUNG CONVERT. L. M.

S. Hill.

Lively.
1. When con-verts first be - gin to sing, Won - der, won - der, won - der,
Their hap - py souls are on the wing, Glo - ry, hal - le - lu - jah.
Their theme is all re - deem - ing love—
2. They won - der why old saints don't sing, Won - der, won - der, won - der;
And make God's earth - ly tem - ples ring, Glo - ry, hal - le - lu - jah!
They view them-selves up - on the shore—
3. The Bi - ble now ap - pears so plain, Won - der, won - der, won - der,
They won - der they should read in vain, Glo - ry, hal - le - lu - jah!
The air is all per - fumed with love,
Glo - ry, hal - le - lu - jah! Fain would they be with Christ a - bove, Sing glo - ry, hal - le - lu - jah!
Glo - ry, hal - le - lu - jah! And think the bat - tle all is o'er, Sing, glo - ry, hal - le - lu - jah!
Glo - ry, hal - le - lu - jah! And earth ap - pears like heav'n a - bove, Sing, glo - ry, hal - le - lu - jah!

EDEN OF LOVE. 12,11,12,11,12,12,12,11.

1. How sweet to re - flect on those joys that a - wait me, In yon bliss-ful re-gion, the ha - ven of rest,
Where glo - ri - fied spi - rits with welcome shall greet me, And lead me to mansions pre-pared for the blest! } En - cir - cled in light, and with glo - ry en-
shroud - ed, My hap-pi - ness perfect, my mind's sky un-cloud - ed, I'll bathe in the o-cean of pleasure un-bound - ed, And range with de-light thro' the E - den of Love.
2. While an - gel - ic le-gions, with harps tuned ce - les - tial, Har - mo - ni-ously join in the con-cert of praise,
The saints, as the flock from the re-gions ter - res - trial, In loud hal - le - lu-jahs their voi-ces will raise: } Then songs to the Lamb shall re - ech - o through
hea - ven, My soul will re-spond, To Im-manuel be giv - en All glo-ry, all honour, all might and do - min - ion, Who brought us thro' grace to the E - den of Love.
3. Then hail, bless-ed state! Hail, ye song-sters of glo - ry! Ye harp-ers of bliss, soon I'll meet you a - bove,
And join your full choir in re - hears-ing the sto - ry, "Sal - va-tion from sorrow, through Je - sus's love:" } Though prison'd in earth, yet by an - ti - ci-
pa - tion. Al - read-y my soul feels a sweet preli - ba - tion Of joys that a-wait me, when freed from proba - tion: My heart's now in heaven, the E den of Love.

THE SHEPHERD'S STAR. 11,10.

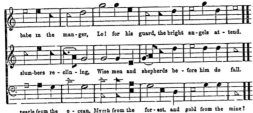

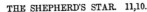

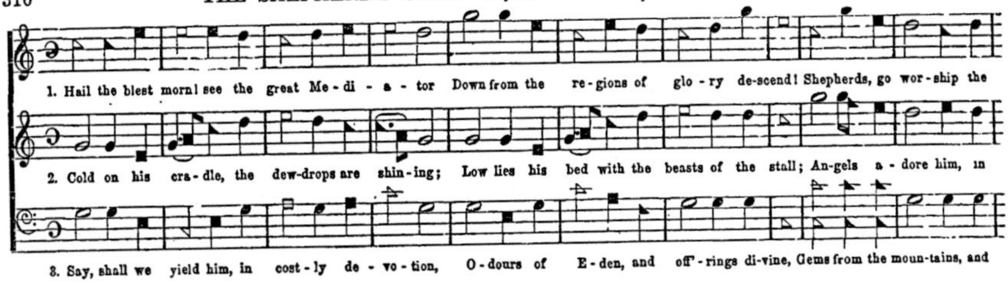
1. Hail the blest morn! see the great Me - di - a - tor Down from the re - gions of glo - ry de-scend! Shepherds, go wor - ship the
2. Cold on his cra - dle, the dew-drops are shin - ing; Low lies his bed with the beasts of the stall; An-gels a - dore him, in
3. Say, shall we yield him, in cost - ly de - vo - tion, O - dours of E - den, and off'-rings di-vine, Gems from the moun-tains, and

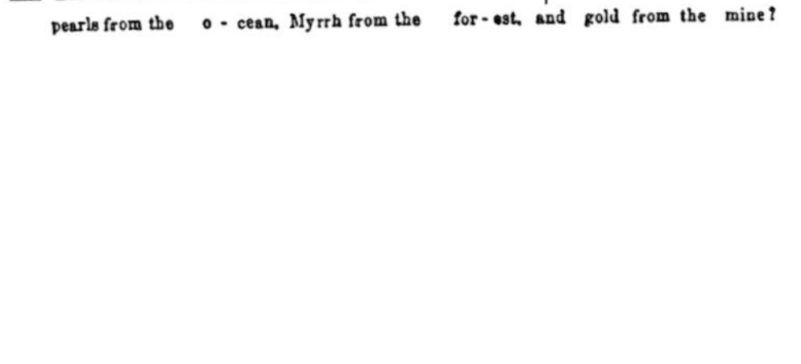
babe in the man - ger, Lo! for his guard, the bright an - gels at - tend.
slum-bers re - clin - ing, Wise men and shepherds be - fore him do fall.
pearls from the o - cean, Myrrh from the for - est, and gold from the mine?

4. Vainly we offer each ample oblation,
Vainly with gold we his favour secure;
Richer by far is the heart's adoration;
Dearer to God are the prayers of the poor.

5. Low at his feet we in humble prostration,
Lose all our sorrow and trouble and strife;
There we receive his divine consolation,
Flowing afresh from the fountain of life.

6. He is our friend in the midst of temptation,
Faithful supporter, whose love cannot fail;
Rock of our refuge, and hope of salvation,
Light to direct us through death's gloomy vale

7. Star of the morning, thy brightness, declining,
Shortly must fade when the sun doth arise:
Beaming refulgent, his glory eternal
Shines on the children of love in the skies

PRECIOUS BIBLE. 8,7,8,7,7,7.

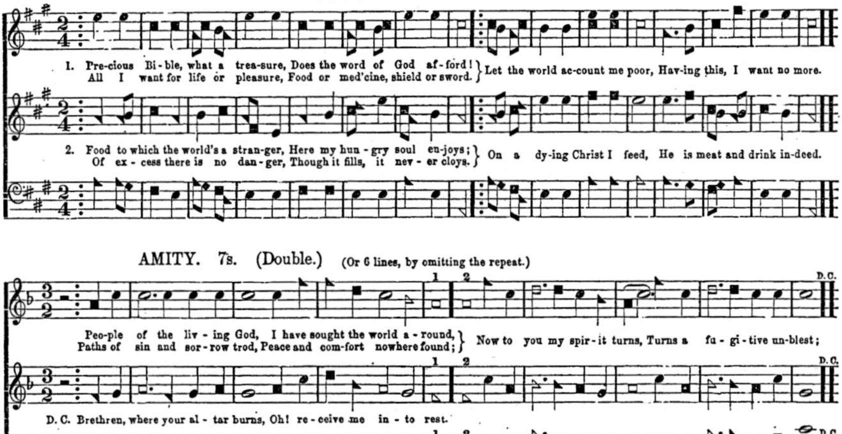
1. Pre-cious Bi-ble, what a trea-sure, Does the word of God af-ford! }
All I want for life or pleasure, Food or med'cine, shield or sword. }
Let the world ac-count me poor, Hav-ing this, I want no more.
2. Food to which the world's a stran-ger, Here my hun-gry soul en-joys; }
Of ex-cess there is no dan-ger, Though it fills, it nev-er cloys. }
On a dy-ing Christ I feed, He is meat and drink in-deed.

AMITY. 7s. (Double.) (Or 6 lines, by omitting the repeat.)

1 2
D.C.
Peo-ple of the liv-ing God, I have sought the world a-round, }
Paths of sin and sor-row trod, Peace and com-fort nowhere found; }
Now to you my spir-it turns, Turns a fu-gi-tive un-blest;
D. C. Brethren, where your al-tar burns, Oh! re-ceive me in-to rest.

CONDESCENSION. C. M.

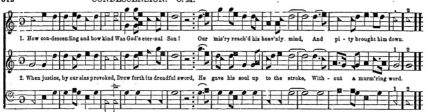

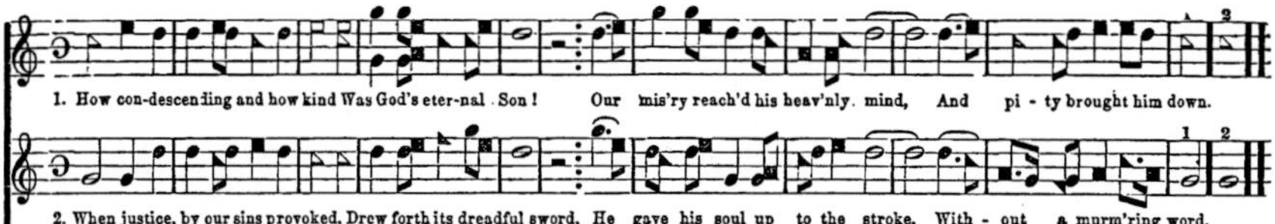
1. How con-descending and how kind Was God's eter-nal Son! Our mis'ry reach'd his heav'nly mind, And pi - ty brought him down.
2. When justice, by our sins provoked, Drew forth its dreadful sword, He gave his soul up to the stroke, With - out a murm'ring word.
1 2

SWEET HEAVEN. L. M.

1. Je - sus, my all, to heav'n is gone, He whom I fix my hopes up - on;
His track I see, and I'll pur - sue The nar - row way till him I view.
Chorus.—O heav'n, sweet heav'n, I long for thee! O when shall I get there?
2. The way the ho - ly pro-phets went, The road that leads from ban - ish-ment,
The king's highway of ho - li - ness, I'll go, for all his paths are peace.
O heav'n, sweet heav'n, I long for thee! O when shall I get there?

TRAVELLING PILGRIM. L. M. 2 lines

Chorus.
Chorus.
1. Farewell! vain world, I'm going home, Where there's no more stormy clouds arising;
My Saviour smiles, and bids me come Where there's no more stormy clouds arising.
To the land, to the land, to the land I am bound, Where there's no more stormy clouds arising.
2. Sweet angels beckon me away, Where there's no more stormy clouds a-ris-ing;
To sing God's praise in endless day, Where there's no more stormy clouds arising.
To the land, to the land, to the land I am bound, Where there's no more stormy clouds arising

LONG TIME AGO. 8s & 4s.

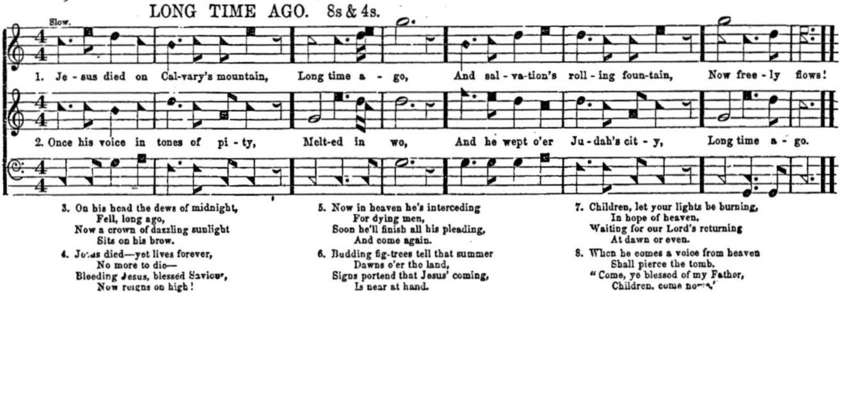
Slow.
1. Je - sus died on Cal-vary's mountain, Long time a - go, And sal - va-tion's roll - ing foun-tain, Now free - ly flows!
2. Once his voice in tones of pi - ty, Melt-ed in wo, And he wept o'er Ju - dah's cit - y, Long time a - go.

3. On his head the dews of midnight,
Fell, long ago,
Now a crown of dazzling sunlight
Sits on his brow.

4. Jesus died—yet lives forever,
No more to die—
Bleeding Jesus, blessed Saviour,
Now reigns on high!

5. Now in heaven he's interceding
For dying men,
Soon he'll finish all his pleading,
And come again.

6. Budding fig-trees tell that summer
Dawns o'er the land,
Signs portend that Jesus' coming,
Is near at hand.

7. Children, let your lights be burning,
In hope of heaven,
Waiting for our Lord's returning
At dawn or even.

8. When he comes a voice from heaven
Shall pierce the tomb,
"Come, ye blessed of my Father,
Children, come no[me]."

CONTENTED SOLDIER. L. M.

Wm. Walker.

1. I've list - ed in the ho - ly war, Till the war-fare is o - ver, hal - le - lu - jah!
Con - tent to suf - fer sol - dier's fare, Till the war-fare is o - ver, hal - le - lu - jah!
Cry - ing a - men, shout
2. The ban - ner o'er my head is love, Till the war-fare is o - ver, hal - le - lu - jah!
I draw my ra - tions from a - bove, Till the war-fare is o - ver, hal - le - lu - jah!
Cry - ing a - men, shout

on till the war - fare is o - ver, hal - le - lu - jah!
on till the war - fare is o - ver, hal - le - lu - jah!

3. I've fought through many a battle sore,
Till the warfare is over, hallelujah!
And I must fight through many more,
Till the warfare is over, &c.

4. I take my breast-plate, sword, and shield,
Till the warfare is over, hallelujah!
And boldly march into the field,
Till the warfare is over, &c.

5. The world, the flesh, and Satan too,
Till the warfare is over, hallelujah!
Unite and strive what they can do;
Till the warfare is over, &c.

6. On thee, O Lord, I humbly call,
Till the warfare is over, hallelujah!
Uphold me or my soul must fall,
Till the warfare is over, &c.

7. I've listed, and I mean to fight
Till the warfare is over, hallelujah!
Till all my foes are put to flight;
Till the warfare is over, &c.

8. And when the victory I have won,
Till the warfare is over, hallelujah.
I'll give the praise to God alone,
Till the warfare is over, &c.

9. Come, fellow-Christians, join with me,
Till the warfare is over, hallelujah!
Come, face the foe, and never flee,
Till the warfare is over, &c.

10. The heavenly battle is begun,
Till the warfare is over, hallelujah!
Come, take the field, and win the crown
Till the warfare is over, &c.

11. With listing orders I have come;
Till the warfare is over, halleluja
Come rich, come poor, come old or young,
Till the warfare is over, &c.

12. Here's grace's bounty, Christ has given,
Till the warfare is over, hallelujah!
And glorious crowns laid up in heaven:
Till the warfare is over, &c.

13. Our Gen'ral he is gone before,
Till the warfare is over, hallelujah!
And you may draw on grace's store,
Till the warfare is over, &c.

14. But, if you will not list and fight,
Till the warfare is over, hallelujah!
You'll sink into eternal night;
Till the warfare is over, &c.

DAYSPRING. 8,7.

1. Chris-tian, see the o - rient morn - ing Breaks a - long the hea - then sky; Lo! th' ex - pect - ed day is dawn - ing,
2. Heath-ens at the sight are sing - ing, Morn - ing wakes their tune - ful lays; Pre - cious off' - rings they are bring - ing,
3. Zi - on's sun, sal - va - tion beam - ing, Gild - ing now the ra - diant hills, Rise and shine till bright - er gleam - ing,
Glo - rious day-spring from on high. Hal - - le - lu - jah! Hal - - - le - lu - jah! Hail the day-spring from on high!
First fruits of more per - fect days. Hal - - le - lu - jah! Hal - - - le - lu - jah! Hail the day-spring from on high!
All the world thy glo - ry fills. Hal - - le - lu - jah! Hal - - - le - lu - jah! Hail the day-spring from on high!

4. Then the valleys and the mountains,
Breaking forth, in joy shall sing;
Then the living crystal fountain
From the thirsty ground shall spring.
Hallelujah :||: Hail. &c.

5. While the wilderness rejoices,
Roses shall the desert cheer;
Then the dumb shall tune their voices,
Blind shall see, the deaf shall hear.
Hallelujah :||: Hail, &c.

6. Lord of every tribe and nation,
Spread thy truth from pole to pole;
Spread the light of thy salvation
Till it shines on every soul.
Hallelujah :||: Hail, &c

ANTIOCH. C. M.

Arranged from Handel. From the Carmina Sacra.

Allegretto Risoluto
Joy to the world, &c.
Let, &c.
1. Joy to the world, the Lord is come! Let earth re-ceive her King; Let ev'-ry heart pre-pare him room,
And heav'n and na-ture sing . . . . And heav'n and na-ture sing.
Ending for 3d Stanza.
Far as the curse is found.
And heav'n and nature sing, And heav'n and na-ture sing, And heav'n, And heav'n and na-ture sing.
Far as the curse is found.
And heav'n and na-ture sing, And heav'n and na-ture sing, And heav'n, &c.
Far, &c.

2. Joy to the world, the Saviour reigns,
Let men their songs employ;
While fields and floods, rocks, hills, and plains
Repeat the sounding joy.

3. No more let sin and sorrow grow,
Nor thorns infest the ground;
He comes to make his blessings flow
{ Far as the curse is found
{ *Second Ending.*

4. He rules the world with truth and grace,
And makes the nations prove
The glories of his righteousness.
And wonders of his love.

BENEVENTO. 7s. (Double.)

S. Webbe.

While, with ceaseless course, the sun Hast - ed thro' the for - mer year, Man - y souls their race have run, Nev - er more to meet us here:
Fix'd in an e - ter - nal state, They have done with all be - low; We a lit - tle long - er wait, But how lit - tle none can know.

JORDAN'S SHORE. C. M.

J. T. White. Psalmist, Hymn 1173.

1. On Jor-dan's storm-y banks I stand, And cast a wish-ful eye On the oth-er side of Jor-dan, hal-le-lu-jah!
To Ca-naan's fair and hap-py land, Where my pos-ses-sions lie, On the oth-er side of Jor-dan, hal-le-lu-jah!
2. Oh! the trans-port-ing, rapt'rous scene, That ri-ses to my sight! On the oth-er side of Jor-dan, hal-le-lu-jah!
Sweet fields, ar-ray'd in liv-ing green, And ri-vers of de-light, On the oth-er side of Jor-dan, hal-le-lu-jah!
3. O'er all those wide-ex-tend-ed plains Shines one e-ter-nal day, On the oth-er side of Jor-dan, hal-le-lu-jah!
There God the Son for-ev-er reigns, And scat-ters night a-way, On the oth-er side of Jor-dan, hal-le-lu-jah!
Chorus.
On the oth-er side of Jor-dan, hal-le-lu-jah, On the oth-er side of Jor-dan, hal-le-lu-jah!

4. No chilling winds, nor pois'nous breath
Can reach that healthful shore;
Sickness and sorrow, pain and death
Are felt and fear'd no more.

5. When shall I reach that happy place,
And be forever blest?
When shall I see my Father's face,
And in his bosom rest?

6. Fill'd with delight, my raptured soul
Would here no longer stay:
Though Jordan's waves should round me roll,
I'd fearless launch away.

IMMENSITY. L. M.

Caldwell.

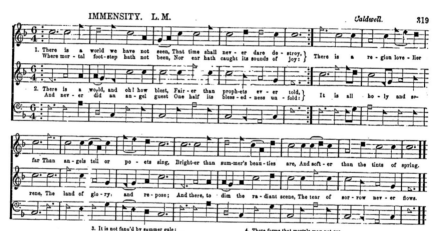

1. There is a world we have not seen, That time shall nev - er dare de - stroy,
Where mor - tal foot-step hath not been, Nor ear hath caught its sounds of joy:
There is a re - gion love - lier far Than an - gels tell or po - ets sing, Bright-er than sum-mer's beau - ties are, And soft - er than the tints of spring.
2. There is a world, and oh! how blest, Fair - er than proph-ets ev - er told,
And nev - er did an an - gel guest One half its bless - ed - ness un - fold:
It is all ho - ly and se - rene, The land of glo - ry, and re - pose; And there, to dim the ra - diant scene, The tear of sor - row nev - er flows.

3. It is not fann'd by summer gale;
'Tis not refresh'd by vernal show'rs;
It never needs the moonbeam pale,
For there are known no evening hours:
No, for this world is ever bright
With a pure radiance all its own;
The stream of uncreated light
Flows round it from th' eternal throne.

4. There forms that mortals may not see,
Too glorious for the eye to trace,
And clad in peerless majesty,
Move with unutterable grace:
In vain the philosophic eye
May seek to view the fair abode,
Or find it in the curtain'd sky:
It is the dwelling-place of God.

BEHOLD THE LAMB OF GOD. 5 lines, L. M., and Chorus.

Air as sung by Mr. T. K. Collins. Arr'd by Wm. Houser.

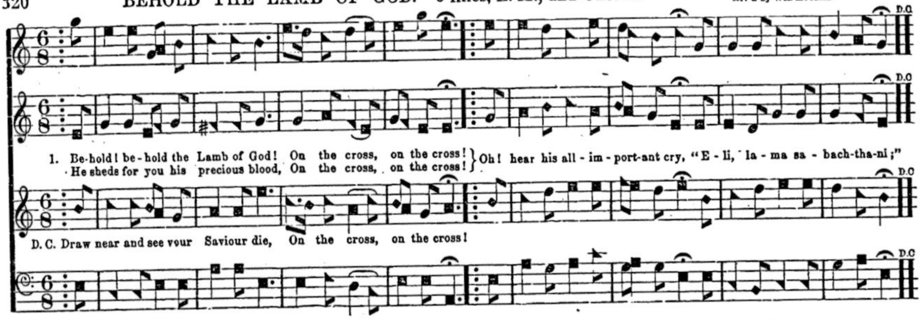
D.C.
1. Be-hold! be-hold the Lamb of God! On the cross, on the cross! } Oh! hear his all - im - port-ant cry, "E - li, la - ma sa - bach-tha-ni;"
He sheds for you his precious blood, On the cross, on the cross! }
D. C. Draw near and see your Saviour die, On the cross, on the cross!

2.

Behold his arms extended wide, On the cross, &c.
Behold his bleeding hands and side, On the, &c.
The sun withholds his rays of light,
The heavens are clothed in shades of night,
While Jesus doth with devils fight, On the, &c.

3.

Come, sinners, see him lifted up, On the, &c.
For you he drinks the bitter cup, On the, &c.
The rocks do rend, the mountains quake,
While Jesus doth atonement make,
While Jesus suffers for our sake, On the, &c.

4.

And now the mighty deed is done, On the, &c.
The battle's fought, the victory's won, On the, &c.
To heaven he turns his languid eyes,
"'Tis finished," now the Conqueror cries,
Then bows his sacred head and dies, On the, &c.

5.

Where'er I go I'll tell the story, Of the, &c.
Of nothing else my soul shall glory, Save the, &c.
Yea, this my constant theme shall be,
Through time and in eternity
That Jesus tasted death for me. On the, &c.

6.

Let every mourner rise and cling, To the, &c.
Let every Christian come and sing, Round the, &c.
There let the preacher take his stand,
And, with the Bible in his hand,
Declare the triumphs through the land, Of the, &c.

1. Ye ob - jects of sense, And en - joy - ments of time, Which oft have de - light - ed my heart,
2. Thou Lord of the day, and thou Queen of the night, To me ye no long - er are known,
I soon shall ex - change you for views more sub - lime, For joys that shall ne - ver de - part.
I soon shall be - hold with in - creas - ing de - light, A sun that shall nev - er go down.

3. Ye wonderful orbs that astonish my eyes.
Your glories recede from my sight,
I soon shall contemplate more beautiful skies,
And stars more resplendently bright.

4. Ye mountains and valleys, groves, rivers, and plains,
Thou earth and thou ocean, adieu!
More permanent regions where righteousness reigns,
Present their bright hills to my view.

5. My loved habitation and gardens adieu,
No longer my footsteps ye greet,
A mansion celestial stands full in my view,
And paradise welcomes my feet.

SAMANTHRA. 11,8.

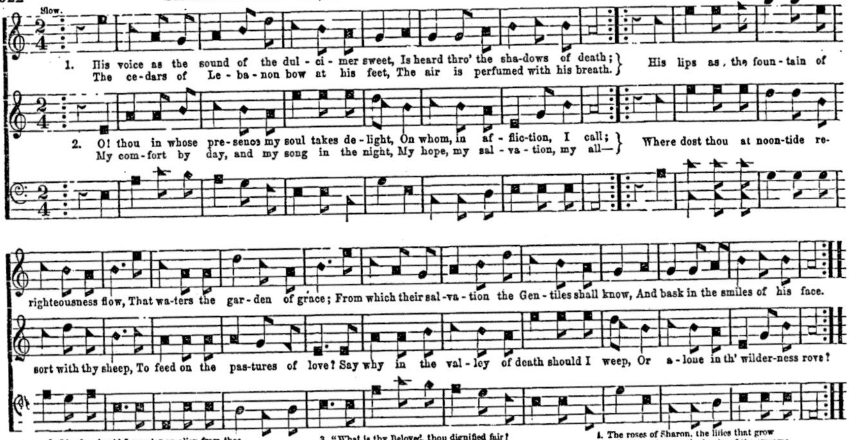
Slow.
1. His voice as the sound of the dul - ci - mer sweet, Is heard thro' the sha-dows of death; His lips as, the foun - tain of
The ce-dars of Le - ba - non bow at his feet, The air is perfumed with his breath.
2. O! thou in whose pre- sence my soul takes de - light, On whom, in af - flic-tion, I call; Where dost thou at noon-tide re-
My com-fort by day, and my song in the night, My hope, my sal - va - tion, my all—
righteousness flow, That wa-ters the gar - den of grace; From which their sal -va - tion the Gen - tiles shall know, And bask in the smiles of his face.
sort with thy sheep, To feed on the pas-tures of love? Say why in the val - ley of death should I weep, Or a - lone in th' wilder-ness rove?

2. O! why should I wander an alien from thee,
And cry in the desert for bread?
Thy foes will rejoice when my sorrows they see,
And smile at the tears I have shed.
Ye daughters of Zion, declare, have you seen
The Star that on Israel shone?
Say if in your tents my beloved has been,
And where, with his flock, he is gone?

3. "What is thy Beloved, thou dignified fair?
What excellent beauties has he?
His charms and perfections be pleased to declare,
That we may embrace him with thee."
This is my Beloved, his form is divine;
His vestments shed odour around;
The locks on his head are as grapes on the vine,
When autumn with plenty is crown'd.

4. The roses of Sharon, the lilies that grow
In the vales, on the banks of the streams,
On his cheeks in the beauty of excellence blow,
And his eyes are as quivers of beams.
His voice as the sound of the dulcimer, sweet,
Is heard through the shadows of death;
The cedars of Lebanon bow at his feet,
The air is perfumed with his breath.

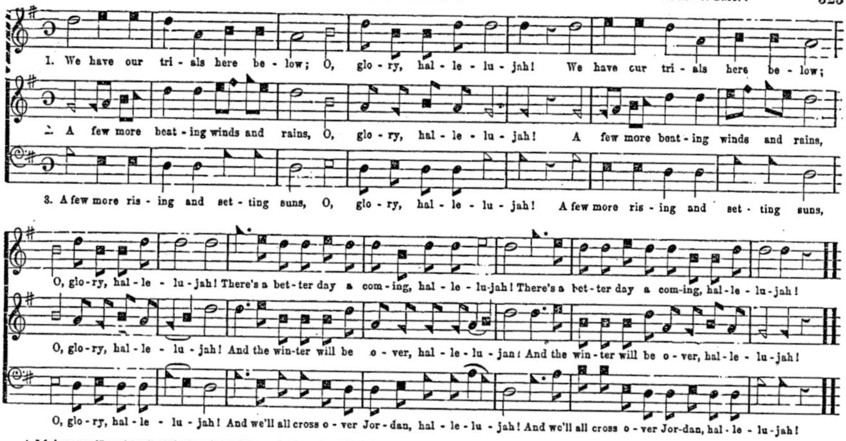
1. We have our tri - als here be - low; O, glo - ry, hal - le - lu - jah! We have our tri - als here be - low;
2. A few more beat - ing winds and rains, O, glo - ry, hal - le - lu - jah! A few more beat - ing winds and rains,
3. A few more ris - ing and set - ting suns, O, glo - ry, hal - le - lu - jah! A few more ris - ing and set - ting suns,
O, glo - ry, hal - le - lu - jah! There's a bet - ter day a com - ing, hal - le - lu - jah! There's a bet - ter day a com - ing, hal - le - lu - jah!
O, glo - ry, hal - le - lu - jah! And the win - ter will be o - ver, hal - le - lu - jah! And the win - ter will be o - ver, hal - le - lu - jah!
O, glo - ry, hal - le - lu - jah! And we'll all cross o - ver Jor - dan, hal - le - lu - jah! And we'll all cross o - ver Jor - dan, hal - le - lu - jah!

4. I feel no ways like getting tired, O, glory, hallelujah!
I am making for the harbour—Hallelujah!

5. I hope to get there by and by, O, glory, hallelujah!
For my home is over Jordan—Hallelujah!

6. I have some friends before me gone, O, glory, hallelujah!
By and by I'll go and meet them—Hallelujah!

7. I'll meet them round our Father's throne, O, glory, hallelujah!
And we'll live with God forever—Hallelujah!

8. O! how it lifts my soul to think, O, glory, hallelujah!
Of soon meeting in the kingdom—Hallelujah!

9. Our God will wipe all tears away, O, glory, hallelujah.
When we all arrive at Canaan—Hallelujah

REMEMBER ME. C. M.

L. J. Jones.

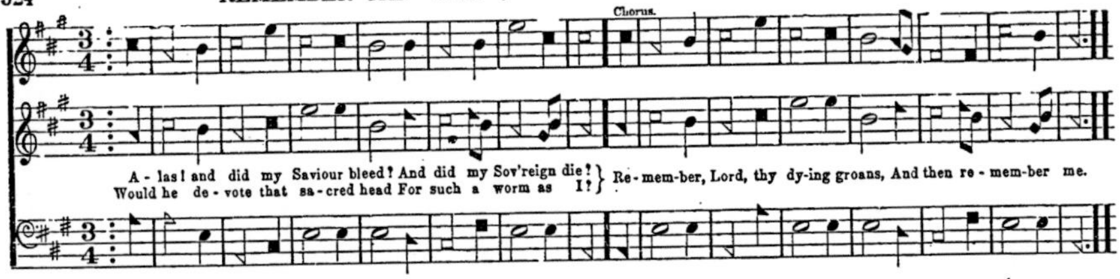
Chorus.
A - las! and did my Saviour bleed? And did my Sov'reign die?
Would he de - vote that sa - cred head For such a worm as I?
Re - mem-ber, Lord, thy dy-ing groans, And then re - mem-ber me.

INTERCESSION. S. M.

T. C. Moffett.

1. The Lord is ris'n in - deed, And are the ti - dings true? Yes, we be - held the Saviour bleed, And saw him liv - ing too.

2. The Lord is risen indeed,
   Then hell has lost his prey,
   With him is risen the ransom seed,
   To reign in endless day.

3. The Lord is risen indeed,
   Attending angels hear;
   Up to the courts of heaven with speed,
   The joyful tidings bear

4. Then make your golden lyres,
   And strike each cheerful chord;
   Join all ye bright, celestial choirs,
   To sing our risen Lord.

FOUNT OF GLORY. 8s & 7s. *R. W. Thompson.*

1. Far from mor - tal cares re - treat - ing, Sor - did hopes and vain de - sires,
Here our will - ing foot-steps meet - ing, Ev' - ry heart to heav'n as - pires.
From the fount of glo ry beam-
2. Who shall share this great sal - - va - tion? Ev' - ry pure and hum - ble mind,
Ev' - ry kind - red, tongue, and na - tion, From the stains of guilt re - fined.
Bless-ings all a - round be - stow-
ing, Light ce - les - tial cheers our eyes, Mer - cy from a - bove pro - claim - ing, Peace and par - don from the skies.
ing, God with - holds his care from none, Grace and mer - cy ev - er flow - ing From the foun - tain of his throne.

HOPEWELL. L. M.

L. J. Jones.

Chorus
1. Je - sus, my all, to heav'n is gone, He whom I fix my hopes up - on;
His track I see, and I'll pur - sue The nar - row way, till him I view.
Hal - le - lu - Jah! Hal - le - lu - jah!
Hal - le - lu - jah! I love the Lord: This note a - bove all oth - ers raise, My Je - sus has done all things well.

2. This is the way I long have sought,
And mourn'd because I found it not;
My grief and burden long has been,
Because I was not saved from sin.
Hallelujah, &c.

3. The more I strove against its power,
I felt its weight and guilt the more;
Till late I heard the Saviour say,
Come hither, soul, I am the way.
Hallelujah, &c.

CUR JOURNEY HOME. 8s & 7s. *L. J. Jones*

1. Come, thou fount of ev'-ry blessing, Tune my heart to sing thy grace; Streams of mer-cy, ne-ver ceas-ing, Call for songs of loud-est praise;
2. Here I raise my Eb-en-e-zer, Hith-er by thy help I'm come: And I hope, by thy good plea-sure, Safe-ly to ar-rive at home
3. O! to grace how great a debt-or Dai-ly I'm constrain'd to be! Let that grace, Lord, like a fet-ter Bind my wand'ring heart to thee!
Teach me some me-lo-dious son-net, Sung by flaming tongues a-bove; Praise the mount—O, fix me on it! Mount of God's un-chang-ing love.
Je-sus sought me when a stranger, Wand'ring from the fold of God; He, to save my soul from dan-ger, In-ter-posed his pre-cious blood.
Prone to wan-der, Lord, I feel it; Prone to leave the God I love—Here's my heart, Lord, take and seal it, Seal it from thy courts a-bove.
Chorus—Hal-le-lu-jah! Hal-le-lu-jah! We are on our journey home; Hal-le-lu-jah! Hal-le-lu-jah! Je-sus smiles and bids us come

MISSIONARY FAREWELL. 8,7,4.

Wm. Walker.

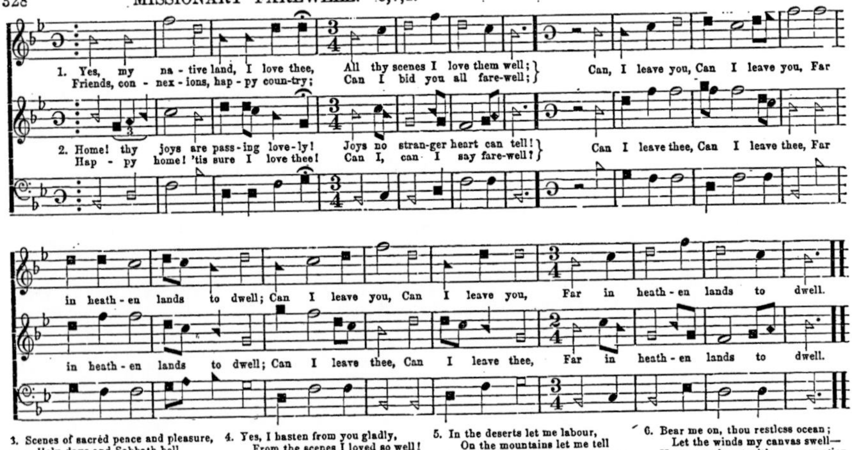
1. Yes, my na - tive land, I love thee, All thy scenes I love them well; }
Friends, con - nex - ions, hap - py coun-try; Can I bid you all fare-well; }
Can, I leave you, Can I leave you, Far
2. Home! thy joys are pass - ing love - ly! Joys no stran-ger heart can tell! }
Hap - py home! 'tis sure I love thee! Can I, can I say fare-well? }
Can I leave thee, Can I leave thee, Far
in heath - en lands to dwell; Can I leave you, Can I leave you, Far in heath - en lands to dwell.
in heath - en lands to dwell; Can I leave thee, Can I leave thee, Far in heath - en lands to dwell.

3. Scenes of sacréd peace and pleasure,
Holy days and Sabbath bell,
Richest, brightest, sweetest treasure!
Can I say a last farewell?
Can I leave you—
Far in heathen lands to dwell? :||:

4. Yes, I hasten from you gladly,
From the scenes I loved so well!
Far away, ye billows, bear me;
Lovely, native land, farewell!
Pleased I leave thee—
Far in heathen lands to dwell. :||:

5. In the deserts let me labour,
On the mountains let me tell
How He died—the blessed Saviour—
To redeem a world from hell!
Let me hasten—
Far in heathen lands to dwell. :||:

6. Bear me on, thou restless ocean;
Let the winds my canvas swell—
Heaves my heart with warm emotion,
While I go far hence to dwell.
Glad I leave thee,
Native land—Farewell—Farewell! :||

THOU ART PASSING AWAY. 11s.

Arranged by Rev. George Coles,
From Russell's "Mind of the Winter Night."

1. Thou art pass-ing a - way, thou art pass-ing a - way, Thy life has been brief as a mid-summer day; Thy forehead is
2. Thou art pass-ing a - way from the beau-ti - ful earth, Thy much lov'd a - bode, and the land of thy birth; From its for-ests
3. Thou art pass-ing a - way from thy kindred and friends, And the last chain that bound thee, the spoiler now rends; And thy last tones

pale, and thy pulses are low, And thy once blooming cheek wears the o-mi-nous glow.
and fields—from its murm'ring rills, From its beau-ti-ful plains and its herbage-crown'd hills.
are falling on love's list'ning ear. And now in thine eye shines the fond, parting tear.

4. Thou art passing away, as the first summer rose,
That awaits not the time when the Winter wind blows,
But hasteth away on the Autumn's quick gale,
And scatters its odors o'er mountain and dale.

5. The light of thy beauty has faded and gone,
For the withering chills have already come on;
Thy charms have departed—thy glory is fled;
And thou soon wilt be laid in the house of the dead.

6. Thou shalt soon be consigned to the cold, dreary tomb,
The lot of all living—mortality's doom:
Thou shalt there sweetly rest in the calmest repose,
Undisturbed by life's cares, and unpierced by its woes.

7. "Who, who would live always away from his God?
Away from yon heaven, the blissful abode,
Where the rivers of pleasure flow o'er the bright plains,
And the noontide of glory eternally reigns?"

OLIVE SHADE. 8,6,8,4.

Col. Daniel Smith.

1. Fa-ther, who in the o-live shade, When the dark hour came on, Didst with a breath of heav'n-ly aid, Strengthen thy son;

2. Oh, by the anguish of that night,
Send us down blest relief,
Or to the chastened let thy might
Hallow this grief.

3. And thou that, when the starry sky,
Saw the dread strife begun,
Didst teach adoring faith to cry,
Thy will be done.

4. By thy meek spirit, then of all,
That e'er have mourned the chief,
Blest Saviour, if the stroke must fall,
Hallow this grief.

AMHERST. H. M. 6,6,6,6,8,8.

Billings.

1. Lord of the worlds a-bove, How pleasant and how fair The dwellings of thy love, Thine earthly tem-ples are; To thine abode My heart as-pires, With warm de-sires, To see my God
2. The sparrow for her young, With pleasure seeks her nest; And wand'ring swallows long To find their wont-ed rest; My spi-rit faints With e-qual zeal, To rise and dwell Among thy saints.
3. Oh happy souls, that pray Where God appoints to hear! Oh happy men, that pay Their con-stant service there! They praise thee still; And happy they, That love the way To Zion's hill

COME, YE DISCONSOLATE. 11,10.

Swan.

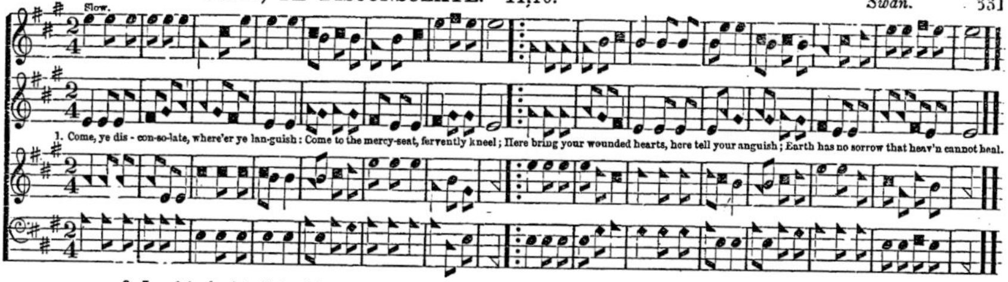
Slow.
1. Come, ye dis - con-so-late, where'er ye lan-guish : Come to the mercy-seat, fervently kneel ; Here bring your wounded hearts, here tell your anguish ; Earth has no sorrow that heav'n cannot heal.

2. Joy of the desolate, light of the straying,
Hope of the penitent, fadeless, and pure,
Here speaks the Comforter, tenderly saying,
Earth has no sorrow that heav'n cannot cure.

3. Here see the bread of life; see waters flowing
Forth from the throne of God, pure from above;
Come to the feast love; come, ever knowing
Earth has no sorrow but heav'n can remove.

TENDER CARE, or SODA. C. M.

P. M. Atchley.

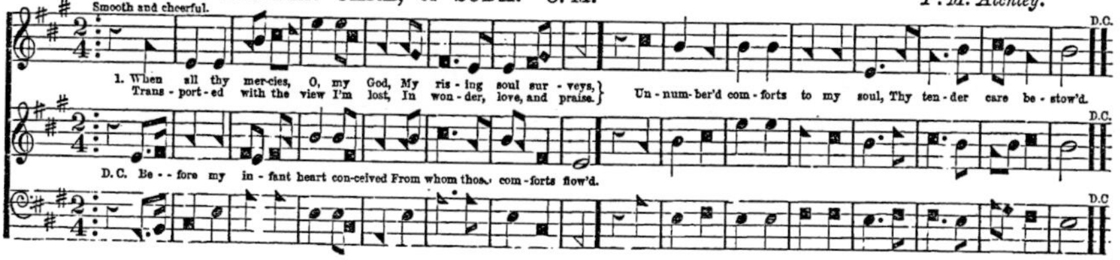
Smooth and cheerful.
1. When all thy mer-cies, O, my God, My ris - ing soul sur - veys,
Trans - port - ed with the view I'm lost, In won - der, love, and praise.
Un - num - ber'd com - forts to my soul, Thy ten - der care be - stow'd.
D.C. Be - - fore my in - fant heart con-ceived From whom those com - forts flow'd.
D.C.

GREENLAND. 7.6.

Swan.

With firmness.
1. Why should I be af - fright - ed At pes - ti - lence and war, The fierc - er be the tem - pest, The soon - er it is
2. With Je - sus in the ves - sel, The bil - lows rise in vain, They on - ly will con - vey me To yon E - ly - sian
3. This world is full of dan - gers, And foes that press me hard; But Je - sus he has pro-mised That he will be my
o'er, The soon - er it is o'er, The soon - er it is o'er, The fierc - er be the tem-pest, The soon - er it is o'er.
plains, To yon E - ly - sian plains, To yon E - ly-sian plains, They on - ly will con - vey me To yon E - ly - sian plains.
guard. That he will be my guard, That he will be my guard, But Je - sus he has pro-mised That he will be my guard

4. Here I shall not be tempted
Above what I can bear,
When fightings are exerted,
His kingdom for to share.

5. From him I have my orders,
And while I do obey,
I find his holy spirit
Illuminates my way.

6. The way is so delightful,
I wish to travel on,
Till I arrive at heaven,
T' receive a starry crown.

RAPTURE. 6, 6, 9.

M. L. Swan.

Cheerful, sweet
* Come a-way to the skies, My be-lov-ed a-rise, And rejoice in the day thou wast born; On this festi-val day, Come ex-ult-ing a-way, And with singing to Zion re-turn.
1
2

* For the balance of this song, see page 88.

NEW YEAR. S. M.

P. M. Atchley.

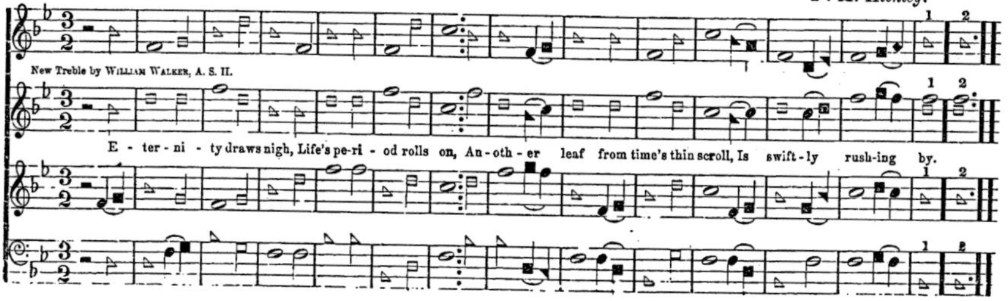
New Treble by WILLIAM WALKER, A. S. H.
E-ter-ni-ty draws nigh, Life's pe-ri-od rolls on, An-oth-er leaf from time's thin scroll, Is swift-ly rush-ing by.
1
2

THE CHRISTIAN'S FAREWELL. 11s.

4. Farewell, trembling mourners, with sad broken hearts,
O hasten to Jesus, and choose the good part!
He's full of compassion, and mighty to save,
His arms are extended, your souls to receive.

5. Farewell, careless sinners, for you I must mourn,
To think of your danger, if still unconcern'd;
I read of the judgment, where all must appear,
How will you stand trembling with tormenting fear!

6. Farewell, my dear brethren, farewell all around,
Perhaps we'll not meet till the last trump shall sound
To meet you in glory I give you my hand,
Our Saviour to praise in a pure social band

GENERAL INDEX.

METRICAL INDEX

Stereotyped by L. Johnson & Co. Phil.